IDENTIFYING AND ANALYZING USER NEEDS

A COMPLETE HANDBOOK AND READY-TO-USE ASSESSMENT WORKBOOK WITH DISK

Lynn Westbrook

Neal-Schuman Publishers, Inc.
New York   London

Published by Neal-Schuman Publishers, Inc.
100 Varick Street
New York, NY 10013

Printed and bound in the United States of America.

ISBN 1–55570–388–7

The paper used in this publication meets the minimum requirements of American National Standard for Information Sciences — Permanence of Paper for Printed Library Materials, ANSI Z39.48-1992.

Library of Congress Cataloging-in-Publication Data

Westbrook, Lynn.
    Identifying and analyzing user needs : a complete handbook and ready-to-use assessment workbook with disk / Lynn Westbrook.
       p. cm.
    Includes bibliographical references and indexes.
    ISBN 1–55570–388–7 (alk. paper)
    1. Library use studies—United States—Handbooks, manuals, etc.
    2. Libraries—User satisfaction—United States—Handbooks, manuals, etc. I. Title.

Z678 .W466 2001
025.5'8—dc 21

00–045220

Dedication

*To my parents
with deep love and abiding respect*

Table of Contents

Identifying and Analyzing User Needs: A Practical Manual on Disk

Table of Contents

Identifying and Analyzing User Needs: A Practical Manual on Disk

Figures and Worksheets

Foreword

As a researcher interested in the measurement and evaluation of library and information resources and services and as an instructor of research methods, I am pleased to write the foreword for this book on community information-needs analysis. There is a need for works such as this that make it more explicit that conducting a sound user needs/community analysis is essentially doing research. Indeed, Lynn Westbrook states in her first chapter that "a community information-needs analysis is a structured, planned, formal study that identifies the information requirements of the people within a library's jurisdiction." Throughout the book she does a commendable job of explaining how good research designs and techniques can be used to make such analyses more effective and reliable. Among the research components that she addresses as they relate to the needs-analysis process are: the proposal; the focus of the analysis, or what would be called the problem in a research study; research questions; data-gathering techniques and instruments, ranging from observation to diaries; reliability and validity; sampling techniques; data analysis; ethical issues; and the report.

On this same theme, I appreciate that Lynn provides somewhat of a theoretical foundation for community information-needs analysis by discussing Brenda Dervin's "sense-making" qualitative-quantitative methodology. The desirability of employing both qualitative and quantitative methods surfaces elsewhere in the book as well. Other evidence of her research perspective includes the consideration of causal relationships, an understanding of which makes it possible for analysts to go beyond mere description and to ex-

plain why certain phenomena occur. The rigorous approach that
she takes to sampling and her reminder that library statistics can
be treated as research data also reflect her view that a community
information-needs analysis is, in effect, research.

At the same time, as someone who has conducted community
analyses as a library administrator and who has taught courses
that include consideration of community analyses and user-needs
studies, I appreciate the extensive attention that she has given to
practical matters such as staffing and training. In fact, much of
the content of this work is based on courses that Lynn taught and
on workshops that she has presented for practitioners. The usefulness of her book is further enhanced by the provision of case
studies, information about the statistical reporting capabilities of
several computerized systems, a glossary, and sample questions.
Her encouragement of long-term, ongoing assessment, her reminder to include nonusers in analyses, and her advice on using
results also reflect her commitment to conducting needs analyses
that will have the maximum practical impact. Other particularly
valuable components of the book include the advice on funding
community information-needs analyses and the lists of suggested
readings.

In this age of accountability for the use of limited resources and
the need to maximize the impact of information services, a work
such as this provides valuable guidance on how to conduct practical, yet rigorous, community information-needs analyses. Its contents and readable style should make it an important addition to
the professional literature.

Ronald R. Powell
Library and Information Science Program
Wayne State University

Preface

Elementary school librarians greet their fledgling readers by name, while "cyber-librarians" work in a virtual space with users they never meet. Public librarians encounter new patron needs with the evolving changes of their locale, while academic librarians struggle to offer students and faculty the benefits offered by each leap of technology. All these professionals share one critical value: they must understand the information needs of their community in order to do their work effectively and efficiently. No librarian today can afford to assume that information-needs are stable, simple, or fully understood. Any library could be replaced tomorrow if another institution meets community needs through another mechanism.

Identifying and Analyzing User Needs: A Complete Handbook and Ready-to-Use Assessment Workbook with Disk provides step-by-step instruction in how to conduct a needs analysis and provides a ready-to-use manual on disk to guide you through completing the process for your library. This package covers the process of information-needs analysis from those initial, tentative steps, into the planning, data gathering, and analysis, and on through changes and recommendations. It also outlines all the major data-gathering techniques, including various forms of questionnaires, several types of interviews and observations, and the use of in-house documents. Finally, it covers academic, public, and school libraries using examples from actual studies to illustrate the major points. Although special libraries vary widely in their nature and mission they can certainly employ this general approach by modifying it for individual situations.

The organization of the book parallels steps in the process.

Chapter 1 covers those first efforts to think about the process and recognize what's involved. Chapter 2 reviews the steps necessary as a prelude to the formal planning process covered in chapter 3. Chapters 4, 5, and 6 examine specific research questions and research tools. Chapter 7 spells out study implementation issues. Analyzing the study results is covered in chapter 8, sharing the results of that analysis is the focus of chapter 9. Chapter 10 outlines mechanisms for acting on the study results. At the end of each chapter, suggested readings are listed to provide further resources on specific topics.

The appendices include three reports of recently conducted information-needs analyses involving a school, a public, and an academic library. The case studies are practical applications and were conducted using the techniques discussed in *Identifying and Analyzing User Needs*. While no single report is likely to match exactly the situation of any particular library, a modest amount of synthesis should produce a practical, useful foundation upon which to build. The final appendix provides information on the statistical reporting capabilities of several major and integrated Online Public Access Computers or OPACs. These reports can, if well used, make an effective contribution to an information-needs study.

Several supplementary pieces support and provide access to the main body of the work. As mentioned above, the study reports in the appendices cover the process in full; included in each report is a portfolio of the documents resulting from the study. Throughout the volume, further readings on specific issues and methods are noted; the full citation of each can be found in the Works Cited section. Particularly useful articles and books are annotated as well as listed in the Suggested Readings section. A glossary provides brief definitions of the more technical and/or uncommon terms. The Index leads the reader to those portions of the text that discuss or mention a particular author's work, as well as various topics, issues, and steps in the process .

The last item in this work is a manual on disk. This manual provides signposts and workspace. Mirroring the book's organizational scheme, the manual helps people move through the stages of a needs-analysis by briefly explaining key points. Filled with worksheets and illustrative figures, it also provides a structure through which people can track their decisions at each stage. Readily opened with any major word processor on a PC or Mac platform, the manual is a searchable, flexible document to be used as needed. For example, use the manual to supplement a full and careful reading of the book. Using your word processor, open the manual and read pertinent sections. Then call up the worksheets as needed, key in your own responses, and print them out for an accessible record of your work. Alternatively, use the book to supplement the full and careful implementation of the manual. Print out the manual, put it in a binder, and follow the stages as they pertain to your situation. Refer to the book only when more information is required on a particular point.

Find what you need in the manual using any of three techniques. First, as with the book, use the subject/author index located at the end of the volume. Second, identify the most relevant chapter, then skim the subheadings until you locate the desired material. Finally, open the manual as a document and use your word processor's "find" command to locate a particular word or phrase, such as "response rate."

Figures and worksheets present a wide variety of useful templates and can be manipulated as needed. (The complete list is reproduced along with the manual's Table of Contents on pages ix–xi.) Since they are available on the disk, the worksheets may be customized to meet the needs of your particular needs-assessment study. For example, completed worksheets may be moved into visual presentations to library advisory boards or printed up as handouts for staff.

For those who want to move straight into conducting an analysis with only minimal discussion and explanation, the manual is the place to start. For those who want to understand the process more fully before applying the techniques, the manual makes a useful support for application work explained in the book.

The reader is assumed to have a thorough understanding of librarianship and a modest understanding of research fundamentals. Should a reader come to this work with an interest in libraries but no actual professional experience in them, it is crucial for that reader to begin by involving a librarian in the process. (Library board members, for example, with an interest in enhancing library service would find the active leadership of a librarian essential.) Similarly, the basics of sampling techniques and simple statistical analysis are covered sufficiently for general use but not explained in great depth, on the assumption that the reader already understands their value and needs only a review of their use in this context.

Finally, those library and information studies educators who share my commitment to the library as a social and cultural institution might find some use for this work in the classroom. If so, I hope to receive commentary and feedback from tomorrow's information professionals, knowledge workers, information specialists, and librarians. Within and beyond its walls, with or without a substantial digital collection, a library must meet the information needs of its community effectively or it has no raison d'être. Understanding those needs is the crucial first step in that process.

Acknowledgments

This book benefits from the thoughtful support of a number of fine people who have been generous with their time and expertise during its development. My deep gratitude goes to Frankie Westbrook for her writing critiques. My appreciation goes to the anonymous reader whose thorough and thoughtful review of an earlier draft of this work inspired critical revisions. I value fully the excellent suggestions provided by Ronald Powell and Charles Harmon.

To all those librarians who attended my workshops on this staff and community centered approach, I owe a profound debt. Their enthusiasm and tough questions helped me hone the work. To the staff of the Library Development division of the sponsor of my workshops, the Texas State Library and Archives Commission, I owe my respect. They genuinely value information-needs analysis, moving from lip service to ready action. To the highly professional Special Services consultant they assigned to me, Wendy Clark, who worked with me and shared the travails of travel, I owe my respect and gratitude. Her suggestions and feedback strengthened each workshop and this book.

To all of those graduate students who took my doctoral courses in this area, I owe a deep appreciation. Their questions, discussions, and analyses helped me find new ways to approach and explain both the overall process and specific procedures.

To those librarians and library board members with whom I've worked on various studies, I am most thankful. Their commitment to their communities exemplifies the best in our field. I owe a special debt to those who graciously permitted me to report the case studies of their analyses in the appendices of this work.

And to Colin McIntyre I offer my warmest thanks for his frequent and essential mom-hugs.

Chapter 1

Getting Involved

Communities give purpose to libraries. School librarians serve communities of students, faculty, and staff. Academic librarians serve communities of undergraduates, graduate students, research faculty, teaching faculty, clinicians, and administrators. Public librarians serve communities of children, genealogists, young parents, retirees, and other people in all walks of life. Although the nature of these communities varies, all effective librarians have a sense of the information needs found in their communities. Meeting those needs provides purpose and direction for daily work and strategic planning in libraries of all types.

Librarians considering the possibility of studying their communities' information needs should ask themselves four crucial questions:

1. What is a community information-needs analysis?
2. What is meant by "user" and "need"?
3. Why conduct the analysis?
4. How does it fit into the planning process?

In a one-person library, the effort to talk through these issues for the first time is well worth the e-mail, telephone, or conference time it takes to contact a colleague. In a larger setting, a few individuals may begin an almost grassroots effort to think through the complexities involved. Any administrator working on a top-down mandate to conduct the study must plan time for middle managers and key staff to consider these four questions.

WHAT IS A COMMUNITY INFORMATION-NEEDS ANALYSIS?

A community information-needs analysis (CINA) is a structured, planned, formal study that identifies the information requirements of the people within a library's jurisdiction. Each of the four words in the term covers a single critical aspect of the process.

The "community" must be carefully prescribed by the library's mission statement. This document identifies the people for whom the library exists. The primary community is generally quite obvious (e.g., a school library serves the students, faculty, and staff of the school). The complexity arises when secondary and subpopulations are considered, particularly if priorities exist among different groups. The degree of service and access accorded to such groups must be determined. A university's Special Collections library, for instance, might admit both academic scholars and high school students while considering the needs of the former far more important than those of the latter. A downtown public library serving a large portion of the business community may concentrate more on the library needs of businesses than on, say, the public demand for best-sellers. Some school libraries include in their mission statement parental information needs. An honest review of "community" may result from updating the mission statement. Of course, in a truly useful study, community members must include both library users and nonusers. In fact, special attention is often paid to nonusers in an effort to understand their needs so that the library may become a productive resource for them.

"Information" must be viewed almost entirely from the individual's perspective. It refers to a wide range of materials, knowledge, data, and resources that entertain, inform, educate, and solve problems. Without entering the long-standing debate on the variant meanings of the term, this type of analysis examines data and materials needed by people, for whatever purposes, that fall within the mission purview of the library.

"Needs" refers to the information requirements of that community. As discussed below, not all needs must be met, not all are recognized, and not all are feasible. The focus, however, is on the information needs, not the actual uses of the library. The thrust of the study centers on any pertinent information need; library use is an incidental piece of the picture.

"Analysis" requires more than organizing the numbers gathered on a questionnaire; it requires placing those data in the context of the library's mission, the community's future, and the possibilities of the immediate environment. A truly practical analysis leads directly and smoothly to identification of priorities among possible changes and initiatives.

WHAT A COMMUNITY INFORMATION-NEEDS ANALYSIS IS NOT

As a contrast, consider what a community information-needs analysis is *not*. Most important it is not a study of what current users are currently doing. A CINA looks at what users and potential users *need*, rather than what current users actually *do*. It may help determine what some users actually do but only as a side effect of the real work.

Neither is a CINA an impact study, which asks, "What impact are we having on the lives of our users?" School librarians may look for higher test scores among those students who have information-literacy work in the library folded into their curriculum. Academic librarians might look for an increased grant-award rate among faculty who receive personalized research support. Public librarians may look for a higher literacy rate among the adults who go through a reading support program cosponsored by the local teachers' union. Those findings indicate the library's impact but say little about the full range of information needs within the community as a whole.

A CINA is also not an evaluation of the library although it may reveal both strengths and gaps in library services or collections. An evaluation asks, "How well are we doing those activities we've chosen to do?" Since the present set of services, programs, and collections is taken as a given, the evaluation questions center on the accuracy, efficiency, and thoroughness of those services. For example, an evaluation might determine the percentage of the answered reference questions or the percentage of filled book requests. An information-needs analysis may reveal that users want more of their book requests met more quickly but it should reveal a great deal more as well.

Although occasionally used for this purpose, a CINA does not support preplanned changes. To have any validity at all, it must be approached as an honest effort to identify and, more important, to understand the needs of the community. In addition to considering how people find information, the study may also examine how they manage what they find. A competent inquiry into those points followed by an open-minded analysis of the data might support a well-planned change, but it might also suggest modifications in an existing plan.

ASSUMPTIONS BEHIND THE PROCESS

Given this expanded definition of an information-needs analysis, perhaps the most critical of several assumptions underpinning the process is the determination of causal relationships. A needs analysis helps librarians gain insight and an understanding of relationships among variables, but it does not "prove" that X causes Y or that providing X service would result in Y benefit. Nevertheless, a change in the library may well mitigate a problem in the community. For example, eliminating age-oriented shelving may make users out of some nonusers in the young adult community.

Almost a corollary to that assumption is the principle that detailed analysis of the community being served is essential. Simply because it is so difficult to identify a causal relationship–much less to effect a change in that relationship–librarians must make every effort to understand their communities. Experience, anecdotes, conversations with "regulars," and circulation statistics tell only part of the story. A properly conducted analysis is more than worthwhile; it is essential to the planning process.

Of course, once the community information needs are understood, the next assumption comes into play, namely that the librarians are accountable and responsible for their services and collections. Complete autonomy and ample funding rarely exist but librarians must be held accountable for their work within the parameters of their situations. Staff who identify previously unknown information needs have done their job well because identification is the first step toward meeting those needs. A needs assessment is threatening to some staff; they worry that simply finding a new need implies a failure on their part. In fact, such a finding is a sign of success. It indicates that they have two elements essential to the provision of excellent service: the research skills necessary to deepen their understanding of community information needs and the open-minded, flexible attitude that allows them to recognize unexpected information needs. Staff who "know everything" about their community, including those nonusers whom they never see, lack the research skills that could uncover the unexpected, the honesty to examine their assumptions about people they never encounter, or both.

The assumptions of "sense-making" are critical. Growing out of her work in communication, Brenda Dervin's original research on "sense-making" lies at the heart of many user-centered studies. In her framework, sense-making is a "process in which individuals encounter problematic situations, identify information gaps that might pertain to the problem solution, and use the information in a way that alleviates the problem. . . . Sense-making is a process; 'sense' is the product of this process" (Waldron and Dervin 1988, 9).

Looking at what people do in their lives provides both a crucial context for their information needs and a deeper understanding of the gaps and barriers they face. Additionally, people may seek information and resources to do more than solve problems. Sometimes people need information as a catalyst, a spark, or general support; those needs are just as important as solving a specific problem (Dervin and Clark 1987, 15–24). Examination of the daily life of individuals, groups, and the community as a whole must recognize the sociological as well as the personal context in which information seeking occurs.

A corollary to this interest in patrons' process of making sense of information is an interest in how they feel, what they think, and what they do. Feelings, thoughts, and activities are too intertwined to separate artificially. Looking at what people do, for example, is limited unless the thoughts and emotions behind the actions are also considered.

Service-oriented librarians tend to focus on the end result, such as finding a book for a patron. Particularly effective librarians recognize that the path to that book is often just as important as the information itself because learning and development can take place during that search process. While every request for the White House e-mail address may not have a complex "process" to explore, more than simple information delivery is often involved.

A final assumption underlying community information-needs analysis is that a snapshot in time is valuable in itself but particularly valuable as part of a series. Everything learned during one CINA has immediate value and use; even more effective analyses, however, develop when data are compared over a number of years.

ISSUES BEHIND THE NEED

A few issues involved in the concept of a "user need" require explanation. Of course, the corollary for "user" is the "nonuser." Those who have the right to access the library and who have an information need falling within the purview of the library are potential users, and their needs are of potential interest to the librarians who might serve them. Those individuals who meet those criteria but never make use of the library are nonusers. Their behavior is crucial because their needs are either unmet or met through an agency other than the library.

More complex is the concept of "need." Green's cogent discussion of the social implications of that often-used but poorly defined term identifies each of the major issues involved. For example, "need is necessarily instrumental" (1990, 65); that is, needs relate to an unreached goal or an end state. In information-needs analysis, an understanding of the users' goals is often as useful as the identification of specific needs.

Additionally, needs are "usually contestable" in that a stated need can be rationally discussed, with one possible result being that some other need may be identified (Green 1990, 66). Reference librarians know this fact of library life well. The patron who "needs" an online public access catalog (OPAC) in order to reach the goal of identifying the name of President James Garfield's vice president might well alter that to a need for an encyclopedia after discussing the goal with a reference librarian.

Not all needs should be or can be met. The patron who needs to identify the people who have borrowed books on abortion has an information need, but no responsible librarian would meet it. Similarly, the person who needs a complete, current, highly detailed demographic analysis of the refugee population of central Africa has a need no one can meet because those statistics simply do not exist, although general estimates of a few demographics are possible.

Finally, information needs can exist without the conscious awareness of the individual (Green 1990, 67). Some patrons need to meet with a librarian, make more effective use of the Internet, or place an interlibrary loan (ILL) request but do not recognize the need as such. Similarly, people can need items they already have because they do not understand the value, flexibility, or purpose of what they have. For example, Welch's examination of information needs among the staff of humanitarian aid agencies revealed that those people "lacked information skills and information infrastructure, leading to a perception that they lacked information itself" (1995, 2).

Needs must also be considered in terms of the values of the library's mission and the values of the library's patrons. There are certain values implied by and involved in certain needs. "People with different values will recognize different needs" (McKillip 1987, 10). The mission statement will incorporate some larger-scale values, but the process of running the study may well raise discussion of more individually held values.

Some needs are simply hidden, unexplored, unknown, or unrecognized. Nonusers may well have information needs that are being met elsewhere or not at all. The local lesbian and gay communities, for example, may go to bookstores when the local public library fails to meet their need for the same type of innocuous romance novels that are provided so plentifully for the heterosexual community.

REASONS FOR CONDUCTING AN INFORMATION-NEEDS ANALYSIS

Any combination of reasons can support and sustain the effort, but the people working on the project should share a common understanding of the reasons behind their effort. There are at least nine viable reasons for librarians to conduct a community information-needs analysis.

- *Planning the general budget.* Both immediate and mid-range planning can be supported. Long-range planning, such as the building development discussed by Cheng-gong (1987), can also be informed.
- *Setting priorities among collection elements, services, and missions.* A careful analysis of the continually growing needs that librarians try to meet assists in identifying those needs that will receive the lion's share of time, equipment, staff training, and funding. Librarians continually deal with the addition of new duties. For example, academic librarians have always provided reference service for on-site students, and now they must also provide that same service for remote-site students. Priorities must often be set among such competing demands.
- *Positioning the library among its competitors.* CINAs provide data that help libraries compete for funding and other resources. Whether within the parent organization or within

the community at large, libraries face competition for users and scarce resources. For example, a public library may compete with bookstores and digital information vendors for users; losing users will eventually mean losing funding. For an academic library the competitors could be other university units competing for authority, funds, and resources such as university computer services. School libraries may compete for volunteer time, administrative support for grant applications, or building space.

- *Determining the optimum allocation of scarce resources.* Considering that most libraries have tight budgets, CINAs can help libraries gather information to help make hard decisions. School libraries, for example, may maximize their collection budgets through careful use of study data on reader interests.
- *Planning for inevitable change.* CINAs can provide information to ease the impact of those changes that take place against the better judgment of the librarians involved. For example, only limited control could be exercised over any of the following: RIFs (a "reduction in force" such as an across-the-board personnel reduction imposed on all units within the city), restructuring services (e.g., moving interlibrary loan in with reference), and consolidating libraries. As economic, political, social, and technological forces combine to dictate change in services, the careful use of a community-needs analysis provides guidance for and means of anticipating these developments. The difficulty here is to keep the study as objective as possible. Be careful to gather data objectively rather than in support of one particular path to change.
- *Helping staff develop a new vision for the library.* CINAs can identify trends, emerging concerns, and unexpected opportunities that can reinvigorate a burned-out staff. Some school librarians, for instance, are looking at the impact of Internet-based information on their programs, services, and collections. Genuinely understanding the needs of those students who use the Internet for homework can help guide the development of Internet resources and services.

- *Supporting long-term growth and development.* Administrators who conduct CINAs with some consistency have solid information to support their decisions. The information allows administrators to track and anticipate trends. The exact focus or specific data-gathering mechanisms may vary over the course of a decade, but the user focus remains steady.
- *Marketing the library.* Although it should never be the primary reason for conducting an information-needs assessment, marketing is a significant side effect of a well-conducted CINA and, therefore, merits recognition early in the process. Simply by contacting individuals in the name of the library, some public relations work is accomplished. People who hear the name, meet the staff, and read about the goals of the library will be somewhat better informed than those who do not.
- *Providing insight on nonusers.* Perhaps the single most crucial purpose for a CINA is to both identify and understand nonusers so that staff have more information to use in designing the changes that might persuade these individuals to use the library.

FITTING INTO THE PLANNING PROCESS

Needs assessment is an ongoing process in that it is part of the planning process. Economic and technological changes continue within the library, the parent institution, and the social environment. Both short-term and long-term planning are often based on the assumption of significant change. One of the best ways to capture relevant data on all of those potential changes is to look at information needs since that area encompasses change in every other area.

A CINA certainly contributes to the planning process in the area of evaluation. After developing an understanding of community users' needs, the library staff might choose to develop services and collections, and to design a user-centered evaluation of those developments. For an evaluation to be viable, the information needs must be incorporated into the standards for staff and services. Quantifiable standards are not a direct product of a CINA, but CINA findings may well support and inform this critical element of the planning process.

Most needs assessments in a well-run library do not produce a large number of completely unexpected findings that would dramatically alter the entire direction of the planning process. The library's mission, the work of the staff, and the needs of the users are generally in sync with each other. Instead, the CINA contributes to the planning process by fine-tuning the knowledge gained through experience, identifying blind spots in staff knowledge, and alerting staff to coming environmental developments.

A CINA can actually be very affirming in that librarians might find that many or even most of their users' needs are being met quite well. Well-met needs are still needs and a confirmation of their status is valuable. The margin of error, however, is slim to none in these days of booming demands and shrinking resources. No one has the luxury of "pretty much" meeting needs; the job must be done well.

As mentioned above, some needs imply values at variance with the library's mission. Beyond that, however, it is neither necessary nor appropriate for the library to provide direct solutions to every CINA-identified problem. For example, faculty almost always need more grant money but actually getting the money is not the library's problem. Nevertheless, the library can help handle this critical need by focusing on the information component in the process. By making grant information and reference support more accessible, librarians may ultimately assist in meeting the need for grant money. Similarly, home-schooling parents might want a well-developed Web site full of curricular materials pertinent to specific lessons. Again, the library can look at the information component of this request or brush it aside as a demand for convenience. Doing the former, the library can help by modifying Web design, collecting and cataloging Web sites, or working in instructional sessions with the parents. Doing nothing misses a great opportunity. Nevertheless, the library has responsibility for meeting some needs and not others; throughout the planning process, administrators must be clear about the distinction.

Finally, a word about timing in relationship to the planning process is essential. Libraries ride the roller coaster of change constantly. Waiting for a season without technology upgrades, staff shortages, new staff-in-training, management restructuring, or environmental developments may mean waiting forever. Acknowledging the continual impact of various forms of change, those interested in an analysis must understand the library planning cycle and step into it. Like stepping into an ongoing dance, this bit of timing requires bold action and great sensitivity. Is the end of a five-year planning cycle approaching? Has some major upgrade or change finally been fully and successfully implemented? Is a new administrator (either at the library or at the institutional level) in place and open to the need for such a study? Are viable grants available to those who can demonstrate needs based on hard research? Are major changes planned with little data available on which to base decisions? When the opportunity presents itself, step in smoothly and quickly.

SUMMARY

Librarians must always take the lead in information provision and management within their communities. The community information-needs analysis is a productive mechanism for staff when taking that leading role. The very act of moving through the process positions the staff more strategically within the environment as new ties with users, potential users, and user groups are formed.

A number of unexpected benefits accrue throughout the process. In some situations, just knowing how much the library staff cares about users' needs begins a modest change in user expectations. (Of course, the well-conducted study accounts for these expectations carefully, insuring that false hopes are not engendered.) Some staff members will develop skills in new areas and some will want to look for other opportunities within the planning process to apply those skills. Communication channels are often improved, upgraded, or established for the first time among staff as well as between staff and patrons. Perhaps of most importance is the opportunity for new partnerships. These can develop out of the process itself and they might be a result of the study. School libraries, for example, may tie in with the PTA more fully. Public libraries may deepen their support among members of the business community. Balancing these complexities and opportunities is essential to a productive needs analysis.

CHAPTER 1 READINGS

Research Methods for Librarians

Powell, Ronald R. 1997. *Basic research methods for librarians.* 3rd edition. Greenwich, CT: Ablex.

Strategic Planning

Himmel, Ethel, William James Wilson, with the ReVision [*sic*] Committee of the Public Library Association. 1998. *Planning for results: A public library transformation process, The guidebook.* Chicago: American Library Association.

Jacob, M. E. L. 1990. *Strategic planning: A how-to-do-it manual for librarians.* How-To-Do-It Manuals for Librarians, number 9. New York: Neal-Schuman.

Robbins, Jane, and Douglas Zweizig. 1992. Planning. In *Keeping the books: Public library financial practices.* Jane Robbins and Douglas Zweizig, eds. Fort Atkinson, WI: Highsmith Press, for the Urban Libraries Council. 217–223.

Library Users and Nonusers

Zweizig, Douglas and Brenda Dervin. 1982. Public library use, users, uses: Advances in knowledge of the characteristics and needs of the adult clientele of American public libraries. In *Public librarianship: A reader.* Jane Robbins-Carter, ed. Littleton, CO: Libraries Unlimited. 189–205.

Introductions to the CINA Process

Assessing your community for library planning. 1987. Ontario: Ministry of Culture and Communications.

Greer, Roger, and Martha Hale. 1982. The community analysis process. In *Public librarianship: A reader.* Jane Robbins-Carter, ed. Littleton, CO: Libraries Unlimited. 358–366.

McKillip, Jack. 1987. *Need analysis: Tools for the human services and education.* Newbury Park, CA: Sage.

Warncke, Ruth. 1975. Analyzing your community: Basis for building library service. *Illinois Libraries.* 57 (2): 64–76.

Zweizig, Douglas. 1992. Community analysis. In *Keeping the books: Public library financial practices.* Jane Robbins and Douglas Zweizig, eds. Fort Atkinson, WI: Highsmith Press, for the Urban Libraries Council. 225–238.

The Planning Process and Its Relationship to Meeting Information Needs

Ruccio, Nancy. 1980. The planning process—Is it for me? *Rural Libraries.* 1 (4, fall): 45–87.

Differences between Various Types of Studies

Hernon, Peter, and Ellen Altman. 1996. *Service quality in academic libraries.* Norwood, NJ: Ablex.

Powell, Ronald R. January 1988. *The relationship of library user studies to performance measures: A review of the literature.* University of Illinois, Graduate School of Library and Information Science: Occasional Paper Number 181.

Zweizig, Douglas, and Eleanor Jo Rodger. 1982. *Output measures for public libraries: A manual of standardized procedures.* Chicago: American Library Association.

Chapter 2

Laying the Groundwork

Given the complexity of a community information-needs analysis (CINA), a moderate amount of time spent on the four elements of groundwork enhances results. First, decisions must be made regarding the level and nature of involvement sought from staff, administrators, and community members. Second, essential logistical procedures are established so that work can begin and continue efficiently. Third, initial communication tasks are completed to bring everyone up to speed on the study. Finally, basic decisions regarding an approach to the study are finalized. Attention to these four points lays a firm foundation to support execution of the study.

INVOLVING OTHERS

Study findings often suggest a number of changes and projects. The library staff members who will be called on to implement those changes and finish those projects need to understand the "whys" and "wherefores." The library director and, on occasion, institutional administrators who will be called on to authorize, fund, and support those changes require the same type of understanding. In certain situations, community members affected or served by those efforts also need to understand some aspects of the study upon which they are based.

Staff, administrators, and community members gain this required understanding in one of two ways. Either the study design and results are explained to them after the fact or they have some level of involvement in the study as it progresses. (The level and nature of that involvement could vary from receiving minimal information to actively gathering data.)

Hiring an outside consultant to run the information-needs analysis and present a report on the findings leads to an after-the-fact approach. Generally consultants involve and inform others, both within and beyond the library, to whatever extent is required of them but no more. Staff and community members may be subjects in the study but are not often partners. Much of the consultants' value lies in the swift efficiency with which they work and the objective authority implicit in their findings. These undoubtedly substantial benefits offset the cost of the consultants' services. When hiring a consultant is not feasible, a similar level of efficiency may be obtained by placing one or two experienced people in sole charge of the work.

On the other hand, another option is available: sacrificing efficiency for the possibility of long-term productivity by involving others in the process. That involvement could move up and down a continuum as needed and appropriate, from simple information to active participation. The long-term products could include any or all of the following: increased enthusiasm and support for implementing change, ability to gather data for other studies (e.g., evaluations or impact studies), ability to analyze data for other studies, and ability to supervise the entire process of running a small-scale study on a departmental level.

Obviously, any involvement of more than the minimum number needed to complete the study entails additional expenditures of time, resources, and energy. The anticipated benefits might fail, in any individual instance, to accrue. The decisions regarding who should be involved, and to what extent, require a great deal of judgment. For example, administrators outside the library interested only in the final report need nothing more. A burned-out staff member interested in a change of pace, on the other hand, may be considered as an investment opportunity. Given training in how to gather and analyze data, the individual might be a valued partner in the process as well as an advocate for any changes required by the work. When an evaluation study of those changes is eventually required, this burned-out staff member may be both able and willing to handle the task of running the study alone. The judgment to balance potential benefits against time invested and authority shared is essential.

GETTING ADMINISTRATIVE SUPPORT

Regardless of the level of involvement sought, getting and keeping administrative support throughout the process is critical. Without administrative support, librarians risk (a) designing an effective study that is then undermined by uninformed administrators and (b) producing findings that demand change but lack authority. The long-term damage to staff morale can be significant. Administrative support can not be taken lightly and must be carefully nurtured throughout the process. Two mechanisms—a written proposal and placement in the planning cycle—can be used to build this support.

Written Proposal

A brief written proposal for the CINA may be used to outline the nature of the study, anticipated benefits, and staff responsibilities. A proposal may mention other types of studies (e.g., evaluation) to clarify the purpose of the CINA through contrast. In any case, the proposal briefly lists reasons for the study and states goals of particular interest to the administration. Included also are sketchy notes regarding initial ideas on the process, procedures, and staffing for the study.

The most common administrative expectations may require discussion of the reasons that a CINA is needed instead of an impact study or an evaluation study. Since many administrators are familiar with impact studies and evaluations but not with CINAs, the proposal might need to explain the purpose and role of a

CINA. Librarians working with an administrator who really wants an impact study can point out why the needs analysis must come first. A productive CINA identifies the areas of need so that modifications can be made to service and collections. Only after those modifications are made should an impact study quantify the differences made by the library. Similarly an evaluation study evaluates library collections and services but the CINA must come first. "Quality" must be judged in terms of the standards valued by the user community. Only a CINA can determine what those standards really are.

Placement in the Planning Cycle

Since successful follow-up is the raison d'être for a community information-needs analysis, a clear statement of its relationship to the present planning cycle can support requests for any changes later suggested by the study findings. A rapidly growing city, for example, may have a five-year goal pertaining to the strength of local small businesses. An analysis of small-business information needs may provide concrete objectives toward that goal, objectives to which the library could contribute. Fitting the study into the annual work plan so that the results can support an Institute of Museum and Library Services (IMLS) or state grant application requires only modest effort.

GETTING MIDDLE MANAGEMENT AND GENERAL STAFF SUPPORT

Ideally, both administrative and staff support develop simultaneously. In larger libraries, however, a concentrated exploration of middle management and general staff support must be made with the same careful focus as that given to administrative support. While "administrators" are those with significant authority over resources and policy, "staff" includes those on the front lines—from volunteer shelvers in a public library to online searchers in an academic library. "Managers" include those whose rank falls between that of the library director and the front-line staff.

Effective changes based on the thoughtful, creative input of the entire staff are more likely to take place when most people feel genuinely invested in the process. That requires the librarian(s) instigating the CINA to sincerely involve and listen to those who want to participate. Involvement means, of course, that the staff gain some level of control over or input into the planning process, even if that control or input is extremely minor. The two simplest means of supporting that involvement are to (1) keep the staff informed and (2) give them the opportunity to provide respected feedback.

Those staff members and managers who do not want much involvement in the overall process may well be content with opportunities to learn about progress or give feedback at various stages. Their varied perspectives and relative objectivity can contribute substantially. They also provide flexibility, allowing other staff to weave planning meetings and data-gathering efforts into their regular duties. Those who lack an interest in the study may develop one later but there is no advantage in pushing them to participate.

As with administrators, staff and managers must see the need for the effort and understand the value of the methodology. This generally requires some education and time. Regular staff meetings, one-on-one chats, carefully selected routed articles, abstracts of persuasive readings, special meetings, and workshops can both persuade and inform. Again, the point is not to involve people against their will or to waste a moment in explaining what will only be ignored. The point is to engage those who will use the study as a significant growth experience, developing professional and research skills at a new level.

Brainstorming sessions, useful as a first step, can help in gathering interested staff to generate ideas on the overall process, question types, and study focus. (An alert librarian will also pick up on any staff concerns.) Fully involving interested frontline staff, regardless of job family, builds on the expertise and experience of people with differing perspectives. In a well-run brainstorming session, shelvers feel just as comfortable in revealing the problems they see patrons encounter in the stacks as instructional librarians feel in revealing the topics they want to cover in class but must drop for lack of time.

In extremely large or noncentralized library systems, another means of initially involving an experienced staff is the e-mail or paper questionnaire. This gives people a chance to identify what they'd like to know about their user community. Simply inviting people to list the top three topics they'd like to see covered in the study may be of use.

Being careful not to imply a promise to cover every topic suggested by staff, librarians beginning this process seriously consider staff input. By talking with selected individuals about why various elements are considered important, librarians develop a feel for the concerns and knowledge areas of the whole staff while gathering useful ideas for the study.

Even at this very early stage, patron confidentiality is crucial. For example, a particular professor's problems with the new OPAC might illustrate a point that someone wants covered. In using the professor's information need as an example, neither the name nor any identifying description should be used. Those used inadvertently are not to be repeated outside of the study context. Similarly, staff should refrain from identifying colleagues in any way. With the focus strongly held to users' needs, the essential ethics of research are not too difficult to maintain.

All of these conversations, readings, meetings, and general groundwork can take place over a couple of days or weeks, depending on staff familiarity with such studies and staff cohesion.

RESPONDING TO STAFF CONCERNS

Once staff and managers are thinking about the actual task ahead, some concerns might resurface or new ones may arise. These concerns should not be treated lightly because they can erupt unexpectedly later on in the process, causing great damage. Using the concerns to get a deeper commitment from the administration and more involvement from the staff is quite productive. Common concerns and possible responses are listed. Librarians and institutional administrators who address these concerns must provide consistent responses.

Common Staff Concerns
and Suggested Responses

Concerns	Responses
"This will be a waste of time; administrators do what they want anyway."	Have an administrator talk with the staff briefly about the importance of the project; get written support from an administrator at various points throughout the process; forward to the general staff all administrators' e-mail notices and memos praising the effort.
"This will just show us what we already know."	It probably will confirm some of what is already known. Some confirmation is likely any time the staff is good enough to build a general sense of users' needs. However, it may also show new directions and will certainly provide depth and detail beyond the general impressionistic level now known. Since the entire staff does not agree about all points of information needs, it will help clear up some areas of confusion. Decisions will be based on data rather than on squeaky-wheel anecdotes.
"I don't know how."	Training, as needed, is part of the process. Individuals will be given the opportunity to learn how to manage the process, gather data, and more. After these skills become part of the regular staff repertoire, they can be used in other projects as needed. The benefits of training everyone who would like to participate are long-term; therefore training is well worth the time it takes to do it well.

Concerns	Responses
"I'm afraid or uncomfortable with handing out surveys or interviewing or doing statistical analysis."	No one will be forced to do anything they find uncomfortable; no benefit comes from requiring people to do that which makes them tense. Likewise, various analytic jobs must be handled by those who can make smooth, rapid progress on them. Training often builds the confidence and interest necessary to overcome some levels of discomfort. Other people get over the discomfort after experiencing the satisfaction of getting to know members of the user community in greater depth.
"We're too busy doing our real job to do this extra stuff."	This project feeds into, supports, and directs everything done in the library. By focusing on the needs of the users, the staff increases the quality of each daily task. That quality is worth the time. This "extra stuff" makes all the regular essentials more effective.
"Okay then, what can we stop doing so we have time to do this?"	Several regular tasks can be dropped, postponed, or reduced for the duration of the study. Some concrete changes must be made. The following task changes might be made for a few months: teach 20 percent fewer classes; postpone implementation of an OPAC upgrade; order only patron-requested materials; have volunteers run story hours. The librarian in charge can also ask for staff suggestions regarding tasks to be temporarily modified. Administrative support for some changes may be essential. When staff are particularly concerned about finding time for the work, a clear schedule can be publicly posted for them to consult.

Concerns	Responses
"This will just show us more things to do that we don't have staff or time or money to handle."	Librarians have long faced the fact that their own success creates more work than their budgets will ever allow them to accomplish. Conducting a CINA does not alter the fact that staff can always identify new services with great prospects for success. The CINA does, however, allow staff to prioritize patron-identified needs. Additionally, the process may identify potential partners who could help provide resources and it may provide data that support a grant application.
"It's too costly. With no money for real raises, how can we find money for surveys?"	This concern can be met on several fronts but may well reflect a deeper problem unrelated to the CINA. From a financial standpoint, it makes good business sense to find out what patrons need, to raise patron awareness of library value, and to identify potential partnerships. A CINA can accomplish all three of those goals with varying degrees of success. While not the primary goal of the study, gathering information ultimately used in grant applications is not an uncommon result. Although successful grant applications and partnerships are not a given, it is possible to plan from the very beginning that efforts to raise money will be included in the follow-up. Also, the out-of-pocket expenses of a CINA can vary widely. Every effort can be made to reduce those costs through donations, the use of volunteers, and making full use of existing data.

Concerns	Responses
"This will be used to evaluate individuals; I'll be evaluated and criticized by my peers."	Since this concern may not be overtly expressed it is helpful to bring it up. Emphasizing that every effort will be made to keep staff names out of the data often helps clarify the intention of the study. Any patron or staff names mentioned inadvertently will be blanked out before any data are shared out for analysis. Positive comments will be shared with the named staff member who may decide to keep them private or share them with supervisors.
"Patrons don't know what they want anyway. We need to decide because we have the expertise."	Two misconceptions are involved in this response. First, some people envision the CINA as a means of creating a patron wish list. A good study identifies a full range of information needs, some recognized as such by patrons but some unrecognized. Second, some staff may fear that anything revealed as a need will be supported without regard for the expertise of the librarians involved in meeting that need. In reality, the judgment of the professional staff is the driving force behind each phase of the process, especially in the final decisions regarding the action plan created in response to the needs identified by the study. The expertise of librarians is not only respected by, but is crucial to, the CINA process.

Each of these concerns may resurface at some point in the process. Individuals may tune out discussions and information on the theory that they will not be involved, only to become interested at a later date. Incidents with patrons, unexpected opportunities, and changes in the information environment may trigger issues for groups or individuals.

SETTING UP LOGISTICAL PROCEDURES

Once there's a general institutional commitment to the information-needs analysis effort, someone must assume responsibility for getting it done. This can be an individual or a team. Assuming that a consultant is not involved and that staffing levels support it, a team of three is preferable because it allows for a range of knowledge areas, skills, and experiences.

In libraries too small to support a team approach, a needs assessment can certainly be accomplished by a single individual, but he or she must be given any assistance available from the parent institution when there are fewer than four full-time employees to help out. A one-librarian public library, for example, might have only two part-time, support-staff members; the township might offer secretarial services for the duration of the project. A school library might have only one librarian and a few volunteers; the principal might offer release time and secretarial services. So small a library requires the full support of administrators and, where possible, some aid from constituents. For example, the principal's aid is useful in a school setting, but faculty willingness to be flexible about library services for a few weeks could be more valuable.

A one-person approach requires special effort in two other areas besides administrative advocacy: judicious determination of the project's scope and active solicitation of alternative viewpoints. As discussed later in this chapter, determining the focus for the study involves a number of options. Obviously a full team provides the support for a wider range of those options than an individual can encompass. In addition, a special effort to obtain extra feedback during the planning stages is important for the lone librarian. Considered comments from colleagues in other libraries provide practical contexts, insights, and ideas.

Throughout the remaining chapters of this book, the entity responsible for the community information-needs assessment is referred to as a team on the theory that even an individual acting alone will seek out input from others.

Forming the Study Team

Team composition requires three attributes: authority, knowledge, and skills. Authority may be temporary so long as it's sufficient; knowledge and skills can develop from workshops, readings, and training sessions.

AUTHORITY

Someone must have the authority to make quick decisions on those occasions when team consultation is simply not possible. Additionally, at least one team member must have the authority to get resources needed for the project, such as staff time, copying, access to volunteers, and approval to publicly distribute documents (e.g., questionnaires).

KNOWLEDGE

Knowledge of three areas must be incorporated into the team. First, knowledge of the study's context is crucial. New librarians will lack a thorough understanding of the library's history. Only long-term staff will understand the nuances of staffing histories, policy changes, service development, community relations, and political connections. The study will be deeply embedded in the history of the library and the community which it serves. Knowledge of that history and a profound understanding of the current situation are essential.

Second, a grasp of data-gathering and data-analysis methodologies is required. Someone may need to train both staff and volunteers and then support them when they need advice during the process. A background in research methodology is also useful when explaining and justifying the data-gathering techniques to staff, administrators, and the community.

Finally, awareness of the changing environment is helpful and, in some situations, essential. Because of rapidly changing technology and telecommunications, many patrons do not even recognize some information needs because they do not know what is possible. When they use a word processor rather than a typewriter, they see an improvement but they do not know to ask for an integrated workstation. Only someone who knows that a workstation is possible would analyze the data with that option in mind. Similarly, such knowledge is crucial in understanding the needs of the sophisticated patron who expects high-end electronic information support.

SKILLS

In addition to authority and knowledge, certain skills make a major contribution to the team. The ability to keep on track is essential. It is particularly important in maintaining the distinction between a community information-needs analysis and an evaluation or an impact study. Without the firm control necessary to remain on focus, sliding into the accepted, more common patterns of an evaluation is all too easy. The ability to remain flexible is always required as plans will have to be adjusted to new circumstances and the unexpected. The ability to manage logistics and detail, a basic job requirement in technical services, is valuable over the course of the study. The ability to synthesize varied data into a cohesive set of patterns, needs, and ideas becomes critical in the data-analysis phase. Finally, the ability to understand the users' perspectives, as well as the perspective of the nonuser, serves the team throughout the study. A frank discussion of the varied skills each person contributes to the team builds a unified expectation of individuals' roles.

Obviously it is rarely possible to choose a team whose members have all the authority, knowledge, and skills ideal for the work. Nevertheless, keeping these elements in mind when choosing the team develops an awareness of missing elements. An effort can then be made to structure work and seek input in such a manner as to mitigate any weaknesses.

Handling Decisions

Once the team has been established, the process for handling decisions must be determined. Must everything be reported to the administration? If so, does that entail the library administration, the parent institution, or both? Do institutional lawyers need to review any decisions for any reason? For example, in working with minors, do institutional policies, confidentiality, or other ethical/legal elements need to pass through a separate layer of authority?

Who controls access to distribution mechanisms? Is the library director allowed to decide what will be sent to whom on what schedule? Quite often the governing board of a public library or an institutional administrator wants to review, revise, and control such decisions. Given the likelihood that a nonlibrarian's understanding of the study is severely limited, that control can be devastating. A university's library committee should not rewrite a well-designed, pretested questionnaire. A well-planned series of community contacts should not be disrupted pending the approval of a city administrator who is off on vacation. The principal should not insist on signing the questionnaire cover letter when the library director is planning to use it as part of a public relations effort. If possible, obtain written permission to inform administrators of the decisions made by the study team and approved by the library director. Keeping administrators informed without relying on them for permission places authority and responsibility together.

Even if administrators require very little reporting from the team, they should be kept informed of major decisions. Information prepares them so they are less likely to balk later. For example, administrators informed early in the study that the CINA will center on information-technology issues will be better prepared to discuss changes in that area at the study's end.

Informed administrators can also alert the team when a separate library project might impact the study. Sensitive budget negotiations, hiring freezes, and personnel discussions might impact timing of the study but ongoing details might also be affected. For example, giving an administrator the schedule of a planned postal mail questionnaire may prompt team notification of a mailed fund-drive request scheduled for the same time. The two are not incompatible but their simultaneous arrival might confuse and frustrate the public; rescheduling one or the other would increase the odds of success for both. While sharing all of the process with administrators is recommended, it is absolutely essential that they be informed about anything connected with legal or financial matters.

ACCOMPLISHING INITIAL TASKS

Once the team and its basic decision-reporting model are established, two initial tasks move the process toward a solid start: conducting a literature review and seeking partners. Both tasks inform and support the next round of decisions. The literature review garners information on the needs of users who share important characteristics with those in the team's population. In addition, the resulting readings can spark ideas and discussions among team members regarding any phase of the process—from instrument design to the final report. Seeking partners, on the other hand, is a concrete, practical step usefully repeated at various stages.

Conducting a Literature Review

One member of the team looks into recent research and practice literature for insights regarding the information-seeking patterns of the population. In-depth studies of information needs in similar communities may well have been completed within the past several years as part of the continual development in information-needs work. Articles such as the one by Leckie et al. (1996) describe the information-seeking behaviors and needs of engineers, lawyers, and others. Using *Library Literature* (and any other pertinent indexes such as *ERIC* or *Business Periodicals Index*), the researcher looks for informative articles and books.

In some cases, the researcher may be lucky enough to find a meta-analysis identifying trends and patterns in several major studies. Others may find research studies on a particularly crucial aspect of their community's situation; academic medical librarians, for example, would probably be interested in a study of how new information technology affects the information seeking of health sciences faculty (Curtis et al., 1997). Similarly, the federal government and other special agencies sometimes undertake a pertinent review. For example, the U.S. Department of Education's survey of services and resources for children in public libraries provides a national benchmark as a comparison for local services (Lewis and Farris, 1990).

Of course, major gaps still exist in the research literature. One such gap, as Virginia Walter points out, is in the area of children's information needs in both school and public library settings (1994, 112). Another wide gap looms in the area of rural public libraries. Shilts reviews one of the few existing studies while pointing out how little is known about their users, much less their nonusers (1991; see also Christensen et al. 1995, and Vavrek 1995). The Works Cited and Suggested Readings portions of this book provide a starting point for further study.

Once the team has made some decisions regarding data-gathering methods (see chapter 4), it is useful to repeat the literature review with an eye for studies utilizing similar tools in similar settings. Team members can write to the authors of such articles asking for copies of their data-gathering instruments. Sometimes it is productive to telephone or e-mail them to discuss the process and ask their advice. Some librarians who have been through the CINA process and written up the results for publication are quite willing to converse with colleagues just beginning that effort.

Similarly, check the World Wide Web for instruments, readings, and colleagues of potential value. Some library and information school faculty Web sites include bibliographies for their courses on different types of libraries and research methodologies.

Seeking Partners

As the team researcher works on readings and Web sites, another member knowledgeable in local politics identifies potential partners for the team to consider approaching. Even at these early planning stages, partners have a good deal to offer, including ideas, supplies, access to subpopulations, and staffing. Partnering with academic computing, for example, may give a university library team ideas about the problems experienced by remote-site users. Public librarians partnering with a copier service could get questionnaires supplied at cost. Partnering with the P.T.A. may pro-

vide a school library team with a cadre of volunteers for a telephone interview campaign. The politically savvy team member
identifies either the broadest range of potential partners or a few
strong possibilities.

In choosing among potential partnerships, the team considers
contact timing, reciprocity, and influence. The ideal timing of that
first contact with a potential partner varies widely. Those who contribute critical ideas need full involvement early in the process.
Those who contribute practical support in the data-gathering stage
require a brief contact initially, but the vast majority of their work
comes later. In school libraries, for example, site-based management of school districts may make it possible to involve faculty,
parents, and administrators on a variety of timetables. Administrators and master teachers may identify major concerns in the
planning stages while active parents provide data-gathering support by distributing questionnaires.

Reciprocity requires consideration not only of what the partner can give the library but a look at what benefits the partner
receives. Thinking about potential benefits for the partner helps
the librarian shape an effective approach. Benefits vary greatly: a
business benefits from publicity, volunteers may enjoy the satisfaction of participating in a worthwhile community effort, and
university faculty may meet some of their service obligations.

Influence involves far more nebulous issues. What expectations
are raised by inviting an individual, group, or organizational unit
to form a partnership with the library? Will members of the county
genealogical society expect to influence questionnaire design or
study results if they volunteer to canvass the general population?
Conflicts of interest may develop in arenas of mutual interest.
School librarians interested in curriculum-design issues pertaining
to information-literacy units, for example, may both partner with
and conflict with faculty on that topic. Someone on the team needs
the tact and political savvy required to move a relationship into a
partnership.

MAKING INITIAL DECISIONS

Building on the background work in research and partnerships, the team moves on to four initial decisions regarding the purpose, focus, use of consultants, and end product of the study. Clearly any of these decisions may be revisited later but both staff and administration benefit from the direction provided by these first decisions.

Purpose

As mentioned earlier, any of several purposes may lie behind a community information-needs analysis and they are not equally valid. Different groups or individuals may have different agendas; therefore, open acknowledgment of, group discussion on, and strong consensus regarding the study's purpose are critical. Poor reasons for the CINA generally tie in to an individual's strongly held opinion or belief. A top administrator may hope to prove that a long-cherished plan will solve some ongoing problem, or librarians in each of two departments may hope to raise the priority given to their own work, or a middle manager may hope to gather data to support a budget request. A study whose purpose is based on the ego or agenda of a staff member is doomed to failure. The purpose must be to gather substantive data on community information needs, not to gather data supporting an extant plan.

Of course in some situations no hidden agenda lurks but no clear, viable purpose is discernible either. Information-needs studies, like Mom and apple pie, are sometimes seen as just plain "good" so that an administrator may order one on general principles. In that case, the team must choose or at least prioritize among the broad purposes for the study.

- Do it to help everyone get a vision of where the library is going in the next few years. A user-centered focus for the library's general direction is a powerful antidote to the feeling common in libraries these days that technological storms obscure what little vision is possible.

- Do it to gather data for making a decision that must be made and could be better informed. Staff cuts, new branches, or consolidated branches may be required by external forces. The CINA becomes a tool for gathering the data necessary to make those inevitable decisions more effective and palatable.
- Do it as a reality check on the assumptions everyone uses in making all those cumulative daily decisions. Complacent, acquiescent, or even disgruntled staff might be reinvigorated and challenged by a CINA, particularly if it explores their most basic assumptions from a patron's perspective.
- Do it as a means of better handling general changes in the library that are either happening or expected. A public library might develop an extensive Web site to serve a large number of home-bound adults and home-schooled children in the community. Exploring the information needs of both groups would guide that ongoing change.
- Do it to establish a baseline to keep track of changing community or environmental trends. Many public librarians find themselves serving communities with rapidly changing demographics. Perhaps an influx of young families with high computer expectations followed the opening of a new IBM plant in town. Perhaps the sudden availability of reliable telecommunications service providers makes remote-site access to the public library more of a patron expectation. A CINA not only provides information for current services but can also provide a baseline—useful, when combined with future CINAs, in tracking trends.

Certainly other general purposes are possible, given individual circumstances. After the team determines the primary purpose, a focus can be determined.

Focus

Five key elements might serve as a focus. Most teams select one, but some teams will choose two or even three elements. This is the time to think honestly about how much time and energy is available for the CINA. As always, good librarians can envision more than is realistically possible to do so a viable focus becomes a touchstone. Any efforts to expand or redefine the study are compared with the focus in order to stay on track. The five common foci are:

- subpopulations,
- specific topics,
- environmental changes,
- library responsibilities, and
- an overview.

Choosing any one of them does not exclude the others.

SUBPOPULATIONS

An open-minded examination of underexamined subpopulations may provide a focus for the study. Certainly some subpopulations require greater understanding than others. Patrons who are on the edge of nonuse merit study. For example, a public library with high attendance at preschool story hours might notice that those same children rarely return to the library after entering public school. Those children and their parents are on the edge of nonuse in that last year before first grade. They use the library minimally and might become strong users if the right changes were made, therefore they merit more work than an arbitrarily demographic subpopulation such as pet-owners.

Obviously, any library team should consider their nonusers and why they do not use the library. Academic libraries often focus efforts on the research faculty. They are strong and powerful users but are far outnumbered by students. A study of that large but underexamined subpopulation, the students, could be quite revealing. How many public librarians have seriously delved into the needs of their young adult patrons? The team must face rationalizations for *not* studying a subpopulation. Choosing to study a subpopulation does not mean that the remaining population will be ignored; it does mean that a concerted effort to examine those needs will lead the study.

SPECIFIC TOPICS

Some specific topics may require in-depth exploration. Technology presents opportunities, raises user expectations, and creates service challenges for librarians. As a specific topic, therefore, technology often provides an excellent focus for an information-needs analysis. The results improve service and can sometimes be incorporated into grant applications.

Another useful topic, patron information channels, builds a deeper understanding of the library's place in patron information seeking. What other individuals, resources, and organizations are utilized by patrons and why? Thinking about other information resources leads the team into a fresh examination of basic assumptions about the "best" way to serve their patrons.

ENVIRONMENTAL CHANGE

A specific environmental change (e.g., new growth in the community) may require particular attention. No community stands still; evolution is the norm. Understanding those ongoing developments allows the library to stay ahead of the curve. When the broad purpose of the CINA is to understand environmental change, the specific focus might be the reading interests or educational needs of the community. Are more members of the public library population looking for financial and medical reading matter than traditional user profiles lead the staff to expect? Do teaching assistants need extensive instruction on information retrieval strategies from their college library?

LIBRARY'S RESPONSIBILITIES

Fourth, a segment of the library's responsibilities (e.g., services or collections) may face new challenges or opportunities. In developing a long-range plan for equipment expenditures or service expansion, library administrators might need a CINA's hard data to inform their decision making. Specific responsibilities worth study include remote-site access, document delivery, off-site reference support, personalized reference service, and instructional services.

OVERVIEW OF COMMUNITY NEEDS

The single most common focus is a broad overview of the community's needs. This is particularly useful when no baseline data from a previous analysis exists and no large-scale changes are in the works. Examining the full population on a broad range of expectations, issues, behaviors, and information-seeking situations requires that particular attention be paid to sampling and instrument design to avoid the "kitchen-sink" syndrome in which everyone's pet topic is thrown into the research design.

Consultants

After the study's broad purpose and specific focus are in place, the team may again consider hiring a consultant for part or all of the process. A good consultant can help with several elements, including research design, staff training, data gathering, data analysis (both statistical and narrative), grant applications, and logistical support. It is obviously quite efficient to place responsibility for all of these elements into the hands of someone who is not meeting the daily demands of running the library.

Using a consultant to run the entire study has the added advantage of giving the team an "out" by having an "objective" uninvolved person make all the decisions. No one can claim that personal relationships or self-interest influenced decisions. (Of course, the team is still responsible for making the major decisions that direct the consultant's work.) A consultant can certainly provide credibility with the staff, community, and administrators.

In some cases, winning a grant to fund the process can mitigate the great expense of a consultant. Some consultants will apply for a grant as part of their contract.

End Product

Whether or not a consultant is used, the team next considers the end product of the CINA and how it will reflect the purpose and focus of the study. Will the study produce a quiet, internal report for the information of staff alone, a set of concrete recommendations for administrators regarding the budget and services, material for a public discussion of the findings, or some other item? Team discussion of this concrete goal provides a forum for ironing out any lingering conflicts in purpose.

The team prepares a brief planning report for staff, managers, and administrators explaining: what the study is expected to accomplish (possibly involving a goals-and-objectives format), what the end product will consist of, and who, at a minimum, will see it. This document informs staff of the team's key decisions and clarifies any administrative goals for the project. (The case studies include examples of such documents.) For example, when the dean of a university library system plans to merge two libraries, then the document makes both the dean's decision and the CINA's purpose clear. It states that the CINA is being conducted primarily to support the many decisions middle managers must make as part of that merger process by analyzing community information needs. In such a case, only the dean and middle managers may see and act on the full report but an abbreviated version may be made available to the full staff. Concise, up-front statements regarding these major initial decisions mitigate staff concerns and provide the team with a focused beginning.

SUMMARY

Since it is not an end in itself, the community information-needs analysis must ultimately be placed in the context of the budget, the library's mission, the parent institution's mission, and the general information environment. The team's decisions throughout the next phases will incorporate those realities more fully. All of this decision making moves quite rapidly with no need for extensive discussion and massive documentation. While important, these broad questions must launch the process, not hold it back.

CHAPTER 2 READINGS

Involving Others

Greer, Roger, and Martha Hale. 1982. The community analysis process. In *Public librarianship: A reader.* Jane Robbins-Carter, ed. Littleton, CO: Libraries Unlimited. 358–366.

Zweizig, Douglas. 1992. Community analysis. In *Keeping the books: Public library financial practices.* Jane Robbins and Douglas Zweizig, eds. Fort Atkinson, WI: Highsmith Press, for the Urban Libraries Council. 225–238.

Public Library Studies

Bolton, W. Theodore. 1982. Life style research: An aid to promoting public libraries. *Library Journal.* (May 15): 963–968.

Harris, Denise. 1989. Community surveys. *The Cape Librarian.* 33: 2–5.

Martin, Lowell. 1944. Community analysis for the community. In *The library in the community: Papers presented before the Library Institute at the University of Chicago August 23–28, 1943.* Leon Carnovsky and Lowell Martin, eds. Chicago: University of Chicago Press. 201–214.

Sarling, Jo Haight, and Debra S. Van Tassel. 1999. Community analysis: Research that matters to a north-central Denver community. *Library and Information Science Research.* 21 (1): 7–29.

School Library Study

Walter, Virginia A. 1994. The information needs of children. *Advances in Librarianship.* New York: Academic Press. 18: 111–129.

Academic Library Studies

Berger, Kenneth, and Richard Hines. 1994. What does the user *really* want? The Library User Survey Project at Duke University. *Journal of Academic Librarianship.* 20 (November): 306–309.

Clougherty, Leo, John Forys, Toby Lyles, Dorothy Persson, Christine Walters, and Carlette Washington-Hoagland. 1998. The University of Iowa libraries' undergraduate user needs assessment. *College and Research Libraries.* 59 (6): 572–584.

McClure, Charles, and Cynthia Lopata. February 1996. *Assessing the academic networked environment: Strategies and options.* Washington, DC: Coalition for Networked Information.

Parrish, Marilyn. 1989. Academic community analysis: Discovering research needs of graduate students at Bowling Green State University. *College and Research Libraries News.* 8 (September): 644–646.

Using Consultants

Green, Joseph. 1989. The ideal consultant. *Library Journal.* 114 (February 15): 133–135.

Matthews, Joseph. 1994. The effective use of consultants in libraries. *Library Technology Reports.* 30 (November/December): 745–814.

Weinberg, Gerald. 1985. *The secrets of consulting: A guide to giving and getting advice successfully.* Foreword by Virginia Satir. New York: Dorset House.

Literature Review

Babbie, Earl. 1998. *The practice of social research.* 8th edition. Belmont, CA: Wadsworth. {See chapter 6.}

Powell, Ronald R. 1997. *Basic research methods for librarians.* 3rd edition. Greenwich, CT: Ablex. {See 205–210 for a number of specialized resources.}

Readings which Illustrate the Value of a Study

Clougherty, Leo, et al. 1998. The University of Iowa libraries' undergraduate user needs assessment. *College and Research Libraries.* 59 (6, November): 572–584.

Westbrook, Lynn. 2000. Analyzing community information needs: A holistic approach. *Library Administration and Management.* 14 (1, winter): 26–30.

Zweizig, Douglas L. 1992. Community analysis. In *Keeping the books: Public library financial practices.* Jane B. Robbins and Douglas L. Zweizig, eds. Fort Atkinson, WI: Highsmith Press: 225–238.

Grant Resources

Barber, Peggy, and Linda D. Crowe. 1993. *Getting your grant: A how-to-do-it manual for librarians.* How-To-Do-It Manuals for Librarians, number 28. New York: Neal-Schuman.

Big book of library grant money, 1998–99. 1998. Chicago: American Library Association.

National Guide to Funding for Libraries and Information Services. 1999. 5th edition. New York: Foundation Center.

National Guide to Funding for Information Technology. 1999. 2nd edition. New York: Foundation Center.

Meta-analysis Example (useful in a literature review)

Harris, Michael, and James Sodt. 1981. Libraries, users, and librarians: Continuing efforts to define the nature and extent of public library use. In *Advances in librarianship.* 11: 110–133. New York: Academic Press.

Chapter 3

Preparing to Conduct a Study

After making the critical, initial decisions, the community information-needs analysis (CINA) team begins actual preparation for the study by examining the resources, identifying the stakeholders, and understanding the ethical considerations of the study. By now some word of the study may be circulating among members of the user population and the staff, who should be fully informed, of course, of the general plan. As these next preparatory steps are being taken, the CINA team insures that all staff members are prepared to answer basic patron questions and make appropriate referrals to those librarians who are fully involved in the project.

RESOURCES

The practical realities of any given situation do much to determine the extent and nature of a particular CINA. As discussed in the previous chapter, hiring a consultant (who may or may not seek a grant to cover costs) is an option for some librarians. Assuming that option is not open to the team, a knowledgeable, thoughtful analysis of the three primary resources must be made immediately. First, staff skills, knowledge, and experience comprise the most flexible resource. Second, determining the time actually available for the project establishes a necessary parameter. Third, funding and materials both provide and limit the avenues open to the team.

A different member of the team should take responsibility for determining the extent of each of the three resources, if possible.

Staff Skills, Knowledge, and Experience

Looking at staff from this perspective requires the ability to look beyond rank and job responsibilities. The team member in charge of this work needs to talk briefly with some staff and, in large libraries, to make a substantial effort to identify individuals with various contributions to make to the study. A quick e-mail note or conversation with a supervisor asking people about their coursework or experience in questionnaire design, interviewing, or data analysis could identify unexpected expertise.

Even in a one-person library, some time might be productively spent in identifying the strengths of volunteers or counterparts in other areas. The administrator who supports the CINA for a one-person library should make available the resources of others wherever possible. Perhaps the office secretary could run a simple statistical analysis on the main computer or manage the basic logistics of a mail questionnaire. A volunteer shelver might have conducted interviews before retiring. Looking beyond rank and job family might reveal untapped resources.

A number of staff skills, knowledge areas, and experiences have potential use in the study, including experience or training with formal questionnaires, interviews, focus groups, observations; the ability to speak easily with strangers; the ability to handle telephone interviews; the ability to manage simple statistical analysis; the expertise to manage narrative data analysis. Managing the flow of data requires the ability to handle detail, keep accurate records, and sort and organize materials. Analyzing the data requires an open mind with few preconceptions as well as the ability to recognize patterns and notice unexpected gaps.

As discussed in coming chapters, staff training of various sorts may be needed. The team might invest in some general training on the management of a needs analysis as one means of identifying staff who have special contributions to make to the process. Through the groundwork already completed, most staff should have a sense of what is happening. A team member might now want to offer an informal but more complete overview for those who are interested in the process. A casual staff meeting, perhaps at a brown-bag lunch, could provide the forum for an explanation of the team, the study focus, and the decision-making process so that people can better understand what they might have to offer. Obviously more training may be needed when specific methods have been chosen but this first step gives people a sense of what is possible and encourages people to think of themselves as potential contributors. For example, talking about how easy it is to conduct exit interviews or distribute questionnaires to groups can be tucked into a regular staff meeting to prime the pump.

Time

Time is a hidden cost that is often underestimated. This work can not be folded into regular duties. As mentioned earlier, the team (and administrators if appropriate) need to decide what work will be stopped or postponed for the duration. The team can certainly complete the study more efficiently by hiring someone to take over routine work for a few weeks if that's an option. (If so, try to get someone who already works for the library or who has completed an internship there. This prevents training from taking a disproportionate amount of the time gained.)

After considering every possible mechanism for gaining time, the team member in charge of this resource must determine a realistic time frame for the entire study. Looking for seasonal, irregular, and one-time interruptions to the regular work flow in the next six months should provide the data needed for this task. Does any department in the library plan new initiatives? Are any building, maintenance, or capital improvements planned? Is the administration or some peer unit relying on the library staff for a special project? The ideal is to identify a six- to eight-week period for data collection and analysis followed by an additional month for the CINA team to complete the final report with recommendations. Of course, the scope of the study, size of the staff, and similar factors dictate variations on that guideline.

Funding and Materials

This review of funding is general, unlike the detailed budget possible after a specific plan of action is completed. By becoming aware of funding elements the team makes maximum use of each resource and begins to keep administrators aware of the costs. Of course, a budget—no matter how modest—must have clearly defined elements. Are unlimited mailing, copying, and stationery costs included along with ten hours of support staff assistance for each of eight weeks? Is a set budget of $1,000.00 available for use as the team sees fit? Are fine-forgiveness coupons, free online searches, or free video loans available as incentives to study participants? The administration, either of the library or of the parent institution, needs to clearly identify exactly what funds and supplies are available for the study.

In addition, the team member in charge of this resource looks for partners to help with costs and activities. For example, will a local copier company help with the layout and/or print questionnaires for free? Will scout troops distribute questionnaires in the local mall? Will the college computer maven distribute an anonymous e-mail questionnaire en masse to faculty with automatic tabulation of results? Will a campus student organization take on the distribution of questionnaires as a group project? This part of the resource analysis requires imagination and a willingness to knock on doors, both metaphorically and literally.

In addition, identifying local costs for common expenses (e.g., copying, mass mailings, telephone questionnaires, meeting space, and newspaper advertisements) provides essential information. Explaining the purpose of the expenditure can sometimes lead to a price reduction if some acknowledgment of the donation is made. Of course, the library administrators must approve any such arrangement; therefore, this is the time to determine their opinion on the matter.

Team members can share the results of their resource investigations informally via e-mail or through brief lists of key factors. Potential staff resources, for example, could be listed with due consideration for privacy. Any limitations on or factors involved in time can be written up in a quick paragraph to share. The funding and materials available to the team should be listed in a memo with a copy sent to administrators—just to keep everyone fully informed.

IDENTIFYING STAKEHOLDERS

Stakeholders, in this context, are those groups, or individuals (whether or not they are library patrons), who have a strong interest in the library and its services. It is important to identify these groups. Some of these interest groups constitute formal organizations or units while others are informal social groupings. School libraries, for example, may identify parents and the P.T.A. library committee as stakeholders even though their information needs fall outside the library's mission statement. Public libraries may identify the local genealogy club, the Parks and Recreation Center's library liaison, and the Chamber of Commerce's Web site designer as stakeholders.

Users may be identified by "systems" as well as by the traditional demographic or organizational groupings. Any of the following systems could substantially supplement more formal means of identifying stakeholders: cultural, political, or membership groups, reference groups, invisible colleges, formal organizations, project teams, legal/economic systems, and information marketplaces (Ford 1977).

Public libraries can identify established groups (e.g., the League of Women Voters and Mothers Against Drunk Driving) as well as ad hoc groups (e.g., coalitions fighting zoning changes) as stakeholders. Citizen groups in the public policy arena require a wide range of information resources and services. These grassroots groups grow out of church affiliations, social concerns, local governmental issues, political convictions, and more. They differ in their duration, local impact, resources, and focus.

Of course, major public-library user groups, such as children and adults, are stakeholders in their own right without reference to any other specific groups or systems they might join. Groups are identified by their specialized interests (such as genealogy), needs (such as large print), or life-situations (such as parenthood or retirement).

School and academic library stakeholder identifications develop readily from the natural groupings within the educational community. Faculty, students, and staff constitute the most obvious groups, although each of these requires significant subdivision. Sometimes a simple annual report for the institution totals the constituents in each group so that a matrix is readily constructed detailing the pertinent numbers.

After identifying the major stakeholders in the community, the team steps back from the list in order to make a special effort to identify any "invisible users" who have a stake in the library but rarely intrude on staff notice. A public library might have a number of patrons who come in almost daily to check the financial news. They never need help, never check anything out, and never request new materials but they are definitely stakeholders. Academic libraries might have invisible users who search the OPAC and other databases on a remote-site basis and drop in to copy articles without ever encountering staff. School libraries might have a population of magazine browsers who drop by before class or during lunch. Since identifying the needs of these invisible users is extremely difficult for obvious reasons, this initial effort at identification is particularly valuable.

After identifying all of these stakeholder groups as fully as possible, the team considers them as potential short-term partners for the duration of the needs assessment, as possible long-term partners, and as valued patrons whose needs must be fully explored in the study. Although full-scale sampling of the population comes later in the study, identifying stakeholders and considering their role in the study is one step in that process.

While identifying the needs of nonusers is important, there is a special value in serving fully the needs of heavy users since they constitute the current support base. One public librarian exemplified this value when she noted that homeschoolers provided "strong, vocal" support of the libraries during a critical referendum (Sager 1995, 204) in her district. Therefore, each of these groups should be identified and their role fully considered.

ETHICAL CONSIDERATIONS

As the final step in preparing to design the actual study, team members review ethical and legal considerations. Particularly if members are inexperienced in research involving people, the CINA team thoroughly reviews these essential points of proper research design. Within the context of informed consent, in every setting, three principles are followed to the letter:

1. the anonymity, or confidentiality, of everyone involved is maintained;
2. library service delivery and quality never even appear to hinge on patron cooperation in the study; and
3. no harm comes to any subject, directly or indirectly, through any aspect of the study.

Confusing anonymity with confidentiality is not uncommon. The team must be able to explain the difference to both staff and patrons. Anonymity means that there is no possible mechanism to tie a particular individual to a particular response. Confidentiality means that at least one member of the study team knows (or could readily discover) exactly who said what but the promise is made that the team member will not reveal that information to anyone outside the team or even mention it unnecessarily to the team. Some methods, such as interviews and focus groups, require in-person contact, destroying anonymity, but the promise of confidentiality (often given both verbally and in writing) is still made.

Obviously, the team has a special obligation to keep patron records confidential. They can not, for example, make a list of all patrons who have checked out books on homeschooling and then call them up to ask if there is any other service they would like to see in that arena. Although very practical in some ways, such a method shatters the expectation that patron borrowing records are private.

In libraries serving children, special care must taken to observe the rights of minors. For any contact that is substantial in nature (e.g., an interview) or might lead to problematic findings (e.g., in-depth questions to teenagers on personal information needs), special care is required. In addition to gaining the permission of their parents or guardians, the team needs to plan on gaining the permission of the children themselves if they are of an age to give it.

Support mechanisms exist for all of these ethical issues. Almost any local college or university has a Human Subject Review Committee. When in doubt, a team member might contact the committee chair to ask for a little quick advice. Of course, if a Library and Information Studies program is available in the community, the program secretary can make a referral to the faculty member who teaches research methods. As a community service, some faculty are willing to meet for a brief discussion of well-considered analysis plans. Some discussion list communities are productive forums for asking about specific ethical concerns. In any case, the issues at hand are sufficiently complex and serious to merit the time it takes to insure strict ethical compliance.

CHAPTER 3 READINGS

Resources

Tygett, Mary, V. Lonnie Lawson, and Kathleen Weessies. 1996. Using undergraduate marketing students in an unobtrusive reference evaluation. *RQ*. 36 (2, winter): 270–276.

Subpopulations

Evans, G. Edward. 1992. Needs analysis and collection development policies for culturally diverse populations. *Collection Building*. 11 (4): 16–27.

Gonzalez, Michael, Bill Greeley, and Stephen Whitney. 1980. Assessing the library needs of the spanish-speaking. *Library Journal*. April 1: 786–789.

Güereña, Salvador. 1990. Community analysis and needs assessment. In *Latino librarianship: A handbook for professionals*. Salvador Güereña, ed. Jefferson, NC: McFarland. 17–23.

Haro, Robert. 1981. *Developing library and information services for*

Americans of Hispanic origin. Metuchen, NJ: Scarecrow Press. {See chapter 2.}

Stenback, Tanis, and Alvin Schrader. 1999. Venturing from the closet: A qualitative study of the information needs of lesbians. *Public Library Quarterly*. 17 (3): 37–50.

Ethics

Krathwohl, David. 1998. *Methods of educational and social science research: An integrated approach*. 2nd edition. New York: Longman. {See chapter 10.}

Sieber, Joan. 1992. *Planning ethically responsible research: A guide for students and internal review boards*. Applied Social Research Methods Series, volume 31. Newbury Park, CA: Sage.

Westbrook, Lynn. 1997. Qualitative research. In *Basic research methods for librarians*. By Ronald R. Powell. 3rd edition. Greenwich, CT: Ablex. {See 145–146.}

Public Library Patrons

Durrance, Joan C. 1984. *Armed for action: Library response to citizen information needs*. New York: Neal-Schuman.

Chapter 4

Framing Questions and Choosing Tools

After basic preparation for the study, the community information-needs analysis (CINA) team moves through a two-step process, framing the research questions for the study and choosing the data-gathering techniques.

FRAMING THE RESEARCH QUESTIONS

Research questions are *not* the actual questions posed to subjects in the study; instead they function like goals in that they are the large questions that the study must answer. The team generates these research questions by considering four points:

- background of the study
- required questions
- probable questions
- possible questions.

Background

Framing the research questions requires the CINA team to determine their own perspective on "information needs" as background for the process. Looking at their library in terms of the library mission, the library functions, information and knowledge needs, user study approaches, and technology shifts, the team quickly establishes a perspective to use in framing the research questions. As explained below, each of these issues contributes to the team's functioning framework. Once that framework is determined, the team moves quickly to determine the actual research questions. The first half-hour of a planning meeting should bring consensus on these points, barring significantly contrasting perspectives.

THE LIBRARY MISSION

A realistic assessment of the library's mission launches the effort to frame the research questions for the study. What is the role of the library within the community? Is the CINA open to redefining that role based on community needs? If so, would the administration and staff be open to such a change? As an example, in a school library adding "curriculum design" and "faculty consultant" to the mission statement would be reasonable if the study revealed that flexible, rather than fixed, scheduling best met the needs of students and faculty. Would the principal be open to such a change? In a public library, would the director be willing to partner with the local P.T.A. and school libraries, adding "support community homework and tutoring programs" to the mission in place of an assumption that all support for school work is the responsibility of the school libraries? If the answer is a definite "no," other areas of focus may produce more useful results. A quick review of the existing mission with an eye to its potential for development establishes one very practical parameter for study questions.

THE LIBRARY FUNCTIONS

The CINA team can consider the basic library functions when the library's mission seems too vague or generalized to be useful. The six traditional library functions involve supporting the archival, cultural, educational, recreational, informational, and research needs of a community (Greer and Hale 1982, 359; see Works Cited for full citations). Does the library have other functions? Should it have others? Are any of those classic functions inappropriate or handled by another unit? For example, an academic library may have no obligation to meet recreational needs, and another administrative unit may carry out the archival function.

INFORMATION AND KNOWLEDGE NEEDS

Yet another means of framing the study's research questions develops from a concentration on the two most common types of information needs, namely "knowledge" and "information." Kim and Little (1987, 7) define the former as an "understanding of a subject matter" and the latter as "a set of facts." To what extent is the library staff responsible for actually developing knowledge in their patrons? What level and type of pure "information" delivery is expected or needed? Using this perspective, Phillips and Zorn, working from a hospital library, found that 69 percent of their community had unmet consumer health information needs (1994, 291). This finding bolstered their successful grant application for funds to use in establishing a consumer health library (1994, 289). The progression from defining to discovering to serving a user need may follow from any open-minded review of basic assumptions.

USER STUDY PERSPECTIVES

In addition to these issues, the CINA team could consider framing their questions in terms of the six traditional perspectives of user studies. Dervin and Clark delineate these perspectives as examinations of:

1. the demands that users place on the library system;
2. the level of community awareness concerning library services and collections;
3. the level of community satisfaction with existing services and collections;

4. the priorities that people place on existing or possible library services and collections;
5. the demographic and environmental components of a community, particularly those affecting information needs;
6. the personal interests and activities of those in the community, particularly those from which information needs may be inferred (1987, 4–5).

Either singly or in some combination, these six traditional approaches to a community information-needs analysis may serve the team well. Care must be taken, of course, to keep the focus on the users' needs rather than on the library's services.

TECHNOLOGY SHIFTS

As a final element, the team can consider the major shifts made possible by technology. For some libraries, the shifts have already taken place and everything else will be a matter of upgrading, moving faster, or moving more efficiently. But for others a really fundamental change in the very nature of the library is yet to be made. For example, is support for and significant service to remote-site users a reality for the first time? Is networking all or part of the school a realistic option? Is a major new service or information format under consideration, such as a shift from a print to a digital periodical collection?

In that case, the team must remember that users may well have needs but not the language or knowledge required to express them, regardless of the library's ability to meet them. Teachers may need access to the OPAC in their classrooms but not mention it because they do not know it is possible. Owners of small businesses in the community may want a single place to access community demographics but not think of the library in conjunction with such a need.

Required Questions

Three kinds of information almost always need to be gathered: demographic data, preferences/attitudes (e.g., reading patterns), and behavior. The team needs to get a clear snapshot of the community in terms of all three areas. Nearly twenty years ago, Zweizig and Dervin urged librarians to look at these basic quantitative community descriptions in terms of users rather than in terms of library activities (1982, 233–235). That advice is still essential.

In some settings, natural divisions cross all three kinds of information. For example, Kim and Little used the division between work and life-coping needs (1987, see Chapter 2). Using that division in public libraries would produce useful information in terms of demographics, preferences, and behaviors. Which demographic groups (e.g., men and women, young families, or retirees) need information for work and which need information for life-coping situations? In universities, there may be a natural division for faculty between teaching and research. Do certain behaviors (e.g., sending research assistants to the library) or preferences (e.g., using table-of-contents services) predominate in reference to teaching needs or research needs? Obviously, some of these divisions have fuzzy edges. Some public library patrons may need computer skills for both work and home. Some faculty combine teaching and research in many of their information searches. As the team considers gathering information on demographics, preferences, and behaviors, use of divisions often creates richer, more meaningful study questions.

DEMOGRAPHICS

Demographics can be misleading when used without context. While relatively easy to obtain, understand, and present, they are not necessarily meaningful on their own. Demographic statistics provide necessary support for the community information-needs analysis but do not constitute a significant finding by themselves. For instance, the research literature suggests that traditional demographics such as age and sex have relatively little value in predicting public library use. (Remember, "sex" is biological and has often been used as a predictor, but "gender" is socially constructed and has not been explored in this context.) To some extent, public library users do tend to be educated females, but confirming that fact in a particular community adds little new information. Far more important are the nontraditional demographic variables, such as perception of the library's accessibility (D'Elia 1980).

Standard demographic variables include first language, race, ethnicity, sex, sexual orientation, age, education level, income, length of time in the community, and physical location. Asking for some of this information can be complex (e.g., listing all possible racial and ethnic groups) and sensitive (e.g., sexual orientation, age). Various techniques exist for eliciting more complete and accurate information on these points. As a first step, the team needs to determine which of the traditional demographic factors are particularly important to the study.

In addition, nontraditional demographic variables may function as predictors, corollaries, or indicators of information need. These variables include such items as the level of community involvement, media use, and distance from the library. In addition, some information on electronic information access is increasingly useful, including home and/or office Internet access, use of e-mail, and even intranet access. In some settings, subjects will be reluctant to admit that they do not have World Wide Web access at home, resulting in deceptive answers or nonresponses. Again, the team determines what is needed at this stage; later efforts will help secure the information.

Demographics help the team to identify subpopulations in order to assess their information needs fully. When in doubt, include the item in ongoing discussions until such time as a final decision can be made. Nontraditional demographics that may help identify information needs in order to "convert" nonusers into users by meeting unrealized needs or increasing access are particularly productive.

Simple descriptive demographics without analysis or application, such as the community's ratio of females to males, are not only useless but can be misleading. Their very familiarity and simplicity entice staff, the study team, and the public into thinking that they mean far more than they do. Carefully choosing the appropriate demographics is the first step; proper application and analysis must follow. For example, the community's ratio of females to males becomes meaningful if it correlates with access to high-end computing equipment. Simply knowing how many women and men exist in the community is of minimal interest; knowing how that ratio correlates with an information need is potentially valuable.

Sample Research Questions: Demographics
- Do sex, age, race/ethnicity, or job family correlate with any information needs, preferences, or behaviors?
- Does use of e-mail correlate with any information-seeking behaviors?
- Do nonusers share any demographic variables such as educational status, distance from the library, employment status?

PREFERENCES

Some data on patron preferences and attitudes are essential to the study. Wherever users have a choice, they often express a preference. Understanding those choices in relationship to information seeking deepens the team's understanding of actual information needs. As the team considers learning activities, work habits, reading choices, and computer-related decisions, they determine those few items actually of primary importance.

Why do users come to the library? In a school library, do the faculty for the upper grades tend to make more use of computers while the faculty for the lower grades tend to browse among the picture books? In an academic library, do students prefer to use the OPACs near a reference desk or to access the OPAC in remote-site computer labs? In a public library, do people tend to stock up on reading matter or just get a few items over a larger number of visits? Why do they take those same needs elsewhere? Why do they take them to bookstores, to the Internet, or to colleagues?

Earlier work on user preferences should be helpful to the team at this point. For example, Marchant's 1994 article on adult public-library users examines a number of the preferences found in that particular segment of the population. Similarly, chapters 2 through 6 of the Kim and Little study (1987) explore various reasons for using public libraries.

As the team considers patron preferences, one member takes particular responsibility for identifying those subpopulations whose preferences are less common, such as users who rely on remote-site access. Again, the research literature supports this exploration. For example, Holt and Hole's 1995 article on a public library's questionnaire of users with disabilities, including the homebound, opens a new window on an often overlooked subpopulation.

Obviously the team considers the preferences of nonusers in an effort to reveal something new about their information needs. Are they finding what they need via bookstores, interpersonal networks, and the Internet? Do they believe or know that they have no information needs? (If so, do they really recognize the full range of possible needs, including recreational needs?) Are they having trouble getting to information resources? Are they concerned about learning to use electronic resources, preferring to abandon needs rather than learn to handle computers? This area of research is only useful if the team can learn more about how nonusers handle their information needs.

As will be seen later, information is often readily available on those most obvious preferences, reading matter and information. What do users and nonusers value in their reading matter and information? Is currency or physical format more important? Eventually, of course, a comparison can be made between what users prefer and what the library has to offer.

BEHAVIORS

The final type of research question required in almost every CINA centers on user behaviors in the library. (Information on nonuser and user behaviors outside of the library is much more difficult to identify and is discussed later in this chapter.) How patrons make use of the library as a physical space is minimal data but useful. The team makes a substantial effort to know what is already being done in the building as well as from remote sites.

What are patrons actually doing in the library? Is the basis of their activity social or does it pertain to one of the more commonly expected areas such as work, learning, exploring, or recreation? The team needs to know more than what items patrons check out; they need to understand the quality of the library use. Is consultation, discussion, personal instruction, or "thinking aloud" part of the behavior that typically occurs during the reference process? If so, simple information seeking is not the only behavior to merit examination.

This type of question may help the team identify needs that patrons do not know they have. For example, teachers might be using the OPAC to create topical bibliographies for their high school students, a behavior the teachers might well characterize as a successful use of the library. Librarians might see that behavior as exemplifying an information need because they know about reference books and Web sites full of such lists. Alternatively, librarians who already create such bibliographies for their teachers may view that behavior as a public relations opportunity.

One final way to think about these three types of questions is to consider an information audit. The purpose of an information audit is to find out what people actually use to get all of their in-

---

Sample Research Questions: Preferences

- What topics are most preferred in terms of: borrowed monographs, in-house periodical use, interlibrary loan requests, and reference questions? (This is useful only for library patrons, not nonusers.)
- What channels do people choose when they have access to reference service via e-mail, in-person, the World Wide Web, and telephone contact?
- Do nonusers share any preferences regarding other means of gaining information on job openings?

formation. This is not to suggest that the team change purpose and actually conduct an audit, but only that the process of thinking about an audit can help to determine demographic, preference, and behavior based research questions worth asking. "All" of user information includes some items for which the library should not take on responsibility, such as personal banking information. But considering the ramifications of an audit might help the team look beyond basic, traditional topics such as users' recreational reading. "Information" begins to include the large and the small, the ready reference and the in-depth. Thinking about how users relate reading to mass media information opens a new perspective. Do patrons use newspapers, the Internet, or television to get their news? Do they have access to but reject mass media as an information source, as suggested by Chatman and Pendleton (1995) in their work on impoverished populations? In any case, examining issues of demographics, preferences, and behaviors needs to be done in almost every information-needs analysis.

Probable Questions

Questions relating to three topics probably need exploration if the team considers them part of the library's environment: specific local issues, community trends, and competitors. In thinking through these issues, team members should focus on the potential value of the information. Almost every library environment encompasses these three points but that does not mean that they are essential, powerful, and complex enough to merit significant space in the community information-needs analysis.

Specific Local Issues

In some libraries, the team might have a particular hypothesis that it wants to test regarding a highly specific, critical issue. For example, an expansion of the main building may be scheduled with most of the new space going to an enlarged children's area. In that case, the CINA might well focus somewhat on testing the assumption that the community's most significant information need cen-

> ### Sample Research Questions: Behaviors
>
> - What do patrons identify as their most successful activity in the library?
> - What type of search (e.g., known item or subject) is most commonly made on the OPAC?
> - What types of information needs are presented at the circulation desk?

ters on children's services or, if that is already determined, the study might provide more detail on the specific elements of that need. What information needs are currently hampered or not met at all due to space considerations? Which of those needs are most important to which groups for what reasons?

Alternatively, the team could examine the library's primary means of serving users. For example, an academic document delivery unit might move all contact to e-mail after implementing an electronic alert system, such as Carl UnCover. The expectation is that faculty and students make ready use of e-mail and prefer (or accept) electronic documents when available. An information-needs analysis would certainly want to focus on the impact of such a policy. Is the basic assumption accurate for all user groups? Are users abandoning information needs that are difficult for them to communicate via e-mail? Are new users picking up the system quickly enough?

Sometimes no highly specific local issue is being considered; sometimes the steady development of the library precludes any major, sudden shift. The team moves on quickly when nothing appears readily in this category.

COMMUNITY TRENDS

Looking beyond the walls of the library, the team next considers any significant trends in the community as a whole. Documents from parent institutions (e.g., the university, school district, or township annual report) might contain statistical analyses, narrative statements, or major goals helpful in identifying and understanding community trends.

Some trends are purely demographic, as when the age or racial ratios in a community change over time. Others have commercial triggers, as when a local Internet service provider first makes full access to the Net a practical possibility for most people in a community. Some trends are almost universal, such as the continually increasing interest in interdisciplinary research in higher education. Major shifts or ongoing trends in the community often affect user information needs down to the individual level; therefore, the team searches out evidence of strong trends.

COMPETITORS

Some librarians are not used to thinking in terms of "competition" because so much of the library culture centers on the premise of sharing information and resources wherever feasible. Nevertheless, the team must take a hard look at other services, organizations, businesses, and individuals who are trying to meet the information needs of the same population. Where else are people going to get information and why? Even the library's steady users may go elsewhere for many of their information needs. These regular users can not be taken for granted. "No social institution . . . is ever guaranteed permanent usefulness and support, in the face of new (perhaps hitherto unknown) and possibly better agencies or products" (Goldhor 1980, 297).

Obviously this section leads to a thorough discussion of nonusers and what they are doing to find their information and meet their reading needs. Again, the research literature may provide insights. For example, Tuominen's study shows that known individuals (e.g., friends and coworkers) and periodicals are used for information more often than public libraries (1996, 8). Convenience and emotional comfort levels are often involved in these decisions, but what else? What is most attractive about these other, competing information providers?

As the team discusses these three types of probable questions (i.e., local issues, community trends, and competitors), they strike a balance among competing priorities. More questions exist than any single study can answer. Recording those questions for future discussion and subsequent studies not only archives the ideas but it also allows team members to set aside questions they find crucial in the assurance that the questions will be reviewed at a later date rather than lost.

Possible Questions

The team might want any of the following ten topics explored depending on the study's focus and the library's resources:

1. satisfaction
2. appreciated services and resources
3. gaps in services and resources
4. funding
5. personal priorities
6. personal changes
7. timing of information seeking
8. remote-site needs
9. information management
10. learning.

To facilitate rapid decision making on these points, individuals may want to divide up the items and make recommendations to the group regarding their inclusion in the study.

SATISFACTION

As mentioned earlier, levels of user satisfaction are often included in information-needs studies, on the theory that anything satisfactory has met a need and anything unsatisfactory has failed to meet a need. There are a number of problems with this approach as a major thrust of the study but it may be useful to seek some information along these lines as a supplement, particularly if any services or collections have been revised recently. The pitfall with this question is the tendency to shift from conducting an information-needs analysis to conducting an evaluation of services. (For a successful balancing of these two issues, see Clougherty et al. 1998.)

APPRECIATED SERVICES AND RESOURCES

Identifying the library's greatest strengths is a particularly useful kind of satisfaction question. Rather than asking for generalities regarding services, resources, collections, and so on, the team might choose to identify those few critical areas of high success. This question is most revealing when asked in relationship to a subset of information needs, that is, in relationship to the most pressing or crucial needs (as defined by the users, not the librarians).

GAPS IN SERVICES AND RESOURCES

The flip side to the previous question, of course, is the identification of gaps in services and resources. Ordinarily this information is difficult to obtain with any validity as patrons naturally report on only what they know already. It does work quite well, however, for one particular subpopulation. A group of people who have been recently exposed to a wider range of library services might have the experience necessary to adequately identify gaps in services and resources. Such subpopulations might include people who have recently moved into a community, faculty who have been at a university for only one or two years, or transfer students.

FUNDING

In some situations, the team might want to be quite blunt about funding questions. Would users be willing to pay more to get more? Asking a simple question can provide ammunition in the ongoing battle for funds. For example, in an academic medical library serving research faculty, one question might gather feedback on the possibility of asking for a cost-recovery fee for online searches. Patrons might approve the idea knowing that such costs would simply be built into grant applications.

PERSONAL PRIORITIES

In some settings, identifying the information priorities of individuals builds a more complete understanding of information needs. Some issues are imposed institutionally (e.g., the university is investing heavily in WebCT as an instructional medium for distance education) or environmentally (e.g., the school district is now networked). Those issues should have been picked up in the earlier work on broad trends. Now the team may want to examine the impact of those trends on individuals. Are materials on course design or course content the top priority? Are lessons on desktop management or a collection of lesson-plan Web sites the greater need?

Are there a few key individuals for whom a special effort would be productive? For example, in an academic music library there might be one faculty member working extensively with electronic composition. Understanding the personal priorities of that individual provides valuable insights that can be acted upon in advance of the instructor's courses on, graduate student work in, and personal research on electronic composition. In a public library with a large number of patrons referred by local social support agencies, it might be worthwhile to meet with a few directors of those agencies to identify their priorities. Are these agency directors most interested in raising literacy levels, identifying employment opportunities, supporting parents, or some other issue? In some cases, one individual instigates the needs of many others by directing their activities; if so, special efforts to understand those needs in some depth are well worth the time invested.

PERSONAL CHANGES

What changes do people note or anticipate in their needs? Again, the general work on trends should get the team some useful information but it is often important to find out how smaller groups differ from the mainstream. Is there a subpopulation of people who think that they will need new job-skill information from the public library or new reading lists from their school library? Sometimes individuals act as harbingers of changes critical to a significant portion of the entire population.

TIMING OF INFORMATION SEEKING

One of the predictors of library use involves the timing of information seeking. The team might want to know if timing is important for this population. Do users get information (from the library or elsewhere) when they are out getting something else? For example, do school faculty check their mail in the office and stop by the library on the way back? Among the larger local businesses, do members of the sales staff ask their close associates for information after the weekly staff meeting? Identifying such use patterns can help librarians position their services more effectively.

REMOTE-SITE NEEDS

What remote-site needs exist? Some people need a professional actually in their home or office to set up telecommunications resources, software, Internet access, and other basics. These needs are often too labor-intensive to meet fully, but they are still critical in some situations. In any case, the team needs to find out what's going on when people access information resources remotely. As discussed in later chapters, various means are available for meeting these needs but the first step is to identify and understand them.

INFORMATION MANAGEMENT

How are users managing the information they get? Librarians can often help with that process if they take the opportunity to get involved. For example, middle-school children can be given basic lessons in organizing and keeping track of information. Faculty can get in-depth work on establishing databases of citations. Almost anyone using the World Wide Web can be taught to manage a bookmark file.

Sometimes known as "knowledge management," this interest in

how people organize and manage their information can be crucial, particularly in contexts where information overload is common. For some users, managing information is a major problem; librarians can help solve the problem but users do not even know to ask for help. (Of course, some librarians do not think to offer. The axiom that the librarian's job ends at information delivery prevents some librarians from diagnosing and solving the information problems that occur after delivery.) The team examination of the whole process from the users' perspective will help determine whether to include this particular research question.

LEARNING

What do people need or want to learn? With the information landscape changing so rapidly, there is often a sense of forever falling behind. Some people want to learn about fully utilizing the Internet, effective searching on the World Wide Web, creating their own bibliographic databases, using desktop commercial services (e.g., FirstSearch, LEXIS, and UnCover), and more. The team might consider asking about basic information-literacy issues.

The preceding ten "possible questions" are so situation-specific that only two guidelines serve the CINA team's discussion of each one. First, when in doubt about including a question, keep it on the table. The next stages of the process will weed out some items when the practical parameters of the study refine the set of research questions. Second, look for ways to combine two or more questions without losing too much. For example, the team might want to look at gaps but only those gaps concerning learning and information management.

Through discussion, the team determines the driving research questions behind the study. These should be written out for ongoing reference. As data-gathering instruments are chosen and designed, the temptation to look for other material will arise. Some data are easy to gather; others are so interesting and revealing that they are hard to resist. When in doubt, the team can always refer to this list of research questions to stay on track. Maintaining the focus of the analysis often becomes the responsibility of one particular team member, with the list serving as a touchstone for many decisions.

WHICH TECHNIQUES FOR WHICH QUESTION

After determining the research questions for the study, the CINA team moves on to choosing one or more of the available data-gathering methods. For every research question the team needs to uncover at least one type of information: (1) what people do, (2) what people remember, or (3) what people think and feel. The temptation is to leap into instrument design without considering how best to gather each of these three types of data.

Which data-gathering techniques answer which type of question? The traditional means of comparing data-gathering techniques reviews their various applications, strengths, and weaknesses. These comparisons demonstrate that some methods of gathering data are practical but often superficial (e.g., close-ended questionnaires). Some are so artificial that they bear little relationship to the users' realities but provide highly specific data (e.g., laboratory studies). Others are extremely time consuming but provide full, complex data (e.g., interviews). Before handling those essential practical questions, however, the team saves time by identifying which methods have even the slightest potential to answer the questions.

As the team determines the most efficient, effective means of answering their research questions, they continually return to the three types of data: what people do, remember, and think. (The following chapter covers actually creating the instruments once the general decisions regarding data-gathering techniques are finalized.)

Getting at What People Do

Research questions hinging on identification of human behaviors require research tools such as observation, exit interviews, in-house records, and diaries. The value of understanding the actual activities and actions of information seekers comes from the complexity and richness of their work. Where do they go for what? What techniques do they try first? Who do they approach and talk with? What types of searches do they enter? What do they read on-site or photocopy or borrow?

The two major problems in gathering these data are rather obvious: honesty and memory. For understandable reasons, people are frequently inaccurate when reporting their activities. They may want to appear more competent, efficient, or knowledgeable than their actual behavior would indicate. They may consider unimportant the activities the team wants most to understand. Even when they want to be as honest as possible, many people have a hard time remembering their actual movements and decisions for any appreciable length of time. The relatively simple act of finding a known item, first on an OPAC and later on the shelf, involves so many small actions that even librarians might find it difficult to report each one. Nevertheless, four data-gathering techniques are productive: direct observations, exit interviews, in-house records, and diaries/journals.

Direct observations allow the librarian to record a complete series of highly specific actions. Observations can also highlight the natural discrepancies between what people claim they do and what they actually do. Observations can range from unobtrusive to participative, with a number of variations in between. (As discussed in the next chapter, ethical issues involved in unobtrusive observations require careful attention.) Observations of remote-site users and nonusers can be particularly revealing.

Exit interviews occur while the actions are still so fresh in people's minds that their reporting is more likely to be accurate. Meeting people as they leave the reference desk, circulation desk, or the building often captures relatively detailed information on recent activities. Of course, these must be extremely brief interviews with a clear focus or people will not stay long enough to complete them. The number of people who are willing to stop for a two-minute interview at even the most hectic season often surprises librarians.

In-house records, while obviously severely limited, cover factual data relating to users. Circulation records, detailed statistics on reference encounters, interlibrary loan requests, and so on can reveal a great deal about patron behaviors within the building. For limited time periods, particularly detailed statistics or records may be kept of the types of questions asked and problems solved at every public service desk. Records of e-mail and telephone queries provide useful data.

Diaries or journals provide a mechanism for the regular recording of personal actions. Because it is so time-consuming, an activity such as keeping a journal is not readily implemented in all libraries, but school and academic librarians have built relationships with faculty to provide opportunities for such work. The "I-Search paper," for example, requires high-school or undergraduate students to record their actions, thoughts, and feelings as they move through their information search process. Some research teams or heavy-user groups might be willing to keep track of their actions for a very limited period of time if convinced of the work's need and value.

Getting at What People Remember

Questionnaires and interviews work as well as anything to identify what people remember. Memories are so overlaid with emotions, intervening events, expectations, and other variables that clarity and accuracy are affected, sometimes severely. How often do people visit the library? How many family members have library cards? How often are secretaries and research assistants sent to find information? What kinds of factual information are most often needed? As mentioned before, a number of problems occur when people try to remember their own actions accurately and honestly, but they also want to "look good" to the researcher. High school students, for example, may not fully realize that they rely on their parents to get most of their research material for them (or the students don't choose to report it if they did). By specifying that people answer a questionnaire or interview in light of a "critical incident" or very limited time frame, researchers can obtain more reliable information about remembered actions and decisions. Questionnaires can pick up some of this information but

---

The Aggie/Longhorn Story

If people want to skimp on this section of the process, tell them this old Aggie/Longhorn (i.e., rival Texas football teams) story using whatever local rivalry would make sense to your audience. (Being Austin-born, I use the Aggie version.) The point, obviously, is to associate poor reasoning with those outside your own team.

Late one night a couple of students were walking home when they encountered a very anxious Aggie searching frantically on the ground under a streetlight. They stopped and kindly offered to help in the search. The Aggie was grateful, explaining that he'd dropped his wallet and couldn't find it anywhere. After a few minutes of fruitless work, one of the students asked the Aggie if he were sure that this was the exact spot at which the wallet had been dropped. The Aggie replied, "No, I dropped it back in that alley but the light is better here."

Of course, the moral for librarians embarking on an information-needs analysis is: don't choose to look where the light is best; look where you need to look, bringing your own light with you. Or, for a more concrete moral: don't do a simplistic questionnaire because it is quick and cheap if you need information that a simplistic questionnaire can't provide.

---

solid interviews, with their effective use of probe and follow-up questions, reveal even more.

Getting at What People Think and Feel

The most useful information is what people think and feel; it is also the most difficult to obtain. Getting people to verbalize their thoughts, decisions, emotions, expectations, desires, needs, wants, frustrations, and so on is difficult under any circumstances. On the other hand, knowing why people do what they do is often more important than knowing what they do.

Just consider, for example, that different groups may have different reactions to the same library service. Jacobson examined the reactions of girls and boys to computers in their school libraries. He found that the use of computers in libraries is somewhat helpful to high school girls in that the nonthreatening library atmosphere reduces their anxiety about computers. On the other hand, the high school boys experienced an increase in their library anxiety only partly mitigated by the opportunity to use computers there (Jacobson 1991, 277). Having computers in the library helped the girls, but the boys would have preferred access outside of the tension-producing library. The implications for instructional design are significant (Jacobson 1991, 278). In many other cases, knowing what people feel and think is essential to fully serving their information needs.

Three techniques work fairly well for gathering this information: in-depth interviews, focus groups, and questionnaires. Choosing the right people to interview and to serve in a focus group is, of course, essential. Since neither data-gathering technique is simple or rapid, it is generally not possible to use a sample large enough to permit generalizing. In-depth interviews conducted by telephone allow a higher level of respondent privacy that may engender more honesty than a face-to-face interview. Questionnaires can, of course, be distributed far more widely. While they have the advantage of providing a private, anonymous forum for emotions and thoughts, questionnaires must be carefully crafted to encourage accuracy, honesty, and completeness.

Triangulation: Mixing Techniques Effectively

In discussing these various means of gathering data, the CINA team generally recognizes that the obvious, simplistic method of sending out one short questionnaire is not going to garner the information they need to answer the research questions. "Triangulation" provides a means of judiciously combining two or more data-gathering methods to maximize results. By combining or sequencing techniques, the team can obtain a fuller picture of their users' needs.

While there is no set technique for triangulation, understanding the principles often helps put it into action. The term refers to the method used to get a fix on a radio signal. By coming at the signal from different directions, a more accurate reading is possible. By gathering information on what people do, what they remember, and what they think, the team creates a more complete understanding of the community's needs.

Triangulation occurs by combining and/or sequencing data-gathering techniques. For example, the team might choose to conduct focus group sessions with three different user subpopulations. Then they could design a questionnaire for mass distribution building on the information gleaned in the focus groups. Alternatively, the team might observe some patrons in action and interview them about their activities. That in-depth work could then be followed by a Web-mounted questionnaire. Looking at what each technique offers determines the initial choices; looking at what each technique fails to gather refines those choices. Triangulation maximizes the effectiveness of the refinement.

CHAPTER 4 READINGS

Triangulation of Methods

Brannen, Julia. 1992. Combining qualitative and quantitative approaches: An overview. In *Mixing methods: Qualitative and quantitative research*. Julia Brannen, ed. Aldershot: Avebury.

Krathwohl, David. 1998. *Methods of educational and social science research: An integrated approach*. 2nd edition. New York: Longman. 617–628.

Chapter 5

Designing Data-Gathering Instruments

After determining a general sense of which data-gathering methods in what combination will best answer the research questions of the study, the community information-needs analysis (CINA) team begins to shift into the next stage. Team members begin the actual design of specific data-gathering instruments, such as questionnaires, interview questions, or observation guidelines. Obviously, this single chapter can not contain the essence of the numerous books available on each separate technique. It does, however, provide enough information to guide initial decisions and facilitate use of the readings suggested throughout the chapter. (For full citations, see the Works Cited section.) For a comprehensive research methodology book of particular use to librarians, see Ronald Powell's *Research Methods for Librarians*, third edition, 1997.

Chapter 6 discusses the use of pre-existing in-house data, such as circulation records and reference statistics, as well as sampling and training. Sampling requires careful consideration of the likely response rate associated with any particular data-gathering method. Once the sample size is determined, the team members may revisit their instrument design decisions in light of the sampling issues. Nevertheless, starting with instrument design keeps the emphasis on the study goals rather than the practicalities that must serve those goals.

Keeping the research questions firmly in mind, the CINA team insures that each element in each instrument garners critical information. (Having the list of research questions literally in sight during the discussions provides a ready checkpoint for everyone.) Recognizing those items *not* needed becomes important. One member of the team might take on that "skeptic" role, just to free everyone else somewhat during the design process. Gathering information just because it is easily obtained muddies the water, causing problems in later data-analysis work.

Simultaneously, the team members with political skills and/or resource access provide valuable insights into the practical opportunities available for gathering more information with greater depth or efficiency. They highlight those data resources on which the team can draw. Since no single data-gathering technique will adequately cover every point, the team maximizes all resources to produce as complete a picture as possible through careful triangulation.

ASKING PATRONS: GENERAL PRINCIPLES

In reviewing the possible mechanisms for gathering data, the CINA team chooses between those methods requiring personal contact, such as an interview, and those that are primarily impersonal, such as a mailed questionnaire. Choosing which of the two is more effective in any particular situation requires careful judgment. The following points can aid in decision making.

Personal Versus Impersonal Contacts

Personal contact produces more complete information when the answers required are generally long or involved. Few people are both willing and able to write down lengthy, complex responses but many will let the researcher write or tape their answers. Personal contact provides the flexibility necessary to handle questions that might require explanations or clarification of terms. Technology and library resources often require this type of intervention. Few high school students recognize "*LCSH*" but some would understand the explanation, "Those big red books next to the online catalog." Some questions require the complexity of a flow chart so that selected segments are answered only if a previous question receives a certain answer. For example, only those who answer "yes" to a question regarding their home use of the World Wide Web would be asked details of that use; everyone else would simply skip those questions. Such complexity might require a personal contact in some situations just to keep subjects from rejecting the entire set of questions on the grounds of complexity. (Of course, a well-designed written questionnaire can accomplish the same goal for a population comfortable with that format.)

Particularly private questions requiring reflection may garner more useful material if asked through an impersonal mechanism. Questions with potentially embarrassing or shameful answers generally do much better when some level of anonymity or confidentiality is assured. Research questions that focus on training or educational needs often involve significant subject discomfort. Few people are willing to admit that they do not know how to find information, use the information technology available to them, or manage their own information needs. In school settings, the real needs of children are difficult to capture due, in part, to the understandable expectation that reporting the need will lead to some blame, extra work, or other negative consequence.

Whether using a person or a form, the team should be prepared for the fact that sometimes people will not be able to supply the requested information until they express themselves fully regarding other matters. In an interview on reading habits, the interviewer may not be able to start on the planned questions until the subject has finished telling the long story of an unjust overdue fine levied months ago. By leaving room for and remaining flexible regarding this "spillover," staff can not only get more information about their planned questions but also unexpected information.

Effects to Avoid

Whether using a form or a person, two different "effects" may color the information provided. Some individuals are reluctant to answer questions in a way that might reflect poorly on the library. This "nice library" effect arises most often when well-meaning people mistake the information-needs analysis for an evaluation of the library. To admit that the library fails to meet a need becomes akin to admitting that Mom really can't bake a decent apple pie—it's just plain rude.

Similarly, some people want to look good themselves. Answer-

Example of Question Wording in a Questionnaire for a Public Library

Question:	"How often do you visit our public library?"
Problem:	Good patron effect—many people won't want to be seen as nonusers so they'll pad the answer.
New question:	"People use the library for a number of different purposes. How often does the library really help you in some way?"
New problem:	Nice library effect—many people won't want to say that the library is not helpful to them.
Final question:	"People visit the library to find hard facts, recreational reading, materials for their families, and more. In the past two months, did you happen to use the library for any reason? If so, what?"

NOTE: This question still centers on library use, appropriate perhaps for some subpopulations but not for everyone. A question on the sources used for different needs might be more fruitful in some settings.

ing questions honestly would not be actually shameful, but stretching the truth a bit would definitely make them more comfortable. Admitting that they only use the library as a shortcut to the mailroom is uncomfortable; therefore, they report using the library daily—technically accurate but definitely misleading.

If possible, counter the "nice library" and "good patron" effects by asking the same question in two ways, carefully wording the question, or providing a context to counter the effect. Ask subjects for specific information rather than general impressions (e.g., ask school teachers where they go first for curriculum-support materials rather than where they go for information). Preface the questions with an explanation of the study's purpose (i.e., clarify the difference between an evaluation of the staff and a needs analysis).

Reliable and Valid Data

In the effort to carefully word each question, a balance must be struck between the need for reliable information and the need for valid information. Reliable information is consistent; ask the same questions of the same group of people next month and the answers remain generally constant. The questions are simple, unambiguous, and absolute. Did you go into the library yesterday? How old are you? Do you subscribe to any magazines? (Always keep in mind, however, that some people will prevaricate about their age and any other simple fact.)

Valid information, on the other hand, provides accurate insights into people's actions, thoughts, and emotions. The questions may not produce the same answers each time they are asked because people change, people's situations change, and people's environments change. The questions will, however, generally produce useful, insightful information. The questions are open-ended and often require follow-up or support. In what ways do you find the library useful? When you need information for your job, what places and people do you consider helpful?

Obviously, reliable information is easier to obtain but it can also be less meaningful than valid information. Straightforward factual questions certainly do contribute to an information-needs analysis. Nevertheless, simple facts alone will not get all of the kinds of information required. The search for valid information produces valuable, meaningful findings that contribute materially to developing a deeper understanding of people's information needs. These more complex questions elicit more complex answers and are well worth the trouble. "Factual questions have a high reliability, but they cannot be used for anything at all subtle" (Line 1967, 48).

Of course, the team balances between the two types of information, gathering some highly reliable information and some highly valid information. The best questions combine both qualities. For example, for research questions centering on people's reading habits, the following questions are possible:

- *Reliable*: Are you currently reading a book or magazine?
- *Valid*: This month, have you been reading any books or magazines? Is that typical for you? In what way?

Imagine answering these two questions. The first question produces a "yes or no" response likely to be pretty accurate as it does not require any great feat of memory and involves little that would shame most people. The second set of questions requires a little conversation. Whether or not reading is taking place this week, a sense of what is typical for the individual begins to appear. "Yes, I read my *Newsweek* and there's a murder mystery I'm working on. That's pretty common for me. I tend to keep up with the movie reviews and headlines through my newsmagazine. I like to have a fun book around to read a bit at night." One other option is available, though; a combination question involving some elements of both qualities.

- *Valid and reliable*: In the past three days, how many books or magazines have you read at least part of? In what way is that typical or atypical of your reading patterns?

The simple facts garnered by reliable questions balanced with the depth garnered by valid questions provide the kind of critical data necessary to an effective CINA.

Neutral Questions

The principle of "neutrality" is critical when wording questions. They must not be "loaded" to elicit a particular reaction or response. Fully open questions—ones that invite every perspective and view—are often more effective than those which limit choices; they are also, however, much more difficult to analyze. Many subjects will pick up on slanted questions and get the impression that the study is designed to confirm the status quo or some preconceived idea. And, obviously, biased data are worse than useless; maximal objectivity is essential in question design.

Critical Incident Technique

Helping people to remember clearly is always an accomplishment. The "critical incident" technique can help to focus subjects' memories by encouraging them to recall particularly meaningful situations (Flanagan 1954). For example, rather than asking about "the last time you needed information," the questions could begin with the injunction to identify a recent, specific example of needing information and to describe it briefly. Then, questions are posed in reference to that critical incident. The problem, of course, is that the situation may be memorable because it differed strongly from the norm in some way. In any case, as a general guideline, do not ask for detailed memories older than six months among adults. (See Fowler 1995, 22–27 for more on stimulating recall.)

Instrument Length

Although short instruments generally deliver a higher response rate than do long ones, the length of the instrument can vary in response to a number of factors. Longer interviews or questionnaires can be used if subjects are convinced of their value and importance. Many people are willing to provide the depth and detail required of a longer instrument when they believe in the contribution they are making to a substantive effort. Of course, "long" means something quite different to a ten-year-old, a mother with three children in tow, and a doctoral candidate.

> ### Question Objectivity
>
> *Topic:* Do high school faculty need help when they are searching the Internet at home for course information? If so, does the school library Web site provide that help?
>
> *Loaded question:* When you're home searching the Internet for class-support material, do you prefer to use the library's homepage as a starting point or to search on your own? [This uses a "satisfaction" approach.]
>
> *Neutral question:* When you're home searching the Internet for class-support material, what do you do to find what you need? [This uses a more open-ended approach.]

Question Wording

Various wording issues merit special attention, such as the use of vague phrases like "use the library." Is an unsuccessful attempt to find a book in the library an example of "using" the library? Is meeting someone in the lobby "using" the library? Even within a homogeneous population, answers vary (Bookstein and Lindsay 1989, 215). The ambiguity of poorly phrased questions lies at the root of many criticisms of library questionnaires.

On another point regarding wording, offering categories, choices, and context can help subjects understand questions more fully. For example, some people will recognize what they cannot recall if given a list of options to browse among. A college senior might not remember all the sources she just searched for her history term paper but looking through a list of choices may help her recognize certain items. Similarly, the injunction to "tell me where you go to get information" may not elicit much from a manager in a large corporation. A more complete explanation including examples could well trigger a lengthy response.

When using this technique in a printed instrument, always (1) offer subjects the chance to add their own choices and (2) use mutually exclusive categories. Leaving the option to write-in additional answers can lead to unexpected insights. It also minimizes the perception that the questions are "loaded" in some way. Mutually exclusive response categories are essential when allowing subjects to "choose all that apply" in their response to a question.

These general guidelines for all instrument designs provide a broad context for the actual design of specific questionnaires, interviews, focus groups, and more. Whether working on person-to-person or person-to-document design, the team should consider these guidelines when making decisions.

PERSON-TO-PERSON

Interviews, focus groups, and observations gather information using a person-to-person format. By their very nature, such instruments require more time and interpersonal energy to administer than do person-to-document instruments; on the other hand, they can also provide great depth, detail, and insight. As mentioned earlier, triangulation techniques may suggest the use of an in-depth, personalized instrument first, followed by the use of a mass-distribution instrument based on the data gathered in the first effort.

In all their variety, interviews are a valuable data-gathering technique. The team determines four characteristics preferred for any interviews: degree of structure, length, timing, and number of subjects per interview. Interviews can function with all the structure of a printed questionnaire being read aloud to the subjects (as one might do with children) or with virtually no structure.

> The structured interview is the mode of choice when the interviewer *knows what he or she does not know* and can therefore frame appropriate questions to find it out, while the unstructured interview is the mode of choice when the interviewer *does not know what he or she doesn't know* and must therefore rely on the respondent to tell him or her. (Lincoln and Guba 1985, 269)

Whatever style of interview is chosen should be appropriate to the setting, questions, and population.

The more formal and structured the interview, the easier it is to analyze the data later. Organizing the resultant data flows more smoothly than it might otherwise when the questions offer a limited array of answers, the topics covered are tightly controlled, and the opportunity to raise new issues is minimal. On the other hand, informal and unstructured interviews provide more opportunities for surprises and detailed insights into unexpected concerns.

Length and timing, two other variables in planning interviews, often go together. Those encounters that interrupt the information-seeking stream (a matter of timing) should be quite brief (a matter of length) so as to maximize response rate while minimizing the impact on subjects. Exit interviews, for example, can take place at the end of an event, such as an online search, while in-depth interviews may take place over the course of an hour. Finally, a choice must be made as to the number of people involved in the interview: one, a small group, or a larger group. In school systems, for example, where the faculty work in teams, it might be useful to conduct a small group interview in the form of a focus group.

There are several strengths to interviewing, not the least of which is that it allows the subject to cover a great deal of time, from the far past to that day's events. The flexibility of the technique al-

---

Variant Wording on an Interview Question

1. Think back to your last big homework assignment, one of those assignments that makes you find a lot of information. What kinds of things worked well for you when you tried to find that information?

2. People get information from bookstores, their friends, the media, their family, the Internet, and lots of other places. What are some of your favorite ways to get information? Why?

3. Doctoral students are often the first ones on campus to really master new research tools and databases. They learn about them from faculty, friends, workshops, and sheer exploration. How do you tend to learn about the information resources in your academic discipline? Are you pleased with those methods?

lows the interviewer to probe, to clarify, and to create new questions based on what has already been heard. Whyte recommended that the interviewer "let the conversation flow naturally but note what aspects of events the informant describes or leaves out so that later the interviewer can phrase questions to fill in omissions or to check his or her understanding of what has been said" (1979, 57). This "flexibly structured" interview style allows the researcher to "recognize statements that suggest new questions or even new lines of investigation" (57).

Although the researcher certainly benefits, the appeal of interviewing to the subjects may not be obvious. Occasionally actual payment is employed as a motivator—using anything from pizza coupons donated by a local business to free database searches. Often, however, subjects choose to participate because they enjoy talking about their experiences and needs with a knowledgeable, interested individual.

As with other data-gathering techniques, specific skills and methods have long been used to strengthen the interview. While thoughtfully adjusting the guidelines of good interviewing to meet the needs of whatever situation is at hand, the interviewer also employs proven techniques. For example, the type of question can vary. "Comparison questions ask people to tell how things are like one another while contrast questions ask people to tell how things differ from one another" (Jorgensen 1989, 88). Interviewers must use probe questions to explore the unknown background on a statement as well as a clarification question to further elucidate what has already been stated. The flexibility provided by the interpersonal interaction allows a great deal of variety in the format of interviews.

The practical matters involved in setting up a series of interviews are not insignificant. The team must

1. design an interview protocol (i.e., the text of the introductory statement as well as the actual questions);
2. arrange for transcription of the notes and/or tapes;
3. allow a good deal of time to set up meetings (unless exit interviews are planned); and

4. prepare to organize the data so as to identify patterns and anomalies.

Some special situations require special consent forms, such as any situation involving minors. Written parental permission is troublesome to obtain but essential when interviewing minors. Just imagine the most worrisome answer obtainable from a child or young adult (e.g., "I need information on how to know if you have VD") to get a sense of why parental consent is essential. Although time consuming, the permission process can be well worth the effort as so little is known about the information needs of children.

Obviously the team must plan to train staff members in the use of probe, clarification, and follow-up questions as well as general interview techniques. As will be discussed in the next chapter, such training is not prohibitively difficult but it must be done well. Interviewers who fail to exercise moderate control over the general flow of the interview can derail the entire process.

The questions do need to be phrased consistently for a needs assessment. While probe and follow-up questions may vary to some extent, the interview protocol requires enough stability to insure that the research questions chosen by the CINA team remain the primary object of each interview and to insure that interviewer impact is minimized.

One factor in the design of the instrument is the potential pool of interviewers. Keeping the interview instrument clean and simple becomes somewhat more important when the team must use a large pool of inexperienced interviewers or a large pool of interviewers who are only modestly informed about the library, for example, shelvers or volunteers of limited experience. (Extremely simple interviews should probably just be changed to a questionnaire.) The interview instrument can be more complex when the team can call on experienced interviewers or can create a small group of well-trained people.

The team considers those people who are both available and who have the qualities of a good interviewer. Sometimes those who talk most readily do not make good interviewers; those who listen well, however, deserve consideration. The team needs people who can engage strangers in conversation easily, who have an air of assurance about the subjects' willingness to participate in the questionnaire, and who have the ability to control the interaction without directing it. Many reference librarians and instructional librarians demonstrate these qualities daily.

The seven primary forms of person-to-person data gathering include focus groups, exit interviews, brief interviews, in-depth interviews, telephone interviews, obtrusive observation, and unobtrusive observation. Each of these techniques is discussed in greater depth below but, in each case, the factors discussed above merit consideration.

Focus Groups

A focus group is

> a gathering of ten to twelve people, usually peers, who are encouraged to talk about specific topics so that their attitudes, perceptions, and language can be analyzed. These gatherings last sixty to ninety minutes and are led by a highly skilled facilitator who ensures that specific topics and issues are explored. The sessions usually are audiotaped, and the transcripts of those tapes along with the facilitator's notes form the raw data that are analyzed. (Mullaly-Quijas et al. 1994, 306)

With some variations, that description of a focus group could suffice for any CINA team. The basic idea is to gather a group of peers for a discussion of their information needs. The number of individuals can range from six to twelve. Any fewer tends to result in dominance by one or two people; any more tends to result in an unmanageable group with some people quite silenced. The length of time varies from forty-five minutes to two hours, depending on the number of participants, their level of interest in the topic, and the complexity of the questions.

The two major advantages of the focus group are time and responsiveness. Individual interviews of ten people take a good deal more time than a single focus group with the same number. More important, however, is the degree of responsiveness a really good focus group generates. Some people share details and examples more fully because the group setting is less intimidating than a one-on-one interview. For many, simply hearing others explain some aspect of their information needs helps facilitate verbalization of their own needs. The contrast and comparisons that naturally occur when people share experiences help bring out detail more fully. People explain the "why" behind "what" they do and those reasons are invaluable.

The practical planning elements involved in setting up a successful focus group all center on insuring full participation. As mentioned before, getting enough people to come is essential and difficult. By looking for times, places, and settings that encourage participation, the team increases the likelihood that sufficient numbers will join the group.

Making all of the logistical arrangements carefully certainly helps increase participation. For example, in a public library the team could advertise that they're looking for participants during the Saturday lunch hour; those who sign up in advance will receive a box lunch during the interview. (Of course, a screening procedure might be put in place to insure that people with varied backgrounds are signed up, rather than only the office staff of the orthodontist next door.) A university library team might advertise in a number of 10:00 a.m. to 11:00 a.m. classes that they will hold a focus group at 11:15 a.m., that they need full participation from students, and that they will provide refreshments. Comfortable timing, a central location, and extensive advertising are needed to garner enough people for a focus group.

Once careful planning and thorough advertising have gathered enough people together for a focus group, a trained facilitator must be available to run it. In this case, having someone from the library to run the focus group can actually hamper progress in that participants may be reluctant to "knock" the library by saying anything negative or explaining why they go elsewhere for information. The team can look for local university business students who have had training in this technique; some may be willing to do this as a class project or community service. Members of the local chamber of commerce may provide names of facilitators in the area. If no one else becomes available, a trained librarian can do the job so long as great care is taken to minimize the "nice library" effect.

Using an excellent tape recorder, the facilitator tapes the full session while taking notes on key points. (Taping is sometimes rejected on the grounds that it inhibits conversation; many people, however, grow used to it rapidly. A reliable tape provides the note taker with a backup system and strengthens the analysis by permitting tone of voice to illuminate a flat transcript.) The team discusses the purpose of the study with the facilitator, providing a list of questions for each focus group. In some situations the facilitator's understanding of the team's research questions may be so tenuous that the risk of inhibiting the group is worth the potential clarification provided by having a member of the team on hand. When several meetings are planned, a team member might sit quietly behind the facilitator for the first few, discussing the direction of the conversations afterwards.

The team needs to determine the necessity of obtaining signatures on written consent forms from participants. While the team must certainly have both minors' and parents' signatures, other participants may need no more than a verbal assurance that the tape recording will be kept confidential with all names and identifying information deleted from the transcript. Given the volatility of focus group discussions, however, an explicit written agreement with the signatures of both parties is generally the best option.

The CINA team's focus group questions, as posed by the facilitator, depend entirely on the nature of their research questions. Since the group is not meant to be representative of the population, any demographic data gathered should be minimal and gathered solely to identify any overwhelming bias due to the accidental gathering of the group. (For example, a group consisting entirely of members of one sex would almost certainly leave out some useful information.) The questions should be open-ended, broad, flexible, and general. Sometimes an experienced facilitator can suggest ways to frame a question to elicit greater response among participants. The heart of the data, however, grows out of the discussion occurring afterwards as the skillful facilitator probes and follows through on various points of interest.

At the end of the session, the facilitator might solicit suggestions from the participants regarding two points. First, do they have any ideas regarding increasing attendance at focus groups? Should flyers be posted in a different place? Should different times or locations be offered? Second, knowing that the librarians are trying to get a handle on the information needs of the community, should other issues be discussed in future focus groups?

As a final means of maximizing contact with these study participants, written materials can be distributed at two points following the actual session. The most direct means of gaining additional information is to hand each participant a small packet at the moment of departure. The packet could contain a small reward (such as a remittance-of-fines coupon), a primarily blank sheet with the request that participants jot down anything else they'd like to add, and a self-addressed stamped envelope (SASE) to return the sheet. As a minor incentive to return the sheet, the packet could include a form for them to request a copy of the findings. A second mechanism for written follow-up is the executive summary of the meeting. Following transcription and initial analysis of the session, a team member can write a short summary (one to two pages) stating the key points. This summary can be mailed to the participants along with a thank you letter, the aforementioned primarily blank sheet, and the SASE. Alternatively, participants might receive this summary of the key points with an invitation to augment, correct, or explain any specific elements of importance to them (Hernon and Altman 1996, 89). In any case, the additional opportunity to contribute may elicit those more personal, private, or sensitive comments that did not surface in the group setting.

In considering the value of information gained from a focus group, the team must look at the size of the group as well as the circumstances of those who participated. Since even very small groups can be quite informative, success should not be judged solely on the basis of group size. On the other hand, the team must consider the type of people who are willing to participate in a focus group. They choose to come to the library for a significant time period and speak in front of strangers about their activities, preferences, and beliefs. The people willing to do that are rarely representative of the population; they may very well differ from the "norm" in some significant way. Their very difference, however, may qualify them to verbalize, explain, and discuss the needs shared with others. Obviously a focus group should be only one part of a study rather than the sole basis of the final analysis.

Possible Focus Group Questions

- What's the easiest way for you to find information? What works the best?
- If you were giving an orientation to someone new in this community, what tips would you give on finding information?
- When was the last time you really needed some solid information? What happened?
- If you could change just one or two things around here to make it easier for you to get the information you need, what would you do?
- What kind of things do you generally want to know? What kind of information do you need?
- What do you do with information once you get it?

Exit Interviews

Exit interviews tend to garner useful details, produce sound readings of satisfaction, and maximize short-term memory. On the downside, they will miss remote-site users and nonusers unless permission is obtained to hold them in a nonlibrary location such as the student center, a shopping mall, or the cafeteria. Exit interviews at the library must take place immediately following some relatively finite, definable interaction with the collection or staff. As people leave a service point (such as circulation or reference) or a major area (such as the children's room) or even the building as a whole, the interviewer steps up to begin the process. Such interviews are generally quite brief so their focus must be crisp and the questions quite clear.

Sometimes people are reluctant to stop for an exit interview due to either individual preference or a corporate culture that discourages such activities. Posting signs at the entrance and flyers at various service points asking for help and cooperation during short exit interviews can prepare people for the possibility of being chosen. The exit interview should be pretested, in part to see if people will cooperate. Just because people look rushed is no reason to assume they won't give an interviewer three minutes. Never underestimate the "nice" law: most people don't want to be seen kicking a dog or refusing to help a librarian. With the right approach, even busy people will often give a librarian a few moments.

Given the brevity of an exit interview, the team should arrange the interviewer's question sheet so that answers can be ticked off quickly. This tight organization facilitates later analysis as well as speed during the interview. Exit interview questions tend to focus on the factual components of what the patron has just experienced or what is commonly experienced. Activities and preferences rather than thoughts form the core of the instrument.

As always, the research questions driving any individual study underpin the selection of actual interview questions.

Brief Interviews

Requiring ten to twenty minutes, brief interviews are particularly useful when a questionnaire is too complex for the subject to complete alone easily or when some particular points of interest are to be pursued in some depth. People who might be unwilling to complete an extensive questionnaire form will sometimes consent to a brief interview on the same points.

Subjects can be approached as they leave an area within the library (as in an exit interview) or appointments can be made for short personal or telephone visits. Obviously the former method fails to reach nonusers and the latter method entails more work for the interviewer. In some settings, arrangements can be made to reach a number of subjects with minimal effort. In a school setting during a day spent on standardized tests, one librarian can move fairly quickly from room to room interviewing teachers with a volunteer who can proctor for the teachers during the interviews. Identifying a setting and time for a number of people to gather in a single place with relatively flexible demands on their time can increase the efficiency of this technique.

Once the subjects agree to participate, the interview needs to move forward swiftly and smoothly. Rather than simply reading the questions in order, the interviewer remains alert for any part of the subject's response that might answer two questions at once. The second question is then asked, with a new wording, simply to invite confirmation or clarification without wasting the subject's time. Alert to any signs of confusion or uncertainty, the interviewer offers to define terms, explain questions more fully, and otherwise smooth the process for the subject. Maintaining a light rapport with the subject allows the interviewer to control the flow of questions while meeting any unexpected concerns.

In training, these interviewers must learn to value the additional comments, the ones that go beyond the expected responses. Recording and, time permitting, asking for a bit more explanation of those comments can lead to useful insights.

In-depth Interviews

Requiring one to two hours each, in-depth interviews produce a great deal of complex, detailed data requiring careful and somewhat difficult analysis. The questions are often open-ended, as in a focus group, so that subjects can readily identify the information-based situations, concerns, and experiences of most interest to them rather than simply responding to a closed list of questions coming from the librarian's perspective. A perceptive, quick-thinking interviewer is needed so that probe and follow-up questions can be used effectively to bring out more complete pictures of the subject's needs. Analysis is a more complex process because patterns most often emerge from the data rather than being set in advance.

Possible Exit Interview Questions

- *On exiting the OPAC:* What kind of question do you generally take to the online catalog? Can you give me an example?
- *On exiting the periodical room:* People use magazines and journals for both recreational reading and specific information. Which was more important to you today?
- *On exiting the building:* Which parts of the library did you visit today? Why?
- *On exiting a grocery store:* People use a lot of different information sources. Where do you tend to go for what kind of information? Can you give me an example?

When relatively little is known about the information-seeking behavior of the community or some subset of the community, then this investment of time and energy is well made. In most CINA studies, however, so much is already known about library users that such depth produces relatively little new information. This technique is quite useful for developing an understanding of non-users. When a community college librarian knows that few political science students use the library, despite repeated assignments requiring library use, in-depth interviews with some of them might reveal their other sources of information, their concerns regarding the library, and other relevant factors. Similar efforts might be appropriate when serving a new subpopulation (e.g., pre-K teachers served for the first time in a school library) or planning a major new service for an established population (e.g., a Web-based ready reference collection established for the business community).

One last group merits use of this labor-intensive approach—community gatekeepers. For example, in public libraries with minimal resources, the difficulties of translating questions may make meaningful data on an ESL population unobtainable. A gatekeeper to that community (such as a community activist, volunteer ESL tutor, or religious leader) may know enough about the information needs to provide useful information. This single interview would not substitute for a full study of the population but it may be the only option available in some situations.

Obviously, it is not possible to conduct in-depth interviews with a reasonable sample of a population of any size. Unlike questionnaires or brief interviews, in-depth interviews are too costly to be used with a fully representative sample. The value of the process, therefore, does not lie in its generalizability. The results often can not be generalized at all. The team will not, for example, be able to say that most nonusers get their information from mass media just because most of the interview subjects do so.

The value of in-depth interviews is twofold. First, they provide a detailed understanding of a few individuals. Understanding even a few people in such depth opens the door for rethinking the needs of others. Even if those interviewed happen to be, in some way, atypical of the population as a whole, the solid foundation of knowing a few so well makes it a bit easier to connect with others. Second, on a more practical front, these interviews provide ideas, suggestions, and possibilities later incorporated into a more precise instrument as the next phase. Interviewing a few nonusers might suggest a few possible questions to be asked of a properly representative sample via a questionnaire. When interviews give people the chance to explain why they make specific choices, the interviewer may glean a number of surprising insights leading to a whole new array of options.

Other than time and data analysis, the three main problems in conducting in-depth interviews are gaining access, establishing rapport, and keeping a focus. People who understand the value of the process are surprisingly willing to talk with an interviewer at length. Initial care must be taken, however, to help them understand that value. A brief in-person contact is most effective in obtaining access because it (a) reassures the subject regarding the professionalism of the interviewer, (b) provides an opportunity for the subject to discuss the purpose and value of the interview, and (c) provides the interviewer with an opportunity to "get a read" on the subject in order to establish rapport more quickly in the actual interview.

Establishing rapport requires a personable, skillful interviewer who is able to put people at ease. This means that the team member who interviews seventh graders well may not be the same one who interviews administrators well. Sometimes the ability to establish rapport with members of a particular group becomes the most critical element in determining who will gather these data. The librarian who has the most contact with the group is often the person least likely to establish a solid interview rapport because subjects have a hard time discussing the situation frankly with someone who is seen as intimately involved in serving them. Issues of authority and sociocultural identity also play a role in establishing rapport. The bottom line is that the interviewer needs to encourage the subjects to reveal their hidden fears, concerns, needs, and more to a relative stranger in an hour or two.

Keeping the focus comes into play once minimal rapport has been established. In line with the research questions underpinning the study, the focus of the interview must be maintained by the interviewer within the boundaries set by the subject. The interviewer, for example, keeps the focus on information rather than opinions about music or chat about sports teams. The subject, however, sets two types of boundaries: first, those information-related topics that are not open for discussion and, second, the definition of information itself. The interviewer attempts to help the subject feel comfortable enough to push back the first type of boundary, as when a nonuser becomes willing to identify unmet information needs. The interviewer attempts to understand the subject's perspective on the second type of boundary, as when it finally becomes clear that the fifth-grader being interviewed identifies certain cartoons as informational in the sense that they provide the definitive description of super powers, data never found in mere books. Within that context, the interviewer must keep the discussion in focus.

When choosing whom to interview, some of the sampling techniques in the next chapter will apply. However, one of the most productive techniques is to identify people known as "key informants." These people are particularly knowledgeable in some area. Understanding their information needs provides special insight into a situation. Some key informants are particularly articulate in an otherwise inarticulate group (e.g., the informal ombudsman in a homeless shelter), have recently moved from one group to another (e.g., new faculty who were recently doctoral students), or have particularly wide-ranging information needs (e.g., the manager in charge of environmental scanning for an entire township). As mentioned earlier, the gatekeepers to a community provide in-depth information as when the manager of a local safe house for gay and lesbian teens provides insight on the information needs of the population whom she serves.

The logistics of in-depth interviewing requires a good deal of personal attention from the interviewer. Each session must be audio-taped and, in the effort to establish rapport, is generally held in the subject's space rather than the library. The interviewer, therefore, must pack a kit containing the tape recorder, spare batteries, the mike, interview questions, pad, pen, and so on. Extensive notes are taken throughout the interview and the tape is checked immediately upon leaving the session. The notes provide at least highlights of the session when an equipment flaw results in a useless tape. Within hours of taping, the interviewer must listen to the tape while jotting down comments regarding (1) possible patterns to be considered in actual data analysis and (2) techniques for strengthening interview skills. (Since pretests are not available to refine this human instrument and since so few interviews are actually conducted, this review of the tape is the interviewer's sole means of improving data-gathering effectiveness.) Since this lengthy process is quite draining, no more than two interviews should be conducted on any one day. After the tapes are transcribed and the transcriptions corrected, the data analysis begins. The original interviewer must take charge of, or at least be central to, that process.

Telephone Interviews

Phone interviews are often simply a different way of delivering brief interviews, although in situations involving extensive service to off-site users (as in support to isolated field labs) it may be the only practical means of reaching users. An advance letter to let people know that interviewers will be calling can significantly improve the response rate. Vavrek cites the "positive effect of mailing introductory letters prior to the phone calls" as one of the reasons his national survey had a response rate six points higher than the national average (1995, 23).

As in the exit interview, this format requires the interviewer to maintain a tight structure. On the telephone, everything seems to take longer. Although the actual time may be no more than that used in a brief interview, the visual and aural distractions faced by the subject combine with the lack of a visual relationship to create a more problematic context for the interview. Careful training can help overcome these problems.

Obtrusive Observation

Obtrusive observation is "a method relying on watching, listening, asking questions, and collecting things" (LeCompte et al. 1993, 196). Participant or obtrusive observation has been used in libraries for some time. Stepping right into the subject's world without disguise, the observer watches, records comments on, talks with, and collects objects from the subjects while remaining "open to the unexpected" (Jorgensen 1989, 82) throughout the process. A school librarian might openly record the search paths of various students; an academic librarian might actually sit next to a patron and discuss the steps taken in an online search. A public librarian might record observations on the information needs that arise during a city council planning session. Given the willing cooperation of subjects, such open observation can combine with judicious interviewing to reveal a great deal about both behavior and thought processes. Each observer must choose a point of balance between observing and participating, supplementing observation with limited interviews.

Understanding observation requires a focus on two points. First, there are four different positions on a continuum of roles that researchers play when using the observation technique: complete participant, participant-as-observer, observer-as-participant, and

> ### Possible In-depth Interview Questions
>
> - What role do computers play in your search for information?
> - What people do you tend to call on when looking for certain kinds of information? Why?
> - Think about the last time you really needed some information for an important project. Tell me about it. What did you do?

complete observer (Gold 1969). This variety allows use of whatever perspective will best answer the research question. Second, as Whyte noted, it is really a "set of methods including interviewing, since any able field worker will supplement what is learned from observing and participating with some interviewing" (1979, 56). The obvious advantage of this method is that it functions as a reality check on what people say they are doing. The CINA team must determine, as with interviews, whether the depth of this information is worth the substantial investment of time taken to gather and analyze it.

Although only unobtrusive observation, with all its attendant ethical and logistical difficulties, can negate the impact of the observer on the observed, much can be accomplished through properly conducted general observation. Of course it must always be kept in mind that, so much as possible, the point of observation is to understand what actually occurs without deliberately introducing new stimuli or manipulating the participants (Adler and Adler 1994, 378). Of necessity, in some settings, the observation must be highly structured. In every case, however, the "intent is to fit into the setting in such a way that the usual behavior of the people being studied is changed as little as possible" (Mellon 1990, 40).

Focusing the observational field in a CINA begins with the research questions. The purpose and consequent setting determine the techniques used in an observation no matter what participants are being studied. Anything from stationing a video camera in front of the reference desk to blending in as a parent at a storytelling session could constitute observation. (In every case the ethical concerns must be carefully addressed.) The setting varies along five parameters:

- number of participants—e.g., settings can be crowded (as in a busy branch library) or sparsely populated (as in a quiet map library)
- public vs. private—e.g., settings can be as public as a reference desk or as private as a professor's office
- size of the observable actions—e.g., settings can be limited to small actions, such as keyboard motions, or they can focus on large actions, such as routes taken through the library building
- staff or public—e.g., settings can involve library staff, the public, or some combination thereof
- individual or group work—e.g., settings can entail individual work, such as one secretary's responsibilities, or group work, such as a planning committee in city government meeting to write a strategic plan.

The settings vary in response to the purpose of the study, as mentioned earlier.

Obtrusive observation requires the researcher to build enough rapport with the participant(s) to mitigate the natural reactions anyone might have to being watched. Observing the strategies employed on OPAC searches by a group of high school students, for example, requires the observer to develop a relationship with each individual informal enough to promote easy conversation yet formal enough to reinforce the nonjudgmental nature of the interaction.

Observations are productive for various types of CINA research questions including the following:

1. those involving problem-solving situations, such as a faculty member teaching a course for the first time with little advance notice;

2. those involving communication, sharing, and distribution of information, such as a research team beginning work on a long-term medical project; and
3. those involving information management entailing a number of resources, such as a community group using private, government, and corporate data to achieve their goals.

Logistical and planning elements of an obtrusive observation are similar to those of an in-depth interview in some ways. The data gathered include tape-recorded interviews, written notes, and even taped notes or videotapes of meetings. The ethical concerns of observing people without seriously affecting their work or inhibiting their willingness to ask for library assistance must be handled through consent forms and adequate support throughout the process. The observer takes on a particularly heavy role in that preparations, contacts, data gathering, and much of the data analysis must be handled personally. Remembering that one of the side benefits of a CINA is the development of patron relations, the team may determine that the time invested in such a technique is worthwhile, in part because of the rapport developed through extended contact between the librarian and a key individual or group.

Unobtrusive Observation

Unobtrusive observation involves special ethical considerations and techniques but can be productive in limited circumstances. The obvious ethical difficulties arise from watching, noting, and even recording the words and actions of individuals who have not given their consent to act as research subjects. Although uncommon, it is even possible to observe someone acting illegally in a library, for example, tearing pages from a journal. Signs, notices, and carefully chosen circumstances can mitigate this problem to some extent. The techniques involved are numerous but most involve blending into the environment, minimizing the effect of the observer on the observed, and capturing sufficiently detailed data.

Relatively few CINA studies utilize unobtrusive observation, however, because it seldom yields appropriate data for this limited purpose. The use of an unobtrusive video camera using time-lapse techniques can identify blind spots, bottlenecks, and heavy traffic times when building-use patterns and general traffic flow around a service desk are central to a research question. The team might, for example, be interested in the reference assistance needs of computer users. Watching desk staff handle the full array of information needs might identify blind spots in the furniture arrangements that make it difficult for patrons to catch the eye of a busy librarian. Since no individuals are purposefully identified, an array of signs and posters can be sufficient public notice. Such items should state the basic facts (e.g., the library staff are watching or filming these areas on these dates for this reason) and should provide an easily available contact person for those with questions. The wording and graphics should invite patrons to read the notice; reading levels and language choices should reflect those used in the community. Small handouts could be available to provide more detail such as the assurance of confidentiality and specifics of the study design.

In each of the seven primary forms of person-to-person data gathering—focus groups, exit interviews, brief interviews, in-depth interviews, telephone interviews, obtrusive observation, and unobtrusive observation—there is a corresponding trade-off between resources expended and depth of the gathered data. A strong application of triangulation in a community information-needs analysis (e.g., using one or two of these methods to generate ideas, possibilities, and suggestions) feeds into person-to-document instrument design.

PERSON-TO-DOCUMENT

Finally, the written word provides excellent data. Materials written by participants vary greatly in their format, content, and impetus. The methodologies involved are well documented elsewhere so only a general overview will be given here.

In all forms of person-to-document data gathering, the team considers means of reaching those who can not read, who are minimally literate, whose disabilities prevent ready written response, whose language skills lie in areas other than English, as well as specific barriers common to their setting. The triangulation of interviews with questionnaires can reach some of those who might otherwise be missed.

Questionnaires: General Guidelines

The questionnaire is perhaps the most thoroughly studied form of data gathering. Hardly a magic bullet, questionnaires are often so badly designed that both staff and administrators may be skeptical of their results (Schlichter and Pemberton 1992). Questionnaires vary on two primary points: (1) means of delivery (personal delivery, postal mail, e-mail, WWW, and point-of-contact) and (2) question format (open-ended questions, Likert scales, multiple-choice questions, and rankings). In addition, issues of wording and layout are critical.

QUESTIONNAIRE DELIVERY OPTIONS

Each means of questionnaire delivery has its advantages and disadvantages. A personally delivered questionnaire allows the researcher to clear up any obvious misunderstandings on the spot and often has an increased response rate, but it is time consuming and may influence the respondent unduly. Mailed questionnaires are relatively simple to distribute but require significant follow-up to produce sufficient response rates. Although they are becoming the bane of discussion lists, e-mail questionnaires are cheap to distribute; of course, they reach a very limited portion of a population. Some WWW sites have embedded questionnaires for their users and those are often productive, assuming all users have equal facility in responding and that individuals do not submit multiple forms. They too reach only a very limited population. Finally, point-of-contact questionnaires (such as in-house questionnaires left at the reference desk or off-site questionnaires left at the senior center) are simple and affordable but do limit responses to those who come to a specific site.

Questionnaire Question Formats

The varying question formats of questionnaires also have their strengths and weaknesses. The use of open-ended questions provides participants with a greater forum for expressing their responses but it can intimidate those who do not feel comfortable or confident in their answers. Those who are minimally literate or particularly rushed for time may be put off by a significant amount of white space left for their replies.

Likert scales use a range of responses along a continuum (e.g., "never, occasionally, sometimes, frequently, always"). The resultant data are simple ordinal (i.e., they can be logically rank-ordered but have no true numeric value since the responses are not discrete, separate items of equal difference with a true zero). There is, for example, no universal consensus on the difference between "occasionally" and "sometimes" in the same way that there is a definite difference between being ten and being twenty years old. While the impact of gathering only simple ordinal-level data will be discussed more fully in chapter 8, the team must consider the weakness inherent in collecting such rough data. Nevertheless, when rough descriptive data is the only game in town, it does move the team somewhat closer to understanding the community's needs.

While also simple ordinal-level data, rankings center on the user's personal preferences and choices. In that sense, it matters less that some people's first choices are far more important to them than their second choices while to others the second choice just barely missed coming out on top. The ultimate decision of ranking one item ahead of another does have meaning and does provide new information.

Finally, multiple-choice questions can be designed to help participants identify their own answers out of a full range of possible answers. The trick here, of course, is to either provide a "full" range or to sufficiently encourage respondents to write in any additional items.

Questionnaire Layout and Production

The team must design the physical layout carefully, using a logo and other means of identifying the library. Positive side effects of good marketing accrue from this professional presentation of the library. Make it easy to write in answers and/or to check off choices. Use boxes for simple check marks but blank lines for writing in rankings. The lettering should be clean, reasonably sized, and simple. Eye-catching devices, such as clip art, bold facing, and font variations, should be very limited. They clutter and detract.

Lacking the strengths of the person-to-person format (such as explanation and motivation), the written instrument must encourage full, thoughtful response through other means. Depending on the question, the layout of the questionnaire can be used to present brief examples, lists of possibilities, and even suggested answers to nourish the respondent's thought process. (Care must be taken, of course, to avoid undue influence on that process.) Informal language and appropriate humor can make the instrument interesting enough to engage respondents.

Production quality will assure respondents that competent professionals will appreciate the effort they expend on the instrument. Given the quality of most copiers, printing is no longer essential for paper questionnaires but the copy quality must still be checked throughout the run. Multiple-page forms require staples or the use of folded paper as well as pagination. If two-sided copying is used, the paper must be heavy enough to prevent words from bleeding through. Return directions should be printed on the actual form, not just on a cover letter, and must be clear. On e-mail forms, directions for responses should be clear to those even with low-end equipment.

Questionnaire Question Wording

Wording questions effectively requires flexibility and care. The obvious, general guidelines apply differently according to the context and type of question being asked. One team member might take on the "quality-control" role by examining each instrument in light of the following points:

- Avoid ambiguous questions, such as "How often do you use the library?" As mentioned before, people define "use" in quite different ways.
- Avoid library and information jargon, such as "CD-ROM" and "OPAC." People know whether or not they've used a computer; only a few know whether the computer entailed CD or online searching. Department names that are clear to librarians are often just nonsense to patrons. Reference, reserve, circulation, information, reader's advisory, and more can confuse respondents.
- Avoid specific titles, such as *Reader's Guide* or *LCSH*. Some titles are available in multiple formats; a library could have *Reader's Guide* available in print, on CD, and via WilsonLine. Asking respondents to identify or recognize titles may simply encourage guessing rather than recall.
- Avoid placing too great a reliance on memory. The greater the detail required, the more recent the memory should be.
- Avoid potentially judgmental questions that are not likely to be answered honestly by those outside the "norm" for the topic. Asking how many books are read each month, for example, assumes the respondent reads, reads books, and reads more than one book each month. If any of those three assumptions is incorrect, the reply may not reflect reality but rather an effort to meet the expectations implied by the question.
- Will all respondents know all the answers? If a questionnaire is to be completed by one adult in a household, will any adult do? For example, could either parent in a two-parent household accurately describe the information needs of the children and young adults living in the household?
- Avoid questions already answerable by in-house data. Rather than asking for the average number of books each individual checks out per visit, analyze circulation records to determine the average and range of books per visit per patron.
- Consider question order carefully. Asking first about the World Wide Web and next about general information needs may lead respondents to think of their general needs only in terms of what the Web offers.

QUESTIONNAIRE PRETESTING

Absolutely essential, the formal pretesting of an instrument takes place in two stages. First, a group of about four to ten people who are within the population complete the instrument just as would anyone in the actual study (i.e., without special explanations or discussion). Second, when possible, brief interviews with members of the pretest group are conducted to elicit their hesitations, concerns, and confusions regarding any aspect of the instrument. Although each questionnaire question was answered, the interview may bring to light any odd interpretations or difficulties and these could be discussed during the revision of the instrument. Based on this information, alterations are made to the instrument. A second pretest should be conducted if the changes are numerous or significant.

Sharing the instrument with colleagues from a similar library might also reveal some areas of ambiguity. The team members must not, however, make the most common pretesting error: to run the pretest on their own library staff, administrators, board, or volunteers. Since these groups are "insiders," are more likely to care about the library, and already know a great deal about the library, their reactions are severely skewed.

The most productive pretest requires the effort needed to find genuinely independent participants. Skipping this part of the process is akin to buying a pair of expensive, nonreturnable shoes without trying them on; if you have a problem later, it's too late. Using library staff for this part of the process is akin to trying the shoes on without standing up; there's no strain on the shoe so you can't really tell if they fit.

QUESTIONNAIRE RETURN INSTRUCTIONS

A simple but often neglected point involves the instructions for returning the questionnaire after completing it. Those instructions must be written on the actual item and placed at the end of the questionnaire. Verbal directions will be forgotten, the enclosed mailing envelope will be lost, and signs will be ignored. Unless someone is going to stand in front of subjects and collect their responses (as might be done in a meeting or assembly), the return instructions must be clearly stated at the end of the questionnaire.

QUESTIONNAIRE DISTRIBUTION TIMING

Respondents require enough time to reply (usually ten days to two weeks) as well as enough of a deadline to keep the questionnaire from being seen as an infinitely postponable task. The team plans for problem periods such as holiday weekends, exams, and seasonal crunches. Additional time for response is provided and plans for additional reminders are made when scheduling forces distribution at an inopportune time. Reminders are mailed out for postal and e-mail questionnaires immediately after the original return date is past. If possible, actual notices are mailed only to those who failed to return the questionnaire; a new letter, fresh copies of the questionnaire, and a new SASE are included. If the response rate is low enough to require it, new signs or distribution points are created for distributed and self-selected questionnaires.

Questionnaires: Increasing Efficiency

Responding to a questionnaire involves several steps: receiving the questionnaire, accepting the questionnaire, deciding to complete it, reading the directions, thinking about each question, indicating an answer to each question, and returning the instrument. Only a well-planned questionnaire will support each of those steps. Once the questionnaires are returned, the team must still track the responses and code the data for analysis. Throughout the entire life cycle of a questionnaire, two factors determine efficacy: a good response rate and well-managed, accurate analysis. As when dealing with layout, the CINA team might choose one member to focus on "quality control" with these points as guidelines.

INCREASING RESPONSE RATES

Particularly when a questionnaire serves as the primary means of data gathering, a strong return rate is important and several techniques are available to encourage it. When calculating the sample size (discussed in the next chapter), the likely response rate should be used as part of the calculation. In a postal questionnaire, for example, as few as 20 percent of the subjects may respond (Patten 1998, 70). Of course, an analysis of nonrespondents is essential to an understanding of nonresponse bias, particularly if one segment of the population failed, en masse, to respond.

To increase response rates, the team must take advantage of the following techniques: attractive, uncluttered layout, high quality production, careful pretesting, clear return directions, appropriate reading level, appropriate degree of formality, minimal use of jargon, effective distribution, and persistent follow-through. Each of these techniques has already been discussed. Specific techniques for increasing response rates for different types of questionnaires are discussed later in this chapter.

MANAGING DATA ANALYSIS

Gathering a relatively large amount of data in a small amount of time is the strongest advantage of a questionnaire; using readily codeable questions maximizes that advantage. Such questions offer a finite number of options to the respondent with devices such as Likert scales, ratings, rankings, and multiple choices. When an open-ended question is essential, a number of likely possibilities might be offered in addition to the opportunity to write in an original response. Even if the final analysis must be done by hand, rather than with a statistical analysis package such as StatView, a simple tally of the number of answers in each category works well. Some research questions certainly demand more user-driven input than others thereby resulting in brief essay and fill-in-the-blank questions, but the use of readily coded answers (where possible) speeds the data-analysis process considerably.

As part of data analysis and, in some cases, to monitor response rates, the instruments can be color-coded. Color can facilitate a rapid separation of the responses when different subpopulations (e.g., students and teachers) are sought or different questionnaire distribution methods (e.g., in-house and at the local teen recreation center) are used. Color can facilitate rapid identification of the site producing the highest response rate when questionnaires are distributed in different places, for example, the main campus and the satellite campus. Simply printing the same questionnaire, or even slightly different questionnaires, on different colors of paper can make the process move more quickly.

The preceding points increase the effectiveness or efficiency of most printed questionnaires. The viability of codeable questions is checked in the pretests, as is the clarity of the return instructions. Techniques for increasing the response rate are numerous. Color-coding facilitates both data analysis and questionnaire distribution. Providing sufficient time to respond before following through with appropriate steps requires planning. In addition to these points, others apply to particular types of questionnaires.

Questionnaires: Various Types

In addition to the traditional postal mail questionnaire, the team might consider other types such as distributed, self-selected, e-mail, and Web-based. Balancing costs and effectiveness with the goal of reaching different subpopulations, the team may well choose to use more than one type of questionnaire.

DISTRIBUTED QUESTIONNAIRES

Distributed questionnaires often generate a high response when a captive audience is well utilized. For example, during a high school assembly, questionnaires could be distributed as students entered and collected as they left. Departmental meetings, staff meetings, and other regularly scheduled groupings provide viable opportunities. Such questionnaires need to be short, taking no more than about five minutes to complete, and permission must almost always be obtained in advance from the meeting organizer. A significant number of people can be reached with relatively little effort if the team identifies various subsets of the population, gains access to group gatherings, distributes questionnaires on site, and encourages questionnaire return before the gathering ends. One strength of this form of distribution method is that it reaches, at least potentially, both users and nonusers alike. The team must make certain that the questions take full advantage of this possible access to nonusers.

The cautions pertaining to distributed questionnaires are self-evident. A significant decrease in response rate can be expected when people are allowed to complete and return the questionnaires later. The groups must be chosen carefully to avoid or minimize the bias that can be generated by any particular group. For example, a group of 300 students in a required Psychology 101 class represents a wider range of first-year students than would 300 students in an elective Women's Studies 101 class.

Another variation on the distributed questionnaire takes place at a point of service. These efforts begin only after the service transaction is complete (i.e., after the reference question is answered or the books have been checked out). Starting after the service is complete helps insure that patrons do not view a completed questionnaire as the price of good service. While point-of-service questionnaire distribution only reaches a subset of library users with no chance at all of reaching nonusers, it is useful for understanding the needs of those who use the library most heavily since those people will be more fully represented than others. The response rate is generally rather high as people are willing to "return the favor" by completing a brief questionnaire and returning it to an easily identified box. Since such people are on-the-go, however, the questionnaire must be quite brief. The team must arrange to keep careful count of the number distributed so that an accurate response rate can be calculated. Although some staff may feel uncomfortable about distributing the questionnaires, the task is simple, and supportive training can insure that most public services staff are at ease during the process.

SELF-SELECTED QUESTIONNAIRES

Self-selected questionnaires can be useful if they reach enough people through the use of various reinforcing mechanisms such as large signs and big return boxes. In public areas within the library and, in some cases, other settings, trays of questionnaires can be placed under large signs next to obvious return boxes. Individuals are self-selected in that they choose to complete the questionnaire on their own with no more encouragement than that provided by the sign. The obvious bias produced by the self-selection method means that it should not be used as the major data-gathering mechanism but it can be useful in controlled settings such as a teachers lounge, the lobby of the only Unitarian church in town, or a dormitory dining room.

To cut down on tampering or vandalism, the trays should be kept near a service desk or within sight of an authority figure of some sort. Although nothing will prevent some people from "stuffing the ballot box" as it were, this method can still be productive. Given the unsupervised nature of this method, a response rate is relatively meaningless. The team might, instead, set a goal for the number of usable responses received based on the population, placement of the trays, and time available. In an effort to reach nonusers, trays might deliberately be placed at points outside of the library. In that case, community partners might be willing to manage the daily housekeeping related to the project.

Mailed Questionnaires

Mailed questionnaires start with a complete list of the members of the population or whatever list will come closest to that goal. A campus registrar's list of all undergraduates, a payroll list of the people who are employed by the school, or city water bill recipients exemplify such lists. The registrar's list will not include every last-minute transfer student or withdrawal; payroll may not have weeded out the person who was laid off last week; the water bill list may not include people who live in apartments. Nevertheless, given the size of the populations and the lack of other available resources, the lists are a reasonable place to start.

The team must determine the levels of access to and accuracy of any list of the population members. If such a list exists, what restrictions are placed on access? Is there a fee? Is it only available in a printed format without preprinted address labels? Even if the list is free and in a useful format, its accuracy must be examined. Is it based on property tax rolls and, therefore, a significant number of apartment dwellers and other renters are omitted? Is it updated annually, leaving out a number of mid-year transfers? Are the addresses likely to be current? No list is perfect but identifying the gaps and flaws in any available list allows the team to compensate wherever possible. Triangulation, for instance, may be used to reach a segment of the population not fully represented on the list.

Planning the logistics of a mailed questionnaire, even when using only in-house mail, requires a great deal of attention. One person should be given control of the operation when the team chooses this method. Those who work with that individual must be able to meet deadlines, plan carefully, and handle details efficiently.

When dealing with smaller populations, a careful record of the distribution process identifies those who fail to return their questionnaires, and these people can be contacted again with a reminder notice. For example, the 370 members on the faculty of a small university can be tracked in this way so that individual follow-up letters can be sent to increase the response rate. When possible, a number is assigned to each person in the sample; that number is written or stamped on the questionnaire as inconspicuously as possible. The number and name of each returned questionnaire are checked off the master list. After a suitable period, usually ten days to two weeks, those who have not responded are sent a follow-up letter. Another round of follow-up letters is sent after a similar interval if the response rate is still too low. The master list is destroyed as soon as the process is complete so that patron confidentiality can be fully maintained.

Mail questionnaires require an engaging cover letter, carefully and concisely worded. Since this letter convinces people to consider the questionnaire it must be persuasive from the beginning. (Using the library's letterhead envelopes gets the letter a hearing since many people are willing to at least consider a missive from that source.) When mailing to homes, particular care must be taken to avoid any implication that money is being solicited. Pleas to "help the library" may well be thrown out before readers notice that the "help" consists of filling out a questionnaire rather than sending in money. In general, the cover letter explains the purpose of the questionnaire, provides contact information for those with questions, and covers return procedures. In some situations, a second cover letter from a sponsoring individual may be used to lend weight, authority, and validity to the instrument. A dean, principal, mayor, or other authority figure might emphasize the value and importance of the questionnaire, encouraging a rapid reply.

To facilitate returns, the usual practice is to provide a self-addressed, stamped envelope (SASE) with each questionnaire. A second SASE is usually included, if fiscally possible, when follow-up reminders are sent out. Some populations can be asked to pay for postage but such a request may lower return rates. Having the return envelopes metered so that the full postage price is paid only on returned items saves money when a large number of questionnaires are sent out. Even when using in-house mail with no postage required, the self-addressed envelope increases the response rate.

In some situations piggyback mailings save money, raise the response rate, and reach a target group efficiently. Putting a questionnaire into some established communication mechanism allows the team to use a well-developed mailing list and an effective communication forum to reach their audience. Anything from an in-house newsletter to the program announcement for a major organization can serve as a conduit for a questionnaire. The questionnaire can be a single-sheet self-mailer enclosed within the primary document or a section within the text of the primary document.

Reminder letters worded with wit and humor often encourage response. There is little point in sending out more than two follow-ups but the team may get a respectable response rate with only one.

E-mail Questionnaires

The obvious problems with an e-mail questionnaire include finding accurate e-mail addresses for individuals, missing all those who do not use e-mail, missing those who do not know how or who are not able to respond to e-mail forms, and, when sending a questionnaire to a discussion list, antagonizing people who resent having their group forum used for that purpose. In addition, the traditional problems with layout and general design are complicated by the fact that the questionnaire will not appear exactly the same to all recipients due to differences in screen size and mailers. The emphasis and structure usually added by font changes are erased by the simplicity of e-mail.

All of these problems aside, an e-mail questionnaire is cheap, simple, and cost effective in certain situations. E-mail lists of individuals within organizations are often available, as are group addresses for en masse distribution. A careful approach to a discussion-list moderator, assuming there is one, can sometimes procure permission to submit a well-designed e-mail questionnaire to the group under a "cover letter" from the moderator. This is particularly worthwhile when a specialized electronic forum reaches a large percentage of the population or an important subpopulation. This e-mailed letter encourages everyone to respond by explaining the potential value of the study to the group as a whole.

Responses should be both printed and saved electronically. The print version serves as a backup should some disaster befall the electronic version. In some cases, the electronic files can be manipulated to fit into various data analysis and data management software files.

WEB-BASED QUESTIONNAIRES

A well-designed, Web-based questionnaire mitigates many of the layout issues found in e-mail and print questionnaires. The opportunity to use color, font, drop-down menus, and graphics can increase both the response rate and the quality of the replies.

The problems, however, still preclude its ready use. Despite the rapid growth of the Internet, a sizeable portion of the population still lacks access, not to mention familiarity and comfort. Within those populations that genuinely have full access, another problem exists in that it is difficult to prevent individuals from sending their responses more than once. That which limits access (such as requiring use of a locally recognized password) raises questions in subjects regarding the true confidentiality of their replies. College students, for example, who must use their campus e-mail account to access such a questionnaire might well consider their confidentiality compromised since the system can link their identities to their replies.

Delphi Study

The Delphi technique was created at the Rand Corporation in the late 1950s as a means of futures forecasting. Throughout the 1960s and 1970s the technique was refined and developed until its efficacy in various situations was well established. Since the 1970s the technique has been used in library research with findings published in journals such as the *Journal of the American Society for Information Science* (Neuman 1995) and the *Journal of Academic Librarianship* (Otto 1982).

This method is potentially useful if the team has a pool of knowledgeable experts within the population able to identify significant information needs within the community at large. Rarely used in CINA studies, the Delphi is most useful when dealing with those few who live on the cutting edge of a major change. For example, those faculty who lead the university in designing distance education courses may know now what will be needed campuswide in the coming year.

Its basic purpose is to support the development of a group consensus. By maintaining the complete anonymity of responses, the technique allows this consensus to be reached without the undue influence (common to group meetings) of rank, power, personality, or persuasive speaking practices (Borko 1970, 27–28).

In general, the technique includes these steps.

1. The first is to ask members of a purposefully selected panel to generate extensive explanations of the information needs they see within the community.

2. The responses are consolidated into a single written instrument designed to elicit panel response to each stated information need.
3. The responses are gathered and the needs sorted to highlight areas of consensus and disagreement.
4. The cycle is repeated until a group consensus on key issues is reached.

Obviously the investigator must remain as neutral as possible throughout the process. The "validity of the resulting judgment of the entire group is typically measured in terms of the explicit 'degree of consensus' among the experts" (Mitroff and Turoff 1975, 22).

The strength of the technique is its validation of experience and expertise in understanding the larger aspects of an amorphous problem. Its tandem weakness is the tendency of some investigators to overanalyze the results. Based on the principle that "the complexity of social systems can be reduced for purposes of analysis without sacrificing realism," the Delphi uncovers the priorities of a community regarding its own concerns (Linstone 1975, 579) but it is not designed for small-scale decisions.

Teams interested in identifying broad trends or prioritizing large issues might find the Delphi appropriate. CINA research questions not susceptible to strict, analytic techniques might benefit from the collective (albeit subjective) judgment of a Delphi. Similarly, when the authority or power of an individual may overly influence the group so that all perspectives are not fully presented, the Delphi may be appropriate (Linstone and Turoff 1975, 4).

Diaries, Journals, and Logs

In addition to questionnaires, participants can sometimes be persuaded to document their activities, thoughts, motivations, emotions, and decisions throughout the life of an information-seeking activity or project through written records. Kuhlthau's work, for example, involved the use of self-reported, written records from high school students. These documents can provide great depth and detail when participants fully engage in the project.

Among their obvious disadvantages are the tendency to reveal only what the participants choose to share with the researcher and the tendency to be incomplete (due to issues such as time, stress, or shame) on those points of extreme difficulty—those very points that are most crucial to the researcher. To minimize these weaknesses, self-reported documents are often used in conjunction with other data-gathering techniques. Kuhlthau, for example, included interviews and observations in her research design.

Finally, the natural end-products of various information-seeking activities can be obtained for research purposes. For example, in the I-Search paper, a fairly common format among high school and college populations, students report the problems and solutions encountered during the information search, as well as the more traditional information on the topic at hand. Those papers lack the artificial nature of a research-induced diary but do include all the problems of an assigned, course-related document. Nevertheless, they can be revealing, particularly when combined with interviews.

All of the preceding people-to-document methods of data gathering produce data that require relatively straightforward analysis because they gather limited data in prearranged forms. One other method of gathering data, the diary or journal, can produce the rich, complex data of an interview or observation. Subjects record their information needs, information-seeking activities, and anything else of potential value.

This method is not generally recommended as a primary means of data gathering in a needs assessment for two reasons. First, it is extremely labor intensive for both the subjects and the librarian. As such, it takes far more time than is generally available. Second, analyzing such open-ended products takes special skills and training far beyond the scope of this work. In an interview or observation, no matter how unstructured, the librarian exercises some degree of control over the focus and subject matter covered. In the completely open format of the journal or diary, even subjects who have been instructed to focus on information gathering will include a vast array of issues, concerns, and topics that can be difficult to organize and analyze. Nevertheless, as a secondary means of data gathering, this technique can highlight a number of issues that can be incorporated into a questionnaire.

Those concerns aside, one variation on the diary can be both extremely effective and efficient in some populations. Some subjects will be willing to identify the information they would like to have, as well as some simple data on it, for a limited period. For example, members of the city council might be willing to record, anonymously, a list of information needs arising during a council meeting. For each need they might be willing to check off a box indicating the urgency of the need and the level of their expectation of actually finding an answer. Finally, they might include a few comments on the information need pertaining to other issues. Is the need new or has it arisen before? If the need were met, how would the information be used? The team can provide them with a form for this. As an incentive to the group and as an aid to data analysis, the reference staff can receive the forms and attempt to provide answers to each need. The process gathers actual examples of information needs on the spot with a clarity and detail that make them highly informative.

SUMMARY

The two primary means of gathering data for a community information-needs analysis are person-to-person and person-to-document. The CINA team must balance the competing objectives of deep data and efficiency as they choose and design their instruments. Semistructured interviews and questionnaires often achieve that balance although many other data-gathering techniques also contribute significantly.

CHAPTER 5 READINGS

Reliability and Validity

Babbie, Earl. 1998. *The practice of social research*. 8th edition. Belmont, CA: Wadsworth. {See 129–135.}

Questionnaires

Assessing your community for library planning. 1987. Ontario: Ministry of Culture and Communications.

Babbie, Earl. 1998. *The practice of social research*. 8th edition. Belmont, CA: Wadsworth. {See chapter 10.}

Bookstein, Abraham. 1985. Questionnaire research in a library setting. *Journal of Academic Librarianship*. 11 (1): 24–28.

Converse, Jean M., and Stanley Presser. 1986. *Survey questions: Handcrafting the standardized questionnaire*. Quantitative Applications in the Social Sciences, number 63. Newbury Park, CA: Sage.

DeVellis, Robert F. 1991. *Scale development: Theory and applications*. Applied Social Research Methods Series, volume 26. Newbury Park, CA: Sage.

Fowler, Floyd, Jr. 1993. *Survey research methods*. 2nd edition. Applied Social Research Methods Series, volume 1. Newbury Park, CA: Sage. {See chapters 5 and 6.}

Fowler, Floyd, Jr. 1995. *Improving survey questions: Design and evaluation*. Thousand Oaks, CA: Sage. Applied Social Science Research Methods Series, number 38.

Kalton, Graham. 1983. *Introduction to survey sampling*. Newbury Park, CA: Sage. Quantitative Applications in the Social Sciences, number 35.

Krathwohl, David.1998. *Methods of educational and social science research: An integrated approach*. 2nd edition. New York: Longman. 361–370.

Marchant, Maurice. 1994. *Why adults use the public library: A research perspective*. Englewood, CO: Libraries Unlimited.

Powell, Ronald R. 1997. *Basic research methods for librarians*. 3rd edition. Greenwich, CT: Ablex. {See chapters 3 and 4.}

Schuman, Howard, and Stanley Presser. 1996. *Question and answers in attitude surveys: Experiments on question form, wording, and context*. Thousand Oaks, CA: Sage.

Wurzburger, Marilyn. 1987. Conducting a mail survey: Some of the things you probably didn't learn in any research methods course. *College and research libraries news*. 11 (December): 697–700.

Individual Interviews

Babbie, Earl. 1998. *The practice of social research*. 8th edition. Belmont, CA: Wadsworth Publishing. {See chapter 10.}

Dewdney, Patricia, and Roma Harris. 1992. Community information needs: The case of wife assault. *Library and Information Science Research*. 14 (January–March): 5–29.

Dresang, Eliza. 1990. Interviewing using micro-moments and backward chaining. In *Evaluation strategies and techniques for public library children's services: A sourcebook*. Jane Robbins, Holly Willett, Mary Jane Wiseman, and Douglas L. Zweizig, eds. University of Wisconsin, Madison: School of Library and Information Studies. 131–134.

Fowler, Floyd, Jr. 1993. *Survey research methods*. 2nd edition. Applied Social Research Methods Series, volume 1. Newbury Park, CA: Sage. {See chapter 7.}

Krathwohl, David.1998. *Methods of educational and social science research: An integrated approach*. 2nd edition. New York: Longman. 284–299.

McCracken, Grant. 1988. *The long interview*. Newbury Park, CA: Sage.

McDonald, Lynn, and Holly Willett. 1990. Interviewing young children. In *Evaluation strategies and techniques for public library children's services: A sourcebook*. Jane Robbins, Holly Willett, Mary Jane Wiseman, and Douglas L. Zweizig, eds. University of Wisconsin, Madison: School of Library and Information Studies. 115–130.

Nicholas, David. 1997. The information needs interview: A long way from library-use statistics. *Education for Information*. 15 (4, December): 343+.

Powell, Ronald R. 1997. *Basic research methods for librarians*. 3rd edition. Greenwich, CT: Ablex. {See chapter 4.}

Focus Groups

Carlson, Lynda, Dwight French, and John Preston. 1993. The role of focus groups in the identification of user needs and data availability. *Government Information Quarterly*. 10 (1): 89–100.

Johnson, Debra Wilcox. 1992. Keeping things in focus: Information for decision making. In *Keeping the books: Public library financial practices*. Jane Robbins and Douglas Zweizig, eds. Fort Atkinson, WI: Highsmith Press, for the Urban Libraries Council. 405–419.

Krueger, Richard. 1994. *Focus groups: A practical guide for applied research*. 2nd edition. Thousand Oaks, CA: Sage.

McKillip, Jack. 1987. *Need analysis: Tools for the human services and education*. Newbury Park, CA: Sage.

Valentine, Barbara. 1993. Undergraduate research behavior: Using focus groups to generate theory. *Journal of Academic Librarianship*. 19 (5): 300–304.

Observations

Glazier, Jack. 1985. Structured observation. *College and Research Libraries News*. 46 (March): 105–108.

Jorgensen, Danny. 1989. *Participant observation: A methodology for human studies*. Newbury Park, CA: Sage.

Krathwohl, David. 1998. *Methods of educational and social science research: An integrated approach*. 2nd edition. New York: Longman. {Chapter 12 provides guidelines and tips on observation.}

LeCompte, Margaret, Judith Preissle, and Renata Tesch. 1993. *Ethnography and qualitative design in educational research*. San Diego, CA: Academic Press.

Powell, Ronald R. 1997. *Basic research methods for librarians*. 3rd edition. Greenwich, CT: Ablex. {See chapter 4 for guidelines on observations.}

Shilts, Thomas. 1991. A study of rural public library patrons by unobtrusive observation. *Rural Libraries*. 11 (2): 27–48.

Whyte, William. 1979. On making the most of participant observation. *American Sociologist*. 14 (1): 56–66.

Wilson, T. D., and D. R. Streatfield. 1981. Structured observation in the investigation of information needs. *Social Science Information Studies*. 1: 173–184.

Zweizig, Douglas, and Debra Wilcox Johnson. 1996. Observation. In *The TELL IT! Manual*. Douglas Zweizig, Debra Wilcox Johnson, Jane Robbins, and Michele Besant, eds. Chicago: ALA. 213–225.

I-Search Papers

Joyce, Marilyn. 1995. The I-Search paper: A vehicle for teaching the research process. *School Library Media Activities Monthly*. 11 (6, February): 31–37.

Joyce, Marilyn, and Julie Tallman. 1997. *Making the writing and research connection with the I-Search process. A how-to-do-it manual for teachers and school librarians*. How-to-Do-It Manuals for Librarians, number 62. New York: Neal-Schuman.

Macrorie, Ken. 1988. *The I-Search paper*. Revised edition of *Searching Writing*. Portsmouth, NH: Boynton/Cook.

Reigstad, Tom. 1997. I search, you search, we all search for I-Search: Research Alternative Works for Advanced Writers, Too. ED 412 545.

Journals and Other Documents

Barry, Christine. 1997. The research activity timeline: A qualitative tool for information research. *Library and Information Science Research*. 19 (2): 153–179.

Comparison of Questionnaires, Laboratory Studies, and Field Studies

Cherry, Joan. 1990. Methods of studying database users: The role of surveys, laboratory studies, and field studies. *The Canadian Journal of Information Science*. 15 (3, July): 17–29.

Demographics Used in a Public Library

Lange, Janet. 1988. Public library users, nonusers, and type of library use. *Public Library Quarterly*. 8 (1/2): 49–67.

In-building Use

Kent, Allen, et al. 1979. *Use of library materials: The University of Pittsburgh study*. New York: Marcel Dekker.

Testing a Particular Model of User Behavior

D'Elia, George. 1980. The development and testing of a conceptual model of public library user behavior. *Library Quarterly*. 50 (4): 410–430.

User Satisfaction Measures

Palmour, Vernon, et al. 1980. *A planning process for public libraries*. Chicago: American Library Association.

Delphi Variations

Richmond, Elizabeth, and Michele McKnelly. 1996. Alternative user survey and group process methods: Nominal group technique applied to U.S. depository libraries. *Journal of Government Information*. 23 (2): 137–149.

Westbrook, Lynn. 1997. Information access issues for interdisciplinary scholars: Results of a Delphi study on Women's Studies research. *Journal of Academic Librarianship*. 23 (3, May): 211–216.

The Term "Library Use" in Questionnaires

Bookstein, A. and A. Lindsay. 1989. Questionnaire ambiguity: A Rasch scaling model analysis. *Library Trends*. 38 (2, fall): 215–236.

Validity

Maxwell, Joseph. 1992. Understanding and validity in qualitative research. *Harvard Educational Review*. 62 (3, fall): 279–300.

Wolcott, Harry. 1990. On seeking—and rejecting—validity in qualitative research. In *Qualitative inquiry in education: The continuing debate*. New York: Teachers College Press, 121–152.

Chapter 6

Using In-house Data and Drawing Samples

While finalizing the instruments, the community information-needs analysis (CINA) team also works on two study elements that support actual data gathering: the use of in-house data and sampling. The in-house data may suggest topics that should be included in the questionnaires, interviews, and other instruments. Sufficient and appropriate samples are essential to the validity of the study.

IN-HOUSE DATA

In-house data may provide useful insights without the work of gathering new information. Although they should never be the sole data for a CINA, these seven types of in-house information are sometimes underutilized: circulation, interlibrary loan, reference, online searching, remote-site use, programming, and instruction. While past use is not necessarily an accurate reflection of future need, it does indicate an active expression of past need.

The team considers such data as automated circulation records, OPAC search records, reference statistics, interlibrary loan data, and transaction logs as possible indicators of patron information need. They look for unsuccessful staff efforts to anticipate a need, such as a children's program with low attendance. Informal means of gathering feedback and suggestions (including idea or suggestion boxes, e-mailed feedback, and program evaluations) provide clues for possible interview items. In-house data describe rather than explain.

This is a good time for someone on the team to quickly review all of the regular methods of collecting these data. If they are in any way inadequate, then the team already has one study finding to report. Some suggested changes might be both obvious and so easy to implement that a quick change allows staff to gather data for the study. For instance, reference statistics might be broken down in terms of the types of need involved in the questions (e.g., instructional or directional or in-depth). Only carefully collected data are worth the effort of analysis, however, so the source of each count requires scrutiny (Walsh 1992).

Monitoring basic functions on a spot-check but routine basis provides useful data. For example, the team might recommend that the library keep one week's statistics on the reshelving rate; knowing the current rate becomes essential if the study determines that patrons need a faster reshelving rate. In addition to data on processing functions, the team might recommend that the librarians in various departments keep track of fill rates on basic requests such as reference, interlibrary loan, and titles.

Through existing in-house data, the team might be able to identify concentrations of use in terms of specific variables. For example, people of a certain age, occupation, zip code, matriculation level, or sex might check out material on a certain topic or in a certain format. Again, past use is not always a clear predictor of future need, but the information does inform other findings and may suggest fruitful lines of inquiry.

As part of the general review of in-house data, the team considers the basic policies and services presently available. Taking an organized inventory of what the library now offers is part of the process of creating a picture of the library's present condition. In writing up the final report, a single-page summary of policy decisions regarding daily management issues, such as hours and OPAC availability, provides an excellent context for the study findings. Pulling together a simplified summary of key policies may suggest questions or topics to be incorporated into focus groups, questionnaires, interviews, or other data-gathering instruments.

Finally, an overview of both library and community history should be placed within the context of the current situation. Knowing the history of the library and community, one member of the team should write up a brief status report to provide a larger context for these seven types of specific in-house data.

Circulation Records

The first of the seven areas of in-house data, circulation records, is usually one of the easiest to maximize due to the flexibility of many automated circulation systems. The team might consider doing a week of spot-checking to look at some basic contrasts. For example, are the most frequently circulated books the same ones that are used in-house? The shelvers can take note of what is used in-house for a week; the team can later contrast those call number ranges with those of the books borrowed that week. If the two do not match, perhaps the library has a group of borrowers and a group of browsers to serve. Looking for what characterizes the information needs of those two groups might become a part of the study.

Although few librarians find time for rigorous, systematic weeding, the team might consider the last weeding project. Which books are not borrowed or used in-house at all? Is there a pattern other than the common one of old and ugly books not circulating? Perhaps the selectors are buying for a population that moved on long ago.

Who borrows what? Are members of one group using information in one format or on one topic area? For example, are undergraduates borrowing books on research methods at an unexpected rate? The crucial point here is to look beyond the flat numbers. Perhaps they have borrowed 100 books on survey design and only 50 books on data analysis but if the library owns 500 books on survey design and 60 books on data analysis, the proportionally greater use of data analysis over survey design indicates a need for more data-analysis books. One out of five survey design books versus five out of six data-analysis books is quite a difference but it does not show up when looking at the flat circulation records. (Of course, patron demographics are not available for some of the analyses that might be desired but those that are should be considered.)

Automated circulation records can be supplemented by reshelving counts, questionnaires, and direct observation. Reshelving counts require little effort beyond setting up the record sheet and a minimal training of shelvers. This gathers data on those materials used in-house and never checked out from any service desk. Questionnaires can be left or distributed in the periodical areas, as discussed in the previous chapter. (See Appendix D for a review of the reports that can be generated by various circulation software packages.)

Interlibrary Loan

Interlibrary loan (ILL) requests are a rich source of data regarding specific items needed by some patrons. (It does nothing for nonusers, those who have no time to wait for delivery, those who are not aware of the service, and those for whom it is too costly.) The team should determine what books and periodicals are requested on ILL in terms of subject matter, publication date, and any other variables pertaining to the library's mission. (If the records are manual or incomplete, one finding of the study should be the need to capture these data more effectively.) Recognizing that no library can house all of the items needed by its patrons, the team considers the data in terms of patron information needs. Is a new topic or discipline cropping up unexpectedly? Are cooperative loan programs actually productive in terms of meeting specific information needs? Do items come in too late to be useful?

In larger libraries, the ILL data may be most effectively mined in a meeting with the ILL supervisor, a few selectors, and the team. The emphasis in such a meeting, however, must stay on the identification of information needs. Selectors must not be made to feel that they have failed patrons by not selecting those items borrowed on ILL. Similarly, the ILL staff must not feel uncomfortable about any items that could not be obtained or that could only be obtained too late or at too high a price for the patron. Starting with the premise that they can not meet all needs, the group may well generate a few key issues or topics that can later be incorporated into the other data-gathering instruments.

Reference

Patterns among reference queries sometimes identify logistical issues. The team learns a great deal by analyzing the timing, content or type, and format of reference questions. (Ideally, someone on the reference staff will actually do this analysis and discuss it with the team at an appropriate point.) Timing issues vary greatly depending on the library mission. Those following the school or academic seasons have more long-term fluctuation than those serving a more stable population. While few librarians keep track of their reference questions by content (e.g., business, art history, or crafts), those who do have a rich data source to mine. Many librarians do keep track of reference questions by type (e.g., long or short, equipment repair or instruction or ready reference or in-depth reference). Finally, the communication mechanism of the question is sometimes crucial (i.e., in-person, telephone, e-mail, WWW form, or letter).

In a school library, are many of the afternoon reference questions really just requests for servicing computer equipment? If so, the community may need functional equipment in the afternoon and any one of several solutions may be proposed to provide that. Do e-mail reference questions in a college library pick up at certain times of the day once the semester is under way? In that case, further analysis may be needed. What kinds of questions come in on e-mail? Requests for citation verification might indicate quite a different need than requests for OPAC assistance. In any case, analysis of reference data is particularly fruitful in the CINA because it represents one of the most direct expressions of information needs.

Online Searching

Online searching involves two formats: end-user searching and mediated searching. Transaction logs often provide valuable data on the problems experienced by end users. For example, if patrons confuse keyword and subject search commands, the team might look further into the possibility of information needs centering on the development of basic search skills. Patterns of confusion or unexpected gaps in the use of more sophisticated search techniques might indicate various instructional needs.

Similarly, librarians who run online searches on behalf of patrons have some detailed information on expressions of information needs. As with all in-house statistics, these do not represent the needs of the entire population, not even the entire population of patrons. They do indicate the past needs of a subset of users. The team looks at who asks for what kind of search when. In a public library, for example, responding rapidly to particularly time-sensitive needs might be more appropriate. In any case, analyzing in-house data to glean insights and identify patterns provides a beginning for the work.

Remote-Site Use

Libraries offering remote-site access to their OPACs, periodical databases, reference service, or other functions may have a separate set of data on this remote-site use. (Even those simply offering networked access throughout the building or campus may have data on which terminals were used by whom for what type of search or activity.) The team can examine these data to identify any gaps between user activity and staff support. For example, are remote-site users dialing up on weekends when no staff are available to provide support? Have circulation staff, who sometimes cover more service hours than do reference staff, kept statistics on the questions they received from remote-site users when reference staff are unavailable? Examine the kinds of questions being asked. Difficulty in dialing-up reflects quite a different need than difficulty in moving from the library's OPAC to the library's homepage. Remote-site users do not generally represent the "average" user but, as a subpopulation, their needs certainly merit special attention.

Programming

Programming efforts, as distinguished from instructional efforts (see below), meet the more general needs of different groups. A public librarian's brown bag forum with guest speakers discussing Georgia O'Keeffe's work attracts community members whose information needs may differ from those of people who attend a story hour, a book discussion group, or a workshop on time management.

Incorporated into many programming efforts are productive data-gathering elements such as attendance records. Many evaluation forms ask patrons to actually name other topics or concerns they would like to see addressed in future programming. Keep a list of books on exhibit, those mentioned in handouts, and those incorporated into the programs so that the team can check to see if the items actually circulated more in the months immediately after the program, as would be expected. If not, perhaps some need remains unmet. Evaluation forms, book lists, and the experiences of programming staff may suggest topics or issues for the team to fold into the data-gathering instruments.

Instruction

Finally, instructional in-house data may highlight some community information needs. When a group within the population requests instruction (such as faculty or genealogists), the team examines those requests as expressions of an information need, being careful to recognize that those who ask for such services are not necessarily representative of the population as a whole. An annual report on instructional activity might summarize recent trends in the timing, delivery method, and subject matter over the past few years.

The team identifies definite trends or anomalies requiring follow-up. For example, if Web access were recently made available to the community but few requests for instructional support are coming in, the team might want to find out why. It could be that the community is generally savvy in this area already or it may be that they know so little that they can not even frame their questions yet.

Knowing what people do in the library with library resources does *not* tell the team what the community needs but it does tell the team what some members of the community will take. It is not the answer by any means but careful use of in-house data can do much toward providing a context for needs and a springboard for solutions. These data often spark questions worth taking into interviews, focus groups, or questionnaires.

COMMUNITY DATA

Just as the librarians may know a great deal about their own operations, someone else may know a great deal about their community. Before gathering community data from scratch, the CINA team asks others to share any available information. These data identify major features of the community served (e.g., the largest majors in a college or the variety of social/civic/religious organizations in a city) and may build an understanding of the community's topography (e.g., the number of specialized computer labs springing up in a school or the new shopping areas being built or new businesses moving into a city).

Depending on the library environment and parent institution, the data can come from a wide range of sources. Computer support staff could have statistics on the number of people who access the library from remote sites. Considering how library access can be dependent on network access, looking for extant data in that area, even if it is outside of their immediate control, serves the team well. The personnel office may provide a profile of a school's faculty. High school teachers might have files of I-search papers that could be analyzed to identify the problems most experienced by students. Social service agencies may have data from their own analysis, as did Beer et al. 1998.

Community data are particularly helpful in identifying and characterizing subpopulations. An academic library's obvious subpopulations include first-year, sophomore, junior, senior, and graduate students. A simple count of these subpopulations is somewhat useful, especially when the team is planning a stratified random sample. However, identifying which portion of each subpopulation is majoring in a natural or social science might provide clues as to their information needs. The team might well assign one person to capture any relevant, immediately available data on the community as a whole.

If community data are unavailable or insufficient, the team may decide to conduct their own community analysis. The steps in this process can be as thorough and detailed as those used by Jo Haight Sarling and Debra Van Tassel (1999) in their work for a Denver public library. Alternatively, a structured review of community environment factors could be conducted by using such items as newspaper reports, maps, local event calendars, lists of local organizations, and projections for community growth. A "neighborhood walk" can be used to identify areas of change, growth, and loss. Conducted in-person (driving or walking) or figuratively, a neighborhood walk entails establishing community boundaries and then identifying the important environmental elements within those boundaries. For example, an academic library team might pin up a map of the campus next to a map of the city in which the campus is located. Using clear plastic overlays on top of the maps, various sites could be marked and viewed in relationship to the library. Sites such as bookstores, computer labs, other libraries, research centers, academic support units, planned computer labs, long-term construction, unofficial departmental collections, and departments could be marked.

SAMPLING TECHNIQUES AND PRINCIPLES

Sampling may be undertaken for either of two distinct and separate purposes; the techniques used to draw a sample vary depending on that purpose. Sampling may be done for accuracy, as when a random sample of university students is drawn with the intention of accurately representing the whole population of university students at an institution. This sampling for representativeness, in which the characteristics of those in the sample represent the characteristics found in the population, is what is commonly understood as the purpose of sampling. Contacting representatives of the population, rather than contacting every member of the population, saves time and resources.

Sampling may also be done for variety, as when a focus group is formed to include people with a wide range of numerous demographic characteristics. A school team, for example, would not hold a focus group of band members to help identify information needs for the entire student body. Team members might, however, identify various student groups and hold a series of focus groups in order to hear from as wide a range of students as possible. They might look at a range of variables, such as activities (e.g., band, theatre, football, tennis, chess, computer club), matriculation levels (i.e., members of each grade), sex, home-language, and race. Putting together focus groups or short interviews, the team members deliberately seek a sample that yields a spectrum of personal and situational characteristics rather than a representative sample.

Sampling for accuracy requires the techniques of probability sampling. Sampling for variety requires that one (or more) of various techniques be chosen in the context of the population qualities and the types of variety sought. In each case, the purpose of the data gathering dictates the appropriate sampling method.

Sampling for Variety

Some extremely labor-intensive data-gathering techniques provide such rich, in-depth data that their use significantly deepens the team's understanding of community information needs. Observations, interviews, focus groups, and written artifacts (e.g., information logs) provide rich data but are far too costly (in data-analysis time, if nothing else) for wide use in most settings. With these labor-intensive data-gathering methods, sampling for accuracy is simply not a viable, practical option. The team must still sample carefully, however, in an effort to maximize variety rather than accuracy. The team cannot claim that all elements of the population have an equal probability of being selected in this type of sample; therefore, the resulting data are extremely weak in reliability although they may be stronger in validity. The results will certainly not support statistical inference and do "not permit generalizing from the sample to the population because the researcher has no assurance that the sample is representative of the population" (Powell 1997, 68). These samples are, however, relatively easy and affordable to draw. Four nonprobability sampling techniques are particularly common in information-needs analysis: self-selected sample, purposive sample, systematic sample, and quota sample. (For more on these and other nonprobability methods, see Powell 1997, 67–69.)

SELF-SELECTED SAMPLE

Participants who respond to a general call for participation form a self-selected sample. Calls range from the general (e.g., a call for focus group participants is published in the local newspaper) to the localized (e.g., a questionnaire is placed in the local senior citizens home) to the focused (e.g., every member of a school's faculty is invited to set up an interview). In each case, the team simply accepts those who volunteer with no assurance that the subjects represent the population. In fact, those who choose to participate in a study almost certainly differ from some members of the population. While acknowledging that particular major weakness during data analysis, the team still gains insights into the variety of information needs experienced by the subjects.

PURPOSIVE SAMPLE

Given the focus of a particular study, drawing a purposive sample may yield useful findings. Based on the team's knowledge of the community, specific individuals could be identified as potential subjects based on their experience or access to a portion of the community. For example, in a small township with a rapidly growing Korean population, the team may work to identify members of the Korean community who have personal knowledge concerning various facets of the community. They might, for example, solicit participation from the ESL instructors, religious leaders, business owners, and parents. Again, regardless of the team's efforts to diversify perspectives, these subjects can not be taken as representative of their community.

Purposive samples also serve to reach into relatively unfamiliar parts of the community. Academic librarians, for example, may tend to see fewer chemistry majors than English majors at the reference desk and may, therefore, feel the need to interview among the former but not the latter. Public librarians may notice that mothers stop bringing their children to the library once the children reach school age and may, therefore, want to hold a focus group with mothers of first-graders. School librarians may be surprised by a strong demand from juniors and seniors for reference resources on the Web and may, therefore, interview several of those students who make the greatest use of this resource. In each case, the team's knowledge or awareness of a particular segment of the community leads to a purposive sampling with no claims of generalizable results.

SYSTEMATIC SAMPLE

Taking advantage of conveniently available subjects lies at the heart of a systematic sample. The team may, for example, distribute questionnaires to every individual or every tenth individual who passes a certain point (e.g., the student commons room or the local post office). The advantage here is that there is relatively little bias in that everyone who passes that point at that time has approximately the same chance of being given a questionnaire. (This assumes, of course, that those distributing the instrument do so to every nth individual without skipping over those who make them uncomfortable.) The weakness, however, remains. The resulting sample in no way represents the population at large because the entire population does not pass the distribution point.

Systematic sampling utilizes events (e.g., local fair) or places (e.g., a shopping mall) over various periods of time. The greater the variety of events, places, and times, the greater the range of possible subjects. The more likely the site or event is to attract a larger portion of the community, the greater the range of possible subjects. The choice of site (e.g., Wal-mart or upscale mall) and time (e.g., weekday morning or Saturday afternoon) usually affects the range of variation among subjects sometimes leading to a strong bias. When dealing with an entire city's population, however, well-chosen and varied site-based distribution can reach many members of a community.

Alternatively, when a fairly complete list of potential subjects is available, then systematic sampling can be employed even more effectively. A random starting point on the list is identified and every nth subject is then selected. This requires an essentially random listing; alphabetical lists can work but those arranged in a hierarchy—such as students by Grade Point Average (GPA)—would not.

QUOTA SAMPLE

Quota sampling requires clearly defined, mutually exclusive, readily totaled subsets of a population. In a school, for example, grade levels generally form subsets that meet those requirements. While some crossover might occur, such as a few juniors taking senior-level mathematics courses, most students fit squarely into a single grade level and the numbers in each level are readily determined. Quota sampling uses any random method of identifying subjects with the addition of an effort to insure that proportional numbers of each subset are included. Exit interviews might be taken at the school entrance until the proportions of each grade were represented in the total number of subjects. While useful for diversifying findings and increasing representation of various subpopulations, the method still lacks the analytic strength of a true probability sample.

Nonprobability Methods to Be Avoided

Convenience and snowball methods of sampling may actually produce such biased results that the team would be better off without the resulting data. The convenience method simply taps the team's existing personal networks in that subjects are selected solely on the basis of the ease with which they can be contacted and persuaded to participate. A focus group can be readily formed from the friends and family of team members but the resulting data would be so limited in perspective and contaminated by the relationships with team members that it would be worse than useless.

The snowball sample has the same flaws but simply uses another personal network. In this technique, one individual is selected; that subject is then asked to suggest one or more people who might also be willing to serve as subjects. Those people are then included and they too are asked to supply names. The pattern continues until a sufficient number of subjects have been obtained. These methods cost too much in biased data to justify their general use in information-needs analysis studies.

There is one exception to this warning. If any subpopulation is difficult to identify, then the snowball sample might help. For example, in many parts of the country it is difficult, even dangerous, for people to discuss their information needs in terms of sexual orientation. Young adults in a school setting and mature adults in the work setting may well be uncomfortable delineating the information needs that pertain to their sexuality. In-depth interviews with gatekeepers could help, but a snowball sample might also gather useful information from a broad range of people in different situations.

Nonprobability Sample Size

Since this sampling's purpose is diversity rather than accuracy, no strict statistical guidelines determine the proper sample size. When a population is genuinely unfamiliar, the ideal is to sample until "saturation" is reached (i.e., until the data begin to repeat well-established patterns with nothing new added).

The practical realities of data gathering, however, often dictate that diversity sampling reach as many subpopulations as feasible rather than reaching for saturation. The team plans for this goal by identifying subpopulations and then using whatever technique will best reach them. Demographic factors (e.g., grade, job rank, discipline, race, ethnicity, language, educational level, age, family structure, or sex) are traditionally used to identify groups within the population as a whole. While useful, those factors are not the only productive possibilities. Library use and support level may also make useful criteria. Those people who make heavy or limited use of library services or who provide special support may also make a useful subpopulation. Each subpopulation is considered, and appropriate ones are sampled to identify a diversity of issues. The sample size in each subpopulation depends on practical limitations such as subject availability, data-gathering time, and data-analysis time. At least two and up to ten individuals in each group should be contacted regarding the information issues that concern them. Those issues are then folded into an instrument that is distributed to a carefully constructed, probability-based sample of the entire population.

Sampling for Accuracy

The details of determining a statistically valid probability sample are beyond the scope of this volume but the following general techniques and principles provide a basis for discussion and further work. Two of the best books on the topic, Kalton's *Introduction to Survey Sampling* and Henry's *Practical Sampling*, are readily available and may well be worth the time needed to read them. Ronald Powell's valuable chapter on sampling provides an overview with some detail (1997, 66–87) as does Arthur Hafner's work (1998, 229–261). Many teams will decide that this is a point at which the learning curve demands far more than is reasonable to give; therefore, an outside expert may be called upon to determine the most appropriate sampling technique and sample size.

The purpose of sampling for accuracy is to sample for representativeness. If the sample does not represent the population, then it is not worth taking. How completely the sample must represent the population is open to some discussion. The realities of time and budget often dictate extremely limited sampling. To some extent it is true that a limited sample may be better than no sample at all, but every effort must be made to insure a meaningful, accurate, appropriate sample within the context of the study. Therefore, probability sampling issues become part of the overall research design and must be considered in designing the data-gathering instruments.

Regardless of the type of probability sample taken, the CINA team (or the outside expert they recruit) handles four tasks: determining the population, identifying the sampling frame, choosing the sampling method, and determining the size of the sample. In some situations, any single task may be judged inappropriate or excessively costly but the team makes those determinations carefully rather than by default.

DETERMINING THE POPULATION

As the first step, the team determines the actual population for the study. The actual population consists of a description of the people who have access to the library. For example, a public university library's population is generally everyone currently affiliated with the university and all taxpayers in the state. A school library's population may be every faculty member, staff member, and student affiliated with the school.

The next step moves from a general definition to a practical reality. The team identifies the sample population, that is, every identifiable member of the actual population. For example, the academic library may be able to identify every currently registered student and currently employed staff member but the people identified in this fashion are not the only ones who are part of the actual population. Transfer students and emergency hires will not be included while recently dropped students would be listed. Taxpayers in the state can be identified but never completely or accurately. The actual population is an ideal in that it is almost impossible to accurately identify every member of it. The sample population includes only those who can definitely be identified and contacted.

Knowing the difference between these two groups is crucial because that difference will certainly affect the outcome of the study. For example, a public library team may determine that identifying the homeless population is simply not possible. Recognizing that fact, the team may decide that involving the staff of the local homeless shelter in the data gathering may be productive even without benefit of a probability sample of the homeless.

Obviously the data-gathering techniques chosen by the team may well become part of this difference between the actual population and the survey population. When an e-mail is the chosen method, the survey population is further reduced to those who have e-mail access and are able to reply to an e-mail. Any written instrument automatically excludes those who can not read at all, those who can not read the language of the instrument, and those who are unable to write down their responses. As a general principle, the team must look for those members of the population who are likely to be missed by their chosen data-gathering methods. They must look for those who are marginalized, such as the illiterate, those who do not read in the language of the instrument, and the homeless, as well as those who are not free to respond.

IDENTIFYING THE SAMPLING FRAME

The sampling frame is a list of as many members of the sample population as possible. As mentioned before in the discussion of the population, obtaining an accurate, complete list of the population is rarely possible. The team must, therefore, identify the sampling frame that will be used along with the flaws inherent in the chosen frame. A secondary aspect of the sampling frame includes contact information on each individual. What level of information is available and how accurate is it? Postal mail, electronic mail, and telephone numbers are rarely completely current.

In academic and school libraries the sampling frames are typically class rolls and employee lists. People who have recently left either list are typically noted on some set schedule. Universities, for example, may revise class rolls on the twelfth day of classes in each term. Employee rolls may be updated on the last workday of each month.

Other variations, however, also confuse the frames. In a university setting, do students who audit classes count as part of the population? Are visiting faculty within the parameters? In a school setting, do parent volunteers who work more than ten hours a week count as staff? Are special education counselors who rotate among various schools in the district included?

Contact information tends to be available within set administrative parameters in academic institutions. School students tend to report to a single homeroom or primary teacher once a day so they can be reached that way even if records of their home contact information are out of date. University students, staff, and faculty must be contacted by postal or campus mail at least once a semester for standard purposes. Gaps and variations will occur but fairly solid sampling frames may be obtained from administrative sources.

Public library teams face a more difficult challenge in forming a sampling frame for their populations. Rather than seeking an elusive ideal, reviewing available formats may prove productive. The team should assign one person to explore the administratively available options. Does the city have a mailing list for all postal customers? Are water bills sent to each residence (home and apartment) and to each business? Is detailed census information available block by block? (A great deal of census information is available on the Internet now.) Tax rolls tend to leave out those who do not own property, and voter registration lists are increasingly incomplete. Telephone books are viable in some communities but they do leave out those with unlisted numbers and those who lack phones. Does the mayor send out a city newsletter to every household and business?

The obvious problem with these household-centered sampling frames is that they leave out entire subpopulations. The homeless, an often-lost group, may be covered by nonprobability sampling in local shelters. Spouses and minors within a household may be reached to some extent through careful instrument design. When one individual responds on behalf of the entire household, however, the findings must be discussed and analyzed with that limitation in mind.

CHOOSING THE SAMPLING METHOD

Several probabilistic sampling methods are available to the team but three methods are particularly useful. The simple random sample determines subjects through use of a random number table, insuring that all members of the population have an equal chance for selection. (The random number table is not the only procedure available for selecting a random sample, as mentioned earlier in the discussion of the systematic sample.) The stratified random sample uses simple random samples of exhaustive and mutually exclusive subpopulations to produce a smaller but equally valid sample. The cluster sample, used in extremely large populations whose elements can not be listed, utilizes natural groups to get down to a level at which identification is possible.

Simple Random

A simple random sample is, in fact, simple but rather tedious to construct. Every person in the sample population is listed and assigned a number. For example, a school library team might print out a list of every student and then simply number each student's name in the order in which it appears on the printout. Using a random number table, students are selected continuously until the proper sample size (discussed shortly) is reached. (For explicit instructions on using a random number table, see Powell 1997, 71–73 or Hafner 1998, 240–244.) Every student is equally likely to be chosen and the task is simple enough to be handled by almost anyone. In larger populations, such as those of public libraries or major university libraries, the tedium of constructing a simple random sample by hand quickly moves it into the realm of the impossible. If an electronic sampling frame permits the application of a computer-generated random sample, then the work is easily completed.

Stratified Random

Two techniques for drawing stratified random samples allow the team to identify the technique that will best represent their population. In a homogeneous community, the proportional stratified random technique requires that (a) the population be divided into exhaustive and mutually exclusive strata and (b) that a set percentage of each strata be drawn at random. A school library team, for example, might determine that the student body varies little along any major demographic variable. In that case, matriculation levels provide ready-made strata into which each student is automatically placed. For example, drawing 10 percent of each stratum (using the simple random sampling technique) insures that an equal percentage of each class is represented. Fewer subjects are required because the use of well-designed strata helps insure that all levels are fully represented.

Most populations, however, are too complex and heterogeneous for this approach. Some strata may be so small and others may be so diverse that proportional sampling fails to present a full picture. In that case, the team chooses disproportional stratified random sampling in which roughly the same number of subjects are chosen from each stratum regardless of the total number available. In a city library system with several branches, for example, the team may determine that the neighborhood communities used as the basis of city council electorates could serve as strata in that they are culturally meaningful, mutually exclusive, and clearly defined. Some, however, are much smaller than others and all lack some degree of homogeneity. Each neighborhood, therefore, might contribute fifty subjects using the city council members' mailing lists for their neighborhood communities as the sampling frames.

Obviously data gathered through disproportional sampling requires special care later in the study. In particular, "when computing estimates of means and estimating standard errors for disproportional stratified samples, one should compute values separately for each of the strata and then weight them according to the relative size of the stratum in the population. . . . In addition, it should be recognized that, in theory, one cannot make legitimate use of various nonparametric statistical tests, test for the significance of correlation, analysis of covariance, etc., without substantial modifications" (Powell 1997, 75).

Cluster Sample

Teams dealing with large populations may find it impossible to list subjects with any meaningful accuracy. Some university libraries who serve a large number of off-site or continuing education students may note that these students slip in and out of the university's rolls every semester rather than moving straight through a program. Some cities keep track of homeowners for tax purposes but have no list of the thousands who live in rapidly expanding apartment complexes. Teams in those cities and universities may want to consider cluster sampling.

Cluster sampling takes advantage of naturally occurring groups or clusters. Cities with no record of apartment dwellers may still recognize an apartment complex as a cluster of people. Since some apartment complexes hold hundreds of people, a two-stage technique may be employed in which buildings within the complex are treated as secondary clusters. A random sample of the actual apartments within the buildings within the complexes yields a two-stage cluster sample.

Variations abound in this technique. At the final cluster stage, the team may select all of the subjects available or only a few. Clustering may occur in one or several stages. A university team, for example, may cluster students by number of credit hours obtained then by address (on campus, in town, out of town). Both probability and nonprobability sampling techniques may be used as needed in multistage sampling although using the latter reduces accuracy.

Cluster sampling requires heterogeneity on one level and homogeneity on another level. At the cluster level, homogeneity is important. That characteristic which defines a cluster, at any given level, should be as similarly applied as possible. Using credit units earned for most of the university but assigned matriculation level for the Residential College unit breaks that homogeneity. At the unit level, that is, the units within any given cluster, heterogeneity strengthens the technique, especially if all units within a given cluster become subjects. (For more on this technique, see Powell 1997, 75–78.) Cluster sampling "usually decreases the precision of the statistics" (Henry 1990, 30).

DETERMINING THE SAMPLE SIZE

Determining sample size requires balancing the realities of subject pools with the requirements of statistical analysis techniques. In a worst-case scenario, the team must simply acknowledge that their resources left them with an inadequate sample size and/or a less robust than ideal sampling technique; therefore, they must use simpler statistical analysis techniques and claim less generalizability for their findings. They may decide that the study is still worth the effort but they should also be willing, if necessary, to stop until they get the resources necessary to make the study more viable.

Six general guidelines affect sample size. Whether using tables, sample size calculators, or formulae to determine sample size, the team considers the following points. (For more on these and other sampling issues, see Powell 1997, 79–87 and Henry 1990, 10–15, 34–46.)

1. The larger the population, the smaller the proportion of it needed in the sample. Alternatively, the more diverse the population, the larger the proportion of it needed in the sample. After a certain critical mass is gained, the proportion of sample to population rises quite gradually unless the population is heterogeneous. Even then, the sample size may rise only slightly if the sampling method can account for the heterogeneity. The corollary here is that a bigger sample is not necessarily a better sample in that it may gain more data than are needed, data which must then be analyzed.

2. Smaller samples, up to a point, are less precise but still viable. Since CINA studies lead to general adjustments in services and collections, rather than to extremely exact alterations, the lack of absolute precision may not invalidate the work. Since all samples produce estimates rather than absolute counts, some range of accuracy in those estimates exists.

3. Variation in the population requires increasing the sample size or separating out the variation patterns. Running a simple random sample on a large, heterogeneous population requires a larger sample size than doing the same on a large,

homogeneous population. Better yet, if possible, the variations could be arranged into strata with smaller samples taken of each stratum. The corollary here is that the sampling technique, as already mentioned, impacts the sample size.

4. Running more precise statistical analyses of data requires that those data come from larger, more accurate samples. Simple descriptive statistical reports, such as an average and a range, require less robust samples than do more complex inferential statistical analyses, such as a linear regression.

5. Sampling bias and sampling variability combine to form sampling error and the level of that error may be mitigated by an appropriate sample size. Sampling bias results when one portion of the population is over- or underrepresented in the sample. Sampling variability occurs in any sample due to the random selection process that yields samples that vary from the population to some extent; that is, no sample can perfectly represent the population.

6. Sample size refers to the number of instruments to be sent out, *not* to the number of instruments that are actually returned and usable. The anticipated return rate must impact the sample size. If, for example, the sample size is 100 for a one-time mailing but only a 20 percent response rate is anticipated, then 500 instruments must be sent out in order to receive 100 returns. If at all possible, the nonresponse bias must be analyzed to better understand the respondents whose input was lost. Low return rates, even when compensated for in this manner, certainly reduce the value of the data.

Since sample size computations take into account a number of variables, no single method covers all situations.

Two mechanisms provide sample sizes without requiring calculations: tables and calculators. Tables are available in the following works: Powell 1997, 80; Hedrick et al. 1993, 78; and Patten 1998, 79. Although not appropriate for all situations, these tables provide a very general, often conservative, guideline. A few commercial and educational entities provide Web-based sample size calculators. The team determines the confidence interval and confidence level required, enters the numbers, and lets the calculator determine the sample size. For Web addresses for a few reputable calculators as well as lucid explanations of key terms, see the readings at the end of this chapter.

Whether using a calculator or a formula, the team must determine the degree of precision required. Those to whom they report may require that particular determination to be made in terms of an acceptable confidence interval and confidence level. The confidence interval is the range of values within which there is a probability that the population parameter will exist over all possible samples; a typical value is plus or minus three. Pollsters note their confidence interval when they report that 60 percent of Americans like chocolate, within plus or minus three percentage points. That is, 57 to 63 is the interval within which they are confident that their report is accurate. As few as 57 percent or as many as 63 percent could actually like chocolate. The confidence level refers to the probability that the true percentage of the population would respond as did those in the sample. A typical value in social science work is 0.05, that is, the team can be 95 percent certain of the responses.

Formulae for calculating sample size vary a good deal depending on the type of sampling technique used, the characteristics of the population, and the degree of precision required. In addition, a number of different formulae estimate the sampling error or the standard error of the mean. The many variations on these two points depend so much on context and specific situations that they fall beyond the scope of this book. For those teams who want to calculate their sample size and sampling error, the works listed below should prove useful. Those teams who want some confirmation that their use of a table or calculator is appropriate or that their application of a formula is accurate could contact a local expert such as a marketing analyst, a statistician, or a survey research company. Understanding the issues involved in sampling will always strengthen those discussions.

CHAPTER 6 READINGS

Analysis of Transaction Logs Data

Nelson, Janet. 1992. An analysis of transaction logs to evaluate the educational needs of end users. *Medical Reference Services Quarterly.* 11(4, winter): 11–21.

Gathering Statistics from Nonlibrary Sources

McClure, Charles, and Cynthia Lopata. February 1996. *Assessing the academic networked environment: Strategies and options.* Washington, DC: Association of Research Libraries for the Coalition for Networked Information.

Community Data

Data from the 1980 census are available at the following sites:
www.censuscd.com/cdblocks/cdblocks.htm
www.geolytics.com/censuscd1980/censuscd1980.htm

In-house Data

Hernon, Peter, and Ellen Altman. 1996. *Service quality in academic libraries.* Norwood, NJ: Ablex.

Massey, Morris. 1976. Market analysis and audience research for libraries. *Library Trends.* 24 (3, January): 473–482.

Price, Anna, and Kjestine Carey. 1993. Serials use study raises questions about cooperative ventures. *Serials Review.* 19 (3, fall): 79–84.

Smith, Mark. 1996. *Collecting and using public library statistics: A how-to-do-it manual.* How-To-Do-It Manuals for Librarians, 56. New York: Neal-Schuman.

Walsh, Anthony. 1992. All the world is data and we but the ciphers in it. . . . William Shakespere [*sic*]. 1992. *Reference Librarian.* 38: 21–30.

Zweizig, Douglas, and Eleanor Jo Rodger. 1982. *Output measures for public libraries: A manual of standardized procedures.* Chicago: American Library Association.

Nonresponse Rates

Fowler, Floyd, Jr. 1993. *Survey research methods.* 2nd edition. Newbury Park, CA: Sage.

Observation of In-house Use

Bustion, Marifran, et al. 1992. On the merits of direct observation of periodical usage: An empirical study. *College and Research Libraries.* 53 (November): 537–550.

Sampling

Babbie, Earl. 1973. *Survey research methods.* Belmont, CA: Wadsworth. 73–110.

Fowler, Floyd, Jr. 1993. *Survey research methods.* 2nd edition. Applied Social Research Methods Series, volume 1. Newbury Park: Sage. {See chapters 2 and 3 for useful advice on sampling and nonresponse.}

Hafner, Arthur W. 1998. *Descriptive statistical techniques for librarians.* 2nd edition. Chicago: American Library Association. {Chapter 8 discusses the differences between probability and nonprobability samples.}

Hedrick, Terry, Leonard Bickman, and Debra Rog. 1993. *Applied research design: A practical guide.* Applied Social Research Methods Series, number 32. 74–80. Newbury Park: Sage.

Henry, Gary. 1990. *Practical sampling.* Applied Social Science Research Methods Series, volume 21. Newbury Park: Sage.

Kalton, Graham. 1983. *Introduction to survey sampling.* Quantitative Applications in the Social Sciences, number 35. Newbury Park: Sage.

Kraemer, Helena Chmura, and Sue Thiemann. 1987. *How many subjects?* Newbury Park: Sage.

Krathwohl, David.1998. *Methods of educational and social science research: An integrated approach.* 2nd edition. New York: Longman. 158–183.

Leedy, Paul. 1989. *Practical research: Planning and design.* 4th edition. New York: Macmillan. 156–166.

Patten, Mildred. 1998. *Questionnaire research: A practical guide.* Los Angeles: Pyrczak. {Table 8.8.1 lists margins of error for various sample sizes while the rest of the chapter provides basic explanations of sampling techniques.}

Powell, Ronald. 1997. *Basic research methods for librarians.* 3rd edition. Greenwich, CT: Ablex. 57–87.

Simpson, I. S. 1988. *Basic statistics for librarians.* 3rd edition. London: Library Association Publishing. 37–51.

Voelker, David, and Peter Orton. 1993. *Statistics.* Lincoln, NE: Cliffs Notes. [If you are comfortable with the abbreviated format of the Cliffs Notes series, then pages 55–67 may provide the quick review needed to clarify the basics of sampling.]

Sample Size Calculators

Freymuth, Casey. The calculator mounted by this author is part of a company (group iv inc.) site: *www.groupivinc.com/resources/ calculator.html.* (accessed 7/5/00)

Martindale, Jim. Martindale's The Reference Desk, Calculators On-Line Center. A "Calculator Center" with eleven subcenters is available at: *www.sci.lib.uci.edu/HSG/RefCalculators.html.* (accessed 7/5/00)

Metrix Matrix. Sample Size Calculator. *www.metrixmatrix.com/ Calculators.asp.* (accessed 7/5/00)

NCS. A company specializing in survey research, NCS provides a sample size and confidence interval calculator along with simple, clear explanations of the basic factors involved. The calculator, glossary, and collection of research notes can be reached at: *www.ncs.com/ncscorp/ research/index.htm.* (accessed 7/5/00)

The "Survey System" by Creative Research System can be accessed at *www.surveysystem.com/sscalc.htm.* Authored by H.G. Zucker, Ph.D., this site explains confidence intervals and confidence levels as well as factors that affect them at *www.researchinfo.com/calculators/ sscalc.htm* and *www.surveysystem.com/sscalc.htm# terminology.* (accessed 7/5/00)

University of California at Los Angeles, Statistics. This array of sample size calculators requires an understanding of the possible variables to be considered in running a calculation since they focus on the power of any given sample size in various situations. If anyone on the team has the expertise to make a choice that fits the situation, then visit *www.stat.ucla.edu/textbook/calculators/powercalc/.* (accessed 7/5/00)

Using a Random Number Table

Hafner, Arthur. 1998. *Descriptive statistical techniques for librarians.* 2nd edition. Chicago: ALA. 240–244.

Kalton, Graham. 1983. *Introduction to survey sampling.* Quantitative Applications in the Social Sciences, number 35. Newbury Park: Sage. 11–12.

Powell, Ronald. 1997. *Basic research methods for librarians.* 3rd edition. Greenwich, CT: Ablex. 71–73.

Value of Measuring Library Activities

Dervin, Brenda. 1977. Useful theory for librarianship: communication, not information. *Drexel Library Quarterly.* 13 (3July): 16–32.

Chapter 7

Launching a Study

Throughout the three stages of data gathering (scheduling, training, and maintaining), the community information-needs analysis (CINA) team relies on the written set of research questions as a guide for decisions growing from the stated plan as well as for those arising from the unexpected. Occasionally new opportunities will arise during the course of the study, such as a university library's chance to add a limited number of items to a university-sponsored questionnaire being sent out to prospective students. Occasionally questionnaires require design changes after pretesting, such as a more complete array of telecommunication choices for remote-site users of a public library. Sometimes staff involvement develops unexpectedly, such as school library volunteers offering to administer exit interviews. For all of these situations and more, the research questions provide focus and parameters for decisions.

SCHEDULING

Scheduling starts with writing down the exact sequence of steps from pretesting and training through the last returned questionnaire, noting carefully any steps that can be accomplished simultaneously. For example, if both a written and an exit interview are to be used as data-gathering instruments, the pretesting for both items could be done simultaneously. The team member most experienced in logistics lays out each step of the process from pretesting through mechanisms for boosting response rates. Which group of volunteers will deliver how many questionnaires to what locations after how much training? Planning on the maximum number of glitches, the team might be able to move ahead of schedule if the process flows smoothly, but they should not make the mistake of leading staff or administrators to expect findings earlier than they can be delivered. Writing down the sequence of steps provides a visual checklist of tasks as well. The entire team can readily see the planned schedule and make adjustments as circumstances warrant when a whiteboard, electronic schedule or other flexible mechanism is available.

After setting up the sequence of steps, the team establishes an actual schedule, writing down how many days will be needed to train staff and volunteers, to distribute questionnaires, conduct interviews, right down to the last detail. Considering the ongoing obligations (e.g., reference desk, classes, and online searches) as well as special situations (e.g., a long holiday weekend or all-day staff meeting), the team lays out the dates for each segment of the work. Pretesting usually takes a few days since it can be difficult to locate suitable members of the population. Training, with few exceptions, takes no more than two hours and often as little as a half hour. Since in-depth interviews are quite wearing, no more than two, or three at the very most, should be scheduled in one day. Postal questionnaires take six to ten weeks, depending on the number of follow-up mailings required; e-mail questionnaires take a couple of weeks less. Observations, exit interviews, and general questionnaire distributions depend on the traffic flow. A Gantt chart lays out the exact schedule and can be readily produced on many office management software packages. It requires, however, nothing more sophisticated than a word processor yet lists each task and delineates each step of the timeline. (For an example, see the manual, Figure 7.1.)

The schedule stops at the last piece of data gathering, before the actual analysis of data or writing the final report. Until the data come in, it is difficult to tell in advance how much time will be needed for those steps. Obviously they will be completed as rapidly and efficiently as possible but it is hazardous to promise administrators a date for the final report prior to gathering the data. Six weeks for analysis and four weeks for writing will generally suffice when a final due date is required for some reason.

Obviously team members must be prepared to change dates either to avoid problems or to take advantage of unexpected opportunities. They might, for example, get all set for a phone survey on the theory that everyone will be snowbound on that February weekend, only to find no one home due to an unexpected thaw. Almost any small-scale postal or e-mail questionnaire will require at least one and often two rounds of follow-up work to build a sufficient response rate. (Since follow-up mailings are not possible with large-scale questionnaire distributions, the number of questionnaires distributed is increased to account for response rate problems. This concern is discussed in the previous chapter's section on sampling.) Individual interviews and even focus groups will need to be rescheduled as subjects' plans change. Likewise the team at a public library might find that the new Chamber of Commerce president is amenable to allowing the team to take a few moments for a questionnaire distribution at the monthly meeting. Such an unexpected opportunity to reach people in a "captive" audience can help immensely.

While there is no set time limit, the schedule for the data-gathering stage generally covers four to ten weeks. The required time depends on the number and type of instruments used, the size and diffusion of the population, and the scope of the study. Balancing the need for steady forward momentum with the time needed for quality data gathering, the team sets out a schedule of steps in some detail and everyone works hard to stay on track.

TRAINING FOR EACH DATA-GATHERING TECHNIQUE

After determining the types of data-gathering instruments to be used in the study, the team considers training people to gather the data. In some situations, of course, extensive training is simply not an option. Sometimes the team members will just have to handle the data gathering on their own without benefit of any additional help due to pressing duties or a lack of support. Sometimes training is not necessary since staff already know enough to handle the required instruments. Finally, training is sometimes simply impractical. If only two focus groups will be used, then another study may well provide a better opportunity for training.

However, when appropriate, the time and effort taken to train staff and/or volunteers in data-gathering techniques pays off in both the short term and the long term. Not only will the current study move more swiftly, but future projects of various types can draw on the skills developed through training.

The team reviews the staff and volunteers available to help in their implementation. Do any staff members already have training or experience in distributing questionnaires, conducting interviews, or observation? Have any staff members expressed an interest in participating in any aspect of the work? Some may want the opportunity to gather data within the population they serve, as when the children's librarian wants to gather data from parents. Not everyone needs to know each technique but the team gains flexibility if one or two people can learn more than one technique. Some people are not good at or temperamentally suited to some methods. Interviewing, in particular, requires interpersonal skills not universally possessed.

The team member in charge of training may choose to give staff enough information about the assistance needed to help them self-select into certain segments of the training. For example, the trainer might explain that exit interviews require the ability to think quickly, take good notes, and connect with people quickly, and that should lead reclusive or shy people to avoid that training. When announcing the schedule to staff, the team could take a few moments to explain what skills are needed. Recruiting people to be trained is the first step. Of course, in some situations, the team or an administrator may need to assign people to certain jobs, just to get the work done in a timely fashion.

As a final option, outsiders can handle some tasks. A consultant may be hired to manage the focus groups, telephone surveys, or questionnaire distribution design. Members of a university research methods class looking for a project might handle pretesting. (Tygett et al. 1996 worked with a marketing research class, for example, on a reference evaluation.) One-time volunteers recruited by the Friends of the Library group might manage questionnaire distribution. The sorting and tabulation of a simple questionnaire might be taken on by a local high school honors organization as a service project. While unskilled outsiders require extensive and careful supervision, their involvement may pay off in the long run if they become library advocates. Whether involving regular staff and volunteers or special one-time contacts, each data-gathering technique chosen by the CINA team requires specific training or skills.

Both interviews and face-to-face questionnaires require one special point during training: staff must know how to handle the situation when people refuse or are reluctant to participate. In that case, staff must be encouraged to use their judgment to some extent. While never insisting or forcing a "hard sell" on the potential subject, they can offer to try at a later time or invite later participation. Those who are personable and can talk easily to strangers will be able to persuade some people to participate.

Interview Training

Interview training generally requires two separate sessions. In the first, staff members are introduced to the purpose of the interviews, the reason for the wording of each question, and the mechanism chosen to approach possible subjects. A productive exercise involves having everyone list on a whiteboard the uncomfortable situations that they fear—such as being refused, being asked to defend the study as a whole, or being asked to provide service in the midst of an interview. The trainer reviews various means of handling those situations, emphasizing that the interpersonal style of each individual subject prohibits the prescription of any single response. At the end of the first session, the trainer might set up two pairs of mock interviews with the class providing feedback for the in-

terviewers. The first session ends with a small "homework" assignment in that everyone must approach one stranger and conduct an interview for real. (A brief discussion of the ethical
implications of this training exercise should help insure that people
are not imposed on unduly and that any meaningful data gathered is utilized properly.)

The second session consists of reports on and discussions of the
practice interviews. Emphasizing the positive, the trainer looks for
multiple solutions to common problems. Some discussions lead to
productive suggestions regarding the implementation of the actual
interviewing. For example, interviewers might benefit from having any of the following: a formal letter from the library director
requesting public participation in the study; an official nametag
to wear while soliciting participation; access to a quiet, more private room in which to conduct longer interviews. This practice
round with its attendant discussion may serve as pretesting if that
activity has not already been completed.

As the training must emphasize, interviewing requires the use
of follow-up, probe, and clarification questions to get a more complete understanding of the answers. (This is particularly true of
the almost ad hoc interviewing involved in participant observation.) Of course, the interviewers can not change the study's purpose but the team must determine in advance how much leeway
is available.

> You can in effect say to the interviewers 'Ask these questions
> exactly as they are written down', or 'Ask these questions in
> wording that each individual will comprehend', or 'Ascertain
> the answers to these questions in any way you like', or 'Find
> out all you can about what people think on such and such a
> topic.' (Line 1967, 63)

Interviewers in even the most formal situations need a certain
amount of flexibility. (If there is absolutely no need for flexibility, the team should be using a questionnaire form.) For example,
if a subject's answer to question one also answers question four
quite clearly, there is no need to ask question four exactly as writ-

ten. Instead, the interviewer mentions the main point of that question and asks the subject for any additional comments.

Observation Training

Observation training requires anything from one to three sessions, depending on the complexity of the behaviors under observation and the experience levels of the investigators. Simple observations (e.g., the number of books actually examined by a child during a single library visit) require less training than more complex observations (e.g., the actions involved in a lengthy reference search). Simple observations are more tightly defined and require fewer interactions with subjects. Complex observations contain a number of possible variables and require that subjects be interviewed.

Of course, in any case, certain qualities enable some investigators to gather the maximum amount of observable data. The ability to concentrate with an intense focus for an extended period of time is crucial. The ability to note and record details quickly and flesh them out more fully at the close of each observation is essential to gathering complete data. In more complex observations of apparently illogical processes, an open-minded flexibility is needed to follow the subjects smoothly.

As in the interview training, observation training begins with an explanation and discussion of the purpose behind the work. Some staff may not see the value in observing a relatively small number of people. Another role must be found for them as their observations will be shallow and incomplete. The most common difficulty in observation is the inability of the interviewer to focus. One of the best training techniques is to share an observation and discuss the notes taken on it. For example, videotape a child's movements through the children's area and have the trainees take notes on it. In discussing the notes, play back the video as needed to illustrate various aspects of focusing the observation. Mock participative observations as class exercises and real observations as "homework" exercises provide fodder for discussing the procedures and honing skills. The ethical guidelines regarding observation require particular emphasis prior to the training exercise.

Questionnaire Design Training

Training for questionnaire design is somewhat paradoxical. On the one hand, individuals design questionnaires more effectively than do committees; therefore, there is little immediate need for training. Whoever would do the training should just go ahead and write the questionnaire. On the other hand, questionnaires are useful in so many situations that, in large libraries, having someone in each department who is capable of writing one is a strength in the long term. The team must determine whether the time invested in a training session is worth the long-range return.

If so, a two-part training session is planned. In the first part, the basics of writing, layout, and response-rate enhancements are covered. People then take the same research questions and draft their own questionnaires. If appropriate, cover letters and follow-up notices are also created. In the second part of the training, the various drafts are shared, discussed, and critiqued by the group.

Questionnaire Distribution Training

Training for questionnaire distribution is much simpler, of course, but still necessary. A simple half-hour session is both critical and easy. Staff must understand the impact of their comments and demeanor on subjects so that they remember to stay as neutral as possible when handing out the questionnaires to groups or individuals. Training should prepare them for both logistical questions (e.g., "Can I turn this in at the library tomorrow?") and content questions (e.g., "Do the questions I answer for my boss count?"). A rapid one-on-one debriefing after the first few distribution rounds can verify the efficacy of the training and provide an opportunity to reinforce or supplement as needed.

Delphi Training

The Delphi, discussed in chapter 5, is also best when handled by an individual rather than a committee but, unlike the questionnaire, is seldom required. The team identifies an open-minded self-starter who can stay on schedule and manage the logistics competently when a Delphi is appropriate for the CINA. A one-on-one review of the phases of a Delphi with someone who has been through the process is the most efficient training method.

Focus Group Training

Focus group facilitation is done, ideally, by someone outside of the library so that subjects are not inhibited or influenced by the presence of a librarian during their discussion of their information needs. If no one is available from the outside, the team identifies a staff member who is personable, at ease with strangers, able to listen well, and able to think quickly. If gathering subjects for focus groups is not too difficult, training a couple of people as facilitators is probably worth the effort. For example, in a large school setting it may be possible to identify and solicit subjects so readily that focus groups will be used for purposes beyond the CINA so that having a few people able to conduct a focus group is worth the training effort.

A single session covers the fundamentals, including the purpose of a focus group, the facilitator's role, encouraging everyone to participate as equally as possible, the use of probe questions to follow through on unexpected insights, means of keeping the discussion on track, taking notes, and use of taping equipment. Videotaping a practice focus group with selected subjects, time permitting, is a very useful means of pretesting the questions while providing practice for the facilitator. The trainer's review of the tape supports feedback for the facilitator.

Ethics in Training

Throughout the training, the basic ethical issues pertaining to confidentiality and authority must be emphasized. Casual discussions of the information revealed during data gathering must be clearly forbidden. Even during data analysis, discussions must not include the names or identifying characteristics of subjects. Training must help staff develop a true understanding of the privacy issues involved in the work. Consider the child who may not want a teacher or parent to know of a reading problem or subject interest. Consider the employees of a local business who do not want their supervisors to know that they have home e-mail and Internet access for fear of having their home-time become work-time. Anonymity is ideal but confidentiality must always be assured.

At no time should anyone feel pressured to participate. Particularly when dealing with minors, participation must be—and must be perceived to be—fully voluntary. Knowing the productive use to which the data will be put, some staff may have a hard time understanding why anyone would choose not to participate, other than the common reasons of being too busy or hurried. The line between encouraging participation and enforcing participation can be thin in some situations; seeing only general good as an outcome, some staff may cross the line unless their training is clear. Others may not recognize themselves as authority figures; some staff believe that people feel free to refuse participation when, in fact, they fear that future library visits will be uncomfortable or that their refusal will become public knowledge.

Finding Trainers

Finally, for all training, the team needs to seek out competent, knowledgeable support. They may look for local experts willing to conduct training sessions for free or at a nominal cost. Local university departments may be willing to post a call for someone to come out and train the staff as a service or class project. Contacting social science, library studies, and information science departments well in advance may lead to graduate students in search of a service or course project. Of course, such an outsider would need to meet with the team to insure compatible goals and perspectives. In some large libraries there may even be staff or retired volunteers with experience in these matters. As mentioned before, consultants (either free-lance or affiliated with state library agencies) may step in to provide careful training as a single service or as part of their cooperative work with a team.

MAINTAINING THE DATA GATHERING

After completing the training and launching the study according to the schedule, the team remains flexible throughout the actual data gathering. The team meets briefly (perhaps via e-mail) to discuss the situation when new opportunities arise suddenly. For example, during the course of an interview, a key informant might raise a new issue worth exploring (e.g., when a teenage, single mother states that she's uncomfortable in the children's area of the public library because the computers are scary). Likewise, early questionnaire returns may show that a major but unexpected issue is important to the community, as when students in a junior high school demand a homework hotline. The team must be ready to go back to the original research questions and make some tough decisions. Should those issues be set aside till the next CINA or should the present effort be temporarily halted while the new issues are incorporated into the data-gathering instruments? Should a special effort be made to go into a closed community, such as that of single parents with little education, in order to follow up on a new issue?

Throughout the process possible new partnerships might come to the notice of someone on the staff. For example, someone distributing questionnaires in the local grocery store might be offered the opportunity to set up a box by the exit. A much larger number of questionnaires could be distributed when the team picks up on such an arrangement. Knowing that such partnerships are one of the many benefits of a CINA, the team trains all staff to handle such offers diplomatically. (Only team members or those they specifically designate should solicit or accept such partnerships, of course.) Maintaining and building on those partnerships can be as simple as sending an appropriate thank you letter or as complex as arranging a formal donation.

Likewise, the decision to recruit, train, support, and reward volunteers builds new partnerships on an individual basis. In addition to supporting the project, this can be a great way to develop a core of supporters. If someone on the library staff generally handles volunteers, that individual should be involved in managing the CINA volunteers so that the opportunity for maintaining contact is increased.

Maintaining the study's momentum keeps everyone's spirits up. The team regularly lets the staff know what has been accomplished so far. Just stating that a set number of interviews has been conducted or that the questionnaire response rate is up to a certain percentage will help. Increasing involvement a bit, such as asking for extra help in passing out questionnaires at the entrance gates, keeps the project from sliding into obscurity. No one should be surprised to hear that the data gathering has ended, because staff and administrators should be aware of the study progress even if they are not participating directly.

Finally, as mentioned earlier, the data must be kept quite private. Aside from the ethical concerns, incomplete and raw data can trigger rumors, gossip, speculation, and problems throughout the staff. Only the team and staff members directly involved in data analysis should review what comes in and even they must keep it absolutely private. The resulting problems can be significant when people on the team start to speculate about findings to even a few chosen associates. At the very least, such speculation may corrupt data gathering and analysis. At the worst, it can generate widespread expectations (for good or ill) which the final report must then actively dispute. As the data come in, one or two team members review them with an eye for any unexpected opportunities or issues meriting follow-up. Other than that, the data are kept private until a thoughtful and complete analysis can be conducted.

CHAPTER 7 READINGS

Support for Interview Training Sessions

Babbie, Earl. 1973. *Survey research methods*. Belmont, CA: Wadsworth. (Pages 176–180 provide guidelines for and information on interview training.)

Fontana, Andrea, and James Frey. 1994. Interviewing: The art of science. In *Handbook of qualitative research*. Norman Denzin and Yvonna Lincoln, eds. Thousand Oaks, CA: Sage. 361–376.

Gorden, Raymond. 1970. Dimensions of the depth interview. In *Reader in research methods for librarianship*. Mary Lee Bundy, Paul Wasserman, and Gayle Araghi, eds. Washington, DC: NCR. 166–171.

Gorden, Raymond. 1975. *Interviewing: Strategy, techniques, and tactics*. Revised edition. Homewood, IL: The Dorsey Press.

McCracken, Grant. 1988. *The long interview*. Newbury Park, CA: Sage.

Support for Observation Training Sessions

Adler, Patricia, and Peter Adler. 1994. Observational techniques. In *Handbook of qualitative research*. Norman Denzin and Yvonna Lincoln, eds. Thousand Oaks, CA: Sage. 377–392.

Bruyn, Severyn. 1970. The methodology of participant observation. In *Reader in research methods for librarianship*. Mary Lee Bundy, Paul Wasserman, and Gayle Raghi, eds. Washington, D.C.: Microcard Editions. 172–185.

Jorgensen, Danny. 1989. *Participant observation: A methodology for human studies*. Newbury Park, CA: Sage.

Schwartz, Morris and Charlotte Schwartz. 1955. Problems in participant observation. *American Journal of Sociology*. 60: 343–353.

Whyte, William. 1979. On making the most of participant observation. *American Sociologist*. 14 (1): 56–66.

Wilson, T. D., and D. R. Streatfield. 1981. Structured observation in the investigation of information needs. *Social Science Information Studies*. 1: 173–184.

Support for Questionnaire Design Training Sessions

Clark, Herbert, and Michael Schober. 1992. Asking questions and influencing answers. In *Questions about questions: Inquiries into the cognitive bases of surveys*. Judith Tanur, ed. New York: Russell Sage Foundation. 15–48.

Converse, Jean, and Stanley Presser. 1986. *Survey questions: Handcrafting the standardized questionnaire*. Newbury Park, CA: Sage.

Croyle, Robert, and Elizabeth Loftus. 1992. Improving episodic memory performance of survey respondents. In *Questions about questions: Inquiries into the cognitive bases of surveys*. Judith Tanur, ed. New York: Russell Sage Foundation. 95–101.

Fowler, Floyd, Jr. 1995. *Improving survey questions: Design and evalu-*

ation. Applied Social Research Methods Series, volume 38. Thousand Oaks, CA: Sage.

Fowler, Floyd, Jr. 1993. *Survey research methods.* 2nd edition. Newbury Park, CA: Sage.

Support for Delphi Training Sessions

Dyer, Esther. 1979. The Delphi technique in library research. *Library Research.* 1: 41–52.

Linstone, Harold A. 1975. Eight basic pitfalls: A checklist. In *The Delphi method: Techniques and applications.* Harold A. Linstone and Murray Turoff, eds. 573–586. Reading, MA: Addison-Wesley.

Westbrook, Lynn. 1997. Information access issues for interdisciplinary scholars: Results of a Delphi study on Women's Studies research. *Journal of Academic Librarianship.* 23 (3, May): 211–216.

Support for Focus Group Training Sessions

Carlson, Lynda, Dwight French, and John Preston. 1993. The role of focus groups in the identification of user needs and data availability. *Government Information Quarterly.* 10 (1): 89–100.

McKillip, Jack. 1987. *Need analysis: Tools for the human services and education.* Newbury Park, CA: Sage.

Mullaly-Quijas, Peggy, et al. 1994. Using focus groups to discover health professionals' information needs: A regional marketing study. *Bulletin of the Medical Library Association.* 82 (3, July): 305–311.

Chapter 8

Analyzing the Results

Analyzing the results of a community information-needs analysis (CINA) involves more than tabulating questionnaire data. Moving from raw data to preparing to write a report is a four-step process: developing an overview of the data, running the statistical analysis, running the narrative analysis, and drawing conclusions. The overview and conclusions involve the whole team but an individual could take on the two types of data analysis, either of which could precede the other.

This is the moment at which an open mind and disengaged ego are essential. People will see as a need that which is already offered. People will make no mention of a carefully nurtured, long-standing service. People will characterize collections as inadequate, staff as unhelpful, and facilities as uncomfortable. Not all people will do so, but even a few can make some members of the data-analysis team uncomfortable.

This analysis process begins a sequence of judgments that eventually leads to specific plans. A defensive attitude undermines the whole process, as does an unquestioning acceptance of most comments. When is a need for a new service really a need to know about a long-standing service? When does a need for polite staff really lead to customer service training? Does a need for a stronger book collection lead to weeding or selecting or both? At the end of this process some libraries "have moved their cultures to a completely user-centered mode. This has changed the way they do things across the board, at the most basic levels of decision making. Other institutions are finding small, incremental ways of solving problems their users have" (De Candido 1997, 6).

DEVELOPING AN OVERVIEW

The overview combines hard data and anecdotal evidence, takes relatively little time, and produces information of both immediate and future value. First, the team examines the response rates for various groups (e.g., users and nonusers, men and women) and the response rates for various data-gathering mechanisms (e.g., postal questionnaires and exit interviews). If the response rates are adequate, they are analyzed on two points: what worked well and what gaps developed? Did e-mail questionnaires reach women effectively? Was there a gap in the returns resulting in little representation of the sophomore student perspective?

Looking at the amount of data gathered in terms of both population and instrument leads naturally to the second overview element, namely a broad look at what mechanisms might be used in future. Perhaps the instrument used to track reference statistics could be used on a regular basis in future. Perhaps a group of hitherto unknown users was identified during a focus group; in future they might become library users or supporters to some extent. In other cases the complete lack of response from a major constituency (e.g., local schoolteachers who refuse to participate in a public library's study) can be crucial. Understanding what lay behind that deafening silence might become a focus of future work.

Finally, the anecdotal input of the CINA team bears discussion. As questionnaires came in and interviews were transcribed, the team members read and absorbed the data to some extent. If anything stood out as a complete surprise, it might be important in the overview. Since good librarians generally have a reasonable grasp of their community's needs, something that comes as a substantial shock deserves attention. Surprises do not always occur but any that do are worth a frank discussion. Perhaps they relate to an instrument, as in finding that busy executives were more than willing to discuss their need for networked information resources. Some may relate to gaps in the responses from subpopulations, as in deans who have no interest in the library's efforts to support distance education projects. Some may come from a single comment on a questionnaire or in an interview, as in the patron who complained at length about an unmet need for electronic document delivery service. In any case, the very fact that these data surprise the team makes them worth consideration but only consideration. They may be isolated anomalies with no impact on the overall study or they may be straws in the wind predicting changes and problems.

This overview generally takes place as an unstructured discussion with informal reports on response rate analysis. A team member should take notes, however, to insure that relevant points are available when the final report is written.

RUNNING THE STATISTICAL ANALYSIS

The process of analyzing statistical data ranges from simply counting responses to determining the relative significance of one set of responses in relationship to a demographic variable. In most cases, the CINA team will not have the data, resources, or expertise to go much beyond a descriptive analysis. This is not a problem since descriptive statistics are all that is generally needed. In any case, the data generally require preparation prior to analysis.

Preparing for the Statistical Analysis

When possible, the team employs a statistical analysis package to track data. Purchasing or using an institutional copy of a package requires that someone learn the program and enter the data. StatView, for example, allows the user to record, track, compare, and run statistical analysis on a complete range of numerical data. The system automatically generates analyses on any appropriate variables, such as the percentage of men who prefer telephone to e-mail in reference service. Given team support and due attention to the ethics of privacy, a volunteer or staff member could readily handle the data entry.

If a statistical package is both unavailable and unobtainable, then the team must plan for the hand tabulation required. Relatively few questions, only essential demographics, color-coded questionnaire forms, and questions with simple, single responses make hand tabulation more feasible. The more advanced calculators permit a number of statistical computations once totals have been generated. Since the statistical analysis packages are useful for a number of research purposes and are available for under $500, the team should certainly try to obtain one rather than go through the laborious tasks associated with hand tabulation.

Basic Terminology

Reviewing six terms, prior to approaching statistical analysis, eases the use of statistical packages and strengthens the effort to apply the correct analysis techniques to the data. Four terms refer to types of data: nominal and ordinal as well as parametric and nonparametric. Two terms refer to types of analysis: descriptive and inferential. All of these terms (as well as "statistic" and "test") are used with varying degrees of specialization in the readings listed at the end of this chapter. If anyone on the team decides to move more deeply into statistical analysis than this modest overview supports, then understanding the context of each term becomes critical.

NOMINAL DATA

Nominal data are non-numeric values. They are simply words to which a number has been assigned; hence the term "nominal" in that they are only nominally numeric. Nominal variables have *only* the characteristics of exhaustiveness and mutual exclusiveness but they can not be rank-ordered. Many demographics are nominal. The variable sex, for example, has two values: female and male. Those values are exhaustive (gender varies but there are only two sexes) and mutually exclusive. They can not, however, be rank-ordered in that one is not greater than the other. In using a statistical package it may be easier to type a 1 for female and a 2 for male but there is no numeric meaning to those numbers; they are just a convenience.

The team could just print the numbers as they appeared on the questionnaire. They could reorder the numbers in descending order and include percentages on each. They could also use a histogram or pie chart to present the information visually but, if so, the actual numbers should also be reported.

Sample Questionnaire Items Yielding Nominal Data

Which of the following have you used to find information in the past two weeks? Check all that apply.

___ e-mail colleague or friend	___ the World Wide Web
___ phone colleague or friend	___ television
___ visit bookstore	___ radio
___ visit Allan Public Library	___ newspaper
___ my own materials	___ other, please explain

In which of the following fiction areas should the Allan Public Library update its book collection? Check all that apply.

___ mysteries	___ fantasy
___ romance	___ modern fiction
___ westerns	___ classics
___ alternative fiction	___ multicultural fiction
___ science fiction	___ other, please explain

ORDINAL DATA

Ordinal data come in three levels: simple ordinal, interval, and ratio. Only simple ordinal and ratio really apply in CINA studies. These are data that can be logically rank-ordered. The degree of accuracy in that ranking marks the difference between simple ordinal and ratio data.

Simple ordinal data come from variables with attributes that can be logically rank-ordered but which do not have a true zero. Typically measured on a Likert scale with the range such as "not very important" to "most important" or in terms of ranking, these data indicate direction but do not have an absolute numeric value. To say that a subject ranks one information need as more critical than another is not to say anything definitive about how much more critical it is; direction is indicated but it is not possible to assign a universally agreed-upon value to that direction.

Ratio data, on the other hand, are based on a true zero. Frequency counts, age, length of residence, number of books borrowed in a given time period, number of searches entered into an OPAC, and number of visits to a bookstore all produce ratio level data. These are the most robust data so they are open to a number of statistical tests, given the proper conditions. On the other hand, only relatively simplistic information-need elements can be expressed in terms of such absolute numbers.

Sample Questionnaire Items Yielding Simple Ordinal Data

Think about the information needs that you've had in this first month of the fall term as well as the ones that you anticipate having in the coming month. Consider every kind of information need from learning to use a new database to finding documents on the Internet to obtaining journal articles for a term paper. Please list and rank your top three information needs below.

Please check the response which best represents your Internet or World Wide Web experience as it pertains to your classwork.

I can find the information I need:

[   ] always   [   ] frequently   [   ] at times

[   ] occasionally   [   ] never

PARAMETRIC

Parametric tests are used when two conditions are met. First, the data gathered must be at the ratio level. Second, either the entire population must be included (e.g., virtually all members of a middle school's faculty complete their questionnaires) or a genuinely sufficient and random sample of a population with a normal distribution must be used (Hafner 1998, 214). To use parametric statistics the analysis requires all the assumptions pertaining to a normal distribution, one that follows the classic Bell curve with the mean, median, and mode falling at the same point and the classic distribution of cases along the standard deviation. "However, if the sample drawn from the population has 100 or more cases, the normality assumptions can almost always be relaxed" (Powell 1997, 192). Often used to determine the existence, strength, and even direction of a relationship between two variables, these techniques provide such useful information that the team may well find it worth the trouble and expense necessary to obtain viable data for their application.

Sample Questionnaire Items Yielding Ratio Data

- In the past two weeks, on approximately how many days have you been able to check your school e-mail account at least once?

- Since the last in-service workshop on using the World Wide Web for curriculum development, some teachers have been encouraged to identify useful Web sites. For some subjects that is much easier to do than for others. Consider the sites, if any, that you have bookmarked both at home and on your classroom computer. Approximately how many Web sites have you currently marked for your classes?

NONPARAMETRIC

Nonparametric tests are used in one of two situations: (1) when the data are at the simple ordinal or nominal level or (2) when the data are clearly based on a nonrandom or nonnormal distribution. Useful for smaller samples, these tests "involve weaker assumptions" and "are less powerful than the parametric tests" (Powell 1997, 194). These tests are best suited to data "that mark or classify observations descriptively rather than quantitatively ... as in assessing attitudes, perceptions, or client satisfaction" (Hafner 1998, 214).

DESCRIPTIVE

Descriptive analyses are numerical and graphical means of identifying and describing patterns among values. Used to identify representative values (e.g., average) and measures of dispersion (e.g., range), they are often applied to nominal and nonparametric data. They are used to describe values or summarize data rather than to draw conclusions from data. Descriptive analyses produce frequency distributions (in both numeric and visual formats), measures of central tendency, measures of variability, and the correlation between two variables. Every CINA will produce a full range of descriptive analyses.

INFERENTIAL

Inferential statistics are a means of drawing inferences from or making judgments on the basis of data by moving from the sample to the population. Using partial measures of a population (i.e., samples), inferential statistics may be used to determine the "significance" of a value. Generally used in hypothesis testing, these statistics may be useful in a CINA when the team needs to "make inferences and judgements about what exists on the basis of only partial evidence" (Powell 1997, 190).

Descriptive Statistics

With nominal, simple ordinal, and ratio level data of a parametric or nonparametric nature, the use of descriptive statistics lays the basic foundation for understanding. Simple frequency counts, standard measures of central tendency, and measures of variability help describe the findings in terms that are generally meaningful to staff and administrators alike. A combination of graphic and numeric representations may prove fruitful; many statistical packages produce both quite readily.

FREQUENCY COUNTS

The simplest and most obvious description of the findings, frequency counts provide more information when given in contrast to each other. Contrast various needs, such as the need for instruction on using the Web with the need for instruction on using the OPAC. Contrast various demographics, such as the number of men and women who need more nonfiction. If there are at least 100 responses, translating the raw number counts into percentages makes it easier for readers to understand the data without misleading people into thinking that the response rate was greater than it really was.

CENTRAL TENDENCY

Finding measures of central tendency means locating the center of the distribution of a set of values. The team must be careful to interpret these statistics in light of each other and in comparison to the range in order to get a sense of the distribution curve shape (e.g., classic Bell curve, bimodal, or skewed). When the mean, median, and mode fall on the same point, the distribution is symmetric. When the pattern runs mode to mean/median to mode, the distribution is bimodal. When the pattern runs mean to median to mode, the distribution is skewed to the left. When the pattern runs mode to median to mean, the distribution is skewed to the right.

The mean, of course, is the arithmetic average of the values in a distribution. Obviously, there's no point in calculating this unless the numbers are real numbers, that is, they have a real zero and real numeric meaning. The ranks and Likert scales, for example, produce nominal data so there's no point in averaging any numbers that are artificially derived from them. The average age of respondents, however, would be reasonable to calculate as would the actual number of Internet information-seeking efforts made in the last week.

The median is the point on the scale of measurement below which 50 percent of the scores fall. The mode is the most frequent score in the distribution, the simplest index of central tendency. Central tendency provides a modest description of the data that may lead the team to consider additional analyses.

VARIABILITY

Measures of variability examine the lengths of intervals that indicate how scores are spread throughout the distribution indicating the variation of scores in a distribution. In one example, ranked items could be marked as 1, 2, 3, 4, or 5. If most respondents chose one response, then that would indicate little variability and merit special attention. An item concerning personal health information, for example, could be ranked 5 by 85 percent of the respondents while an item concerning parenting could be ranked as 1 by 70 percent of the respondents. In both cases, the lack of variability indicates a stronger consensus.

The range, mean deviation, variance, and standard deviation are commonly used and readily provided by not only statistical packages but also by many calculators. Each measure provides a different insight regarding the data.

The range is the distance between the highest and lowest scores; it is seriously limited by the influence of extreme scores. The mean deviation is the average of the absolute differences (i.e., without regard to the negative nature of some scores) of each score from the mean. If respondents vary in age from 15 to 79, then the range for age is $(79 - 15) + 1 = 65$.

Although useful, the mean deviation is not robust enough to use in some other calculations. Variance, on the other hand, is another way of getting to the absolute deviations and it allows the later application of inferential statistics (Hafner 1998, 187). Variance is basically the standard deviation squared. Most commonly used, the standard deviation is the positive square root of the variance. (See Krathwohl 1998, 401, for instructions on determining the standard deviation without a calculator.) "It is a useful measure of dispersion, because in many distributions of scores we know what percentage of the score lie within plus or minus one, two, and three standard deviations. Its usefulness is enhanced because its units of measure are the same as those of the original data. The standard deviation is useful for comparing groups" (Powell 1997, 188).

Inferential Statistics

When moving beyond basic description into analysis, the team may employ inferential analysis if the size and nature of the sample support inference. Inferential statistics generally examine the correlation between two variables or the significance of the findings.

CORRELATION

One of the most commonly used measures of correlation, the Chi-square test, determines whether a statistically significant relationship exists between two variables. It does not indicate the direction or strength of the relationship, only whether it exists. Used most readily on two nominal variables that may (or may not) be parametric in nature (e.g., sex and e-mail use or home Internet access and library card ownership), the Chi square is a function available on some advanced calculators. For example, looking at the variables of sex and heavy Internet use might lead the team to wonder whether the difference in use between the two sexes is meaningful or just chance. Running a Chi-square test can determine the answer.

Another more familiar measure of correlation, a *scatterplot*, can produce dramatic results on occasion if at least one of the variables is ordinal. For example, plotting age against number of bookstore visits in the past month might indicate that as age increases, so too do bookstore visits. In cases of extreme correlation, the simple visual record of that plotting will demonstrate both the existence and direction of a correlation. For example, if the relationship between Internet use (as measured by number of uses made in the past week) and grade level were plotted, then the rate of Internet use would go along the vertical axis and the grade level along the horizontal axis.

6				x	xxx	xxx	xxx
5				x	xx	x	x
4			xxx	xxx			
3		xx					
2	x						
1		x	x				
0	xxx						
	6th	7th	8th	9th	10th	11th	12th

Of course, the table as a whole and each axis should be properly labeled to fully clarify the information. In addition, given the resources, a variety of inferential statistics could be run to quantify the strength and direction of the correlation.

When the correlation is not so obvious or when a statistical determination of its strength is required, then several measures of correlation are available. A Pearson product-moment correlation (also known as Pearson's r) can be calculated on ratio level data that are parametric in nature (Hafner 1998, 215–216). When nonparametric or simple ordinal data are available, the Spearman rank-order correlation coefficient may be appropriate. It can still determine the existence and strength of a relationship (Hafner 1998, 218–222).

SIGNIFICANCE

The idea of "statistical significance" is that findings might be genuinely meaningful or simply due to random chance. As mentioned before, the Chi-square test can be used to determine significance with parametric or nonparametric nominal data. A number of other, more complicated tests are also available but their use will require the team to either make use of a statistical package or fairly sophisticated calculations. Assuming parametric data, the team might use a Z test if the standard deviation of the population is known or a student's t-test when it is not known. Analyses of variance (ANOVA and MANOVA) test "for differences among the means of more than two samples or groups" (Powell 1997, 193).

Choosing the most effective statistical test depends on two very different sets of criteria: statistical and practical. To learn more about the statistical criteria, the team can either call in an expert or have one member explore some of the readings listed at the end of this chapter. To apply the practical criteria, the team considers two points. First, what resources and expertise are available for ready application? Second, what levels of statistical analysis will be expected, welcomed, and understood by those to whom the final analysis will be reported? There is no point in expending tremendous effort in running a Pearson r when the Library Board wants to read percentages. Alternatively, it can be detrimental to present simple descriptive statistics to people who expect, use, and understand inferential statistics.

RUNNING THE NARRATIVE ANALYSIS

While the statistical analysis follows highly formalized rules, the narrative analysis develops with guidelines. The interviews, focus groups, observations, and open-ended questionnaire items yield narrative data. Any portions deriving from a sufficient and random sample may be worth counting but, for the most part, the analysis requires coding.

Coding requires skills as sophisticated as any used in inferential data analysis, and librarians have experiential background that often makes the learning process less intimidating than it might be otherwise. Their experience may come in the form of reference or cataloging work. Those in reference generally understand the following experience. After leaving the reference desk at the end of a busy shift, a librarian pauses a moment to chat in the hall with other colleagues about the type of questions she handled. Five questions on the Shawnee prompt her to announce that the fifth-graders have their annual Indian assignment. A few questions from some of her regular patrons on the stock market lead her to wonder whether or not Mr. Greenspan has been in the news that morning. One question on using the Web for home schooling reminds her that this question is still rare but cropping up with greater frequency. This librarian has, in fact, informally coded the experience she has just had on the reference desk. That is, she has identified the patterns and anomalies found in the questions. Alternatively, catalogers use "codes" when they apply subject headings to a book. They look at the narrative text (the book) and apply codes (the subject headings) that best represent the book's content.

In narrative data analysis, however, there is rarely a preset list of codes. The CINA team does not know exactly what subjects will say; therefore, no absolutely complete list of codes is available. Rather, the data analyst must create the codes. In a CINA, many of the patterns will emerge rapidly, but greater nuance requires greater skill. It is well beyond the scope of this work to develop that skill but the readings at the end of this chapter support further growth in this area.

The general steps for the process are reiterative. Only by tentatively applying the codes will their gaps and ambiguities become obvious. Once those weaknesses become apparent, changes are made in the codes, and the process begins anew. The following steps provide a broad plan.

1. *Read and reread the data.* Keeping the user's perspective in mind, try to understand what was said without interpreting it any more than necessary. Accept the fact some responses were simply too vague to understand fully.
2. *Identify and verbalize the patterns.* What comes up more than once? What stands out as an issue for one person alone?
3. *Generate codes from the patterns in the data.* Since the codes come from the data, the wording reflects the user's perspective. The following response to a questionnaire question, "I have to find stuff on the WWW all the time for my boss

and the others on my management team. They expect me to find the sites and it takes me much too long," might be coded as "I need to learn to search the Web for my job."

4. *Define the codes.* Write a clean, simple definition so that someone else doing this coding would be able to recognize what is meant by each code. Adding an example from the data helps clarify the explanation. If one person is doing this alone, it still helps to write down the code definitions so that future studies will have the codes ready for use. Doing it well this first time will cover a hefty percentage of what is needed in future studies.

5. *Put the codes into a hierarchy.* This allows for directional coding and relationships. Rather than a code of "internet," make directional codes such "I need to use the Internet" and "I never need to use the Internet." Following basic cataloging principles, put codes in relationship to each other with broader, narrower, and related headings. For example, codes on the Internet might include the following:

Internet (mentioned but nothing more specific available)
Broader:
   Computers
Narrower:
   I use the Internet for work
   I use the Internet for my daily living
   I use the Internet for education
   I use the Internet to help other people
   I avoid the Internet when possible
   I never use the Internet
   I need to learn to use the Internet
   I need to learn to search the Web
   I need to learn to manage my bookmarks
Related:
   I need to learn to use computers in general

6. *Apply the codes.* Narrow questions that yield only a dozen or so codes can be applied by hand if that is preferred. Simply number them, keep the definitions and examples handy, and write the number next to the piece of text to which it

applies. More often, however, the complexity of the data requires far more codes than can be readily handled this way. In that case, use a piece of data management and analysis software specifically designed for narrative data. HyperResearch and Nudist are two of the more common packages. Have the content transcribed as a simple text file, and use the software to apply and manage the codes. These programs allow ready printouts of every example of any code, of reports on which codes were shared, and more. For example, a report might highlight the fact that social science faculty (a demographic easily entered with the coding) need more work on searching multiple databases than on searching the Web.

7. *Test the coding for accuracy and consistency.* A 90 percent code-recode rate is generally required (Miles and Huberman 1984, 64). To achieve this, take substantial and random portions of the text, put them in separate files, and recode them from scratch. If possible, have another person apply the codes. Then compare the two sets of codes. Any codes that are inconsistently applied require review and revision.

If possible, try to have two people look at the entire body of data. Even if one person does the coding, a second mind deepens the discussion of possible codes. Working together to shape definitions, two people may be able to more fully represent user perspectives and mitigate the influence of the library's perspective than could one person alone.

Once the analysis is complete, pull out those exemplars of various needs, ideas, and issues that bring life and reality to the code. Look for those that might bring statistical data to life or illustrate a point effectively. Being careful to fully protect subjects' confidentiality, go back to the original words and set aside those tales for possible use in the final report.

DRAWING CONCLUSIONS

The final step in data analysis is to move from findings to conclusions. After the team analyzes the community's information needs, it then begins to identify and create means of meeting those needs. Since these solutions are the primary reason for going through this entire process in the first place, this part of the work is particularly satisfying. Those who worked on the data gathering deserve to share something of this stage, if only the news that it is under way.

The complex issues involved in moving from *identifying a need* to *meeting that need* prevent any single approach. Two characteristics of each need, however, generally combine to provide a structure for decision making: potential impact and resources. Meeting some needs would have such a strong impact on the community or on one portion of the community that those needs stand out from the others. Similarly, some needs require so few resources that meeting them is an obvious choice. For example, an academic library team might find that a large number of faculty need automated alert services, something that could be provided with a minimal investment of staff time and relatively little cost. The combination of high need with low cost leads to a relatively easy decision. Consequences of that decision, however, require careful consideration. Will alert services increase the demand for interlibrary loan? If so, are systems in place to support that increase in terms of base budget and staff time?

Similarly, some needs pertain to only a very small number of people and would entail a major cost. A public library team, for example, might find that the 0.05 percent of their population that speak a particular language need a substantial collection of books and magazines in that language. To even begin to meet that need through direct purchase would severely limit collection development in other heavily used areas. In that case, the team might examine alternative means of meeting the need for reading matter. They might, for example, look into building a special interlibrary loan arrangement with another library, seeking a sponsor from within the community for a donation program centered on those materials, or identifying Web sites in that language which could provide some of the required materials. Again, consequences of the decision require consideration. Is that small portion of the community affecting the overall environment substantially? Is it, for example, growing? Would cooperation with the school or an ESL agency provide special resources that could lead to a core of devoted, regular library users? Would a small-scale partnership provide the leverage for a substantial grant? If so, would the ongoing connection provide the community support required to maintain the specialized language collection and provide meaningful cataloging for it?

Those needs that have moderate impact and cost require more careful balance. Looking at community partnerships, grant sources, and special funding opportunities helps in making those decisions. Careful perusal of the literature and judicious use of well-chosen discussion lists can sometimes unearth different mechanisms that colleagues have used to meet these needs.

Involving Others

In some large libraries the team will not be involved in making any decisions about handling the opportunities presented by the study findings. It may be that the needs pertaining to reference, for example, will simply be passed on to the reference staff with the team bowing out immediately. The needs pertaining to capital improvements may be passed on to the library administrators for their sole consideration. The significant difficulties caused by this type of sequencing make it extremely problematic, however, and it is certainly not recommended. Without the insights and fuller information of the study team, the newly involved staff may well miss critical subtleties. In addition, the learning curve on all the material is steep so that a good deal of time is wasted in simply relearning what others already know. The ideal situation in a large library is to have the CINA team draw in those staff members who are likely to be involved in the implementation of study results. The team can brief their colleagues, answer their questions, participate in initial discussions, and gradually step out of the work as their input becomes less crucial. Even administrators benefit from in-person discussions with written reports as support.

In any setting, however, soliciting staff input and ideas from all levels and departments involves everyone in the process. The balance between efficiency and results must again come to the fore. Those who are involved must know the boundaries of their involvement. No suggestion will be implemented just because its originator worked on the project or works in the affected department. The discussion is not for the purpose of reaching consensus, although consensus building may result. Those in authority make the final choices. Nevertheless, knowledgeable and committed staff are more likely to carry out any proposed changes with greater efficacy if they participate in the decision-making process.

The momentum rises as different minds work to tackle the problems. The simplest way to initiate activity is to distribute and present a basic report of preliminary findings. The team selects easily explained findings for an uncomplicated forum, looking particularly for work needed in departments that are staffed by people who are open to new ideas. They encourage input by e-mail, personal conversation, and other mechanisms without undue regard for formality. For example, the team report might note that a large number of transfer students are coming in to the college at the semester break and that these students have reported great difficulty in finding what they need for upper-division courses. Staff would then be encouraged to think of practical, feasible means of helping those students make the transition more smoothly.

Another means of generating ideas is to call on colleagues via discussion lists, conferences, and other means. Especially in one-person libraries, the expertise and experience of the professional community are an invaluable resource. One team member could take charge of posting a few select messages to the appropriate discussion lists and tracking the responses. The team will have two resources to offer the library community in exchange for this help: their needs-analysis techniques and their instruments. Additionally, of course, the team can post a compilation of the responses to their query for the benefit of all.

Using the Literature

Finally, one team member can scan the literature for "how-I-did-it-well" articles on the problem at hand. The authors of these articles can be contacted to discuss details, if appropriate. A column in *Public Libraries*, for example, presents the expertise of four librarians who work with homeschoolers (Sager 1995). Their insights and experience certainly would provide valuable information for any public library whose community information-needs analysis has just revealed a growing interest in homeschooling.

SUMMARY

The four-step process of analyzing the data includes developing an overview of the data, running the statistical analysis, running the narrative analysis, and drawing conclusions. While all of the team must be involved in the first and last of these, one person could do each of the remaining steps alone. Ideally, though, a number of minds looking at the data would be worth the time and effort as they could generate more possibilities, capture more of the nuance, and handle more perspectives than could any individual. Particularly when examining the narrative data (e.g., interview transcripts, open-ended questionnaire questions, and observation notes), having different approaches to the data is productive.

CHAPTER 8 READINGS

Example of Statistical Analyses in Action

Kim, Choong Han, and Robert David Little. 1987. *Public library users and uses: A market research handbook*. Metuchen, NJ: Scarecrow Press.

Graphic Data Display Formats

Voelker, David, and Peter Orton. 1993. *Statistics*. Lincoln, NE: Cliffs Notes. [If you are comfortable with the abbreviated format of the Cliffs Notes series, then pages 9–25 may provide the quick review needed to compare the merits of various graphic formats.]

Nominal Data Analysis

Chambers, John, William Cleveland, Beat Kleiner, and Paul Tukey. 1983. *Graphical methods for data analysis*. Belmont, CA: Wadsworth International Group.

Hafner, Arthur. 1998. *Descriptive statistical techniques for librarians*. 2nd edition. Chicago: ALA.

Krathwohl, David. 1998. *Methods of educational and social science research: An integrated approach*. 2nd edition. New York: Longman. 387–418. [See also 488–489 for a lucid explanation of the Chi square and an example of how to calculate it.]

Powell, Ronald. 1997. *Basic research methods for librarians*. 3rd edition. Greenwich, CT: Ablex. 183–190

Reynolds, H.T. 1984. *Analysis of nominal data*. 2nd edition. Quantitative Applications in the Social Sciences Series, number 7. Newbury Park, CA: Sage.

Voelker, David, and Peter Orton. 1993. *Statistics*. Lincoln, NE: Cliffs Notes. [If you are comfortable with the abbreviated format of the Cliffs Notes series, then pages 27–40 may provide the quick review needed to manage measures of central tendency and variability.]

Ordinal Data Analysis

Hildebrand, David, James Laing, and Howard Rosenthal. 1977. *Analysis of ordinal data*. Quantitative Applications in the Social Sciences Series, number 8. Newbury Park, CA: Sage.

Krathwohl, David. 1998. *Methods of educational and social science research: An integrated approach*. 2nd edition. New York: Longman. 455–494.

Powell, Ronald. 1997. *Basic research methods for librarians*. 3rd edition. Greenwich, CT: Ablex. 190–198.

Narrative Data Analysis

Krathwohl, David. 1998. *Methods of educational and social science research: An integrated approach.* 2nd edition. New York: Longman. 302–325. [See also pages 320–323 for insights and suggestions on data-analysis software.]

Westbrook, Lynn. 1997. Qualitative research. In Ronald Powell's *Basic research methods for librarians.* 3rd edition. Greenwich, CT: Ablex. Chapter 6, 143–164.

Nonparametric Techniques

Downing, Douglas, and Jeff Clark. 1997. *Statistics the easy way.* 3rd edition. Hauppauge, NY: Barron's. 240–251

Leedy, Paul. 1989. *Practical research: Planning and design.* 4th edition. New York: Macmillan. 208–209.

Grants

Barber, Peggy, and Linda D. Crowe. 1993. *Getting your grant: A how-to-do-it manual for librarians.* How-To-Do-It Manuals for Librarians, number 28. New York: Neal-Schuman.

Big book of library grant money 1998–99: Profiles of private and corporate foundations and direct corporate givers receptive to library grant proposals. 1998. Prepared by The Taft Group. Chicago: American Library Association.

Chapter 9

Sharing the Results

All of this hard work culminates in the opportunity to share the results with everyone involved. After all the data gathering and analysis are complete, the team creates strong support for their proposed changes by communicating effectively with the public, administrators, and staff. Team members present their decisions regarding the opportunities, solutions, partnerships, and developments in the context of the study.

FRAMEWORKS FOR SHARING

Three points form a crucial framework for the presentation: the library's services, standards, and needs. Taking care not to surprise any interested parties, the team uses communication effectively throughout this stage. Avoiding the formality of the research article format and carefully relating major points to community issues, the team works together to gradually inform everyone and answer their questions.

The process of sharing results may require multiple stages and a number of mechanisms for communication. In the early stages, administrators receive brief, informal verbal updates on major findings as they are uncovered. In later stages, groups of nonlibrarians, such as school library boards, may receive a single written report as part of a formal presentation. Staff may prefer an overview of the entire process with special, discussion-based meetings on the issues most immediately affecting their work. Hitting the highlights and leaning toward brevity, the team can make it clear that more detailed information is available for those who would like to see it, as are individual discussions. At some point, having a brown bag lunch and discussing what was learned about the research process (as opposed to the actual findings) may be fruitful.

The intentions are always to inform, interest, and involve with complete accuracy. No single method is recommended because situations vary so greatly, but a combination of the oral and written is essential. The oral allows for discussion, questions, and nuance. The written provides a public acknowledgment of the findings, plans, and decisions; referring to such a document will be necessary as changes are implemented.

Put Findings in the Context of Services

In any presentation, the team provides a fundamental context for the findings by discussing them in terms of actual services and collections. Obviously some basic data on the library are essential for this step, but the earlier work on in-house data should provide almost everything that is needed. Occasionally an unexpected finding may require a bit of additional data but even that should already be available from the analysis work.

One simple format for providing this type of context is a two-part listing of what users need and what the library already possesses to meet those needs. Tearle followed this pattern in the first part of her article on information needs in academic law libraries (1994, 75–77). Noting which unmet needs are to be handled in what way, as shown in the sample below, provides a sense of direction and establishes priorities.

Some needs may not be met at all on the grounds that they are outside of the library's mission. Nevertheless, the people with those needs may be referred elsewhere in the community. For example, a school library team might determine that some immigrant parents need English lessons in order to support their children's use

Sample Reporting Document for a Public Library	
Users' Need	**Means of Meeting the Need**
To learn to search the Web	Create basic handout on navigation
	Train two volunteers to hold classes
To find books for preschoolers	Reorganize "easy" books by topic
	Clarify signs in picture book area
	Put lists on commonly needed topics into our bookmark series
Support for homework	Short-term: add a homework help page to our Web site and send out PR on it to schools, etc.
	Long-term: liaison with school librarians, PTA committees, and principals to build more support for joint programs

of the library better. The team may well decide that taking on adult ESL work is far beyond their mission, budget, expertise, and staffing. They might, however, make a partnership arrangement with ESL services in the community to help their patrons' parents hook up with the services they need.

Some needs may be partially met now as plans are made for additional resources or services at a later stage. Others may be acknowledged as being so far beyond the scope of possibility that funding issues must be explored fully prior to any planning.

Finally, this aspect of the reporting provides ample opportunity to warmly acknowledge the library staff who are currently meeting many needs so well.

Put Findings in the Context of Standards

When the team has written standards for the services and collections available, placing the findings in terms of those standards provides a concrete, thorough framework for discussion. Of course, setting new standards or revising old ones in light of the study findings may be a major task suggested by the team.

Various versions of accepted standards are available if the team wants to use this approach but lacks a statement of in-house standards of their own. The RLG Conspectus, for example, provides some libraries with guidelines regarding collections. Others are suggested by various experts, such as the 1994 work *Assessment and the School Library Media Center* edited by Kuhlthau. Pritchard provides a substantial review of major approaches to measuring quality in academic libraries, many of which would work in any setting (1996). Performance measures and guidelines for their measurement are published by the American Library Association, such as the slightly dated but admirable work by Van House et al. (1987). For a list of all ALA standards, guidelines, and criteria, see: *www.ala/work/standards.html.* The various Association of College and Research Libraries (A.C.R.L.) standards are available at the association's Web site. For benchmarking purposes, the U.S. Department of Education's National Center for Education Statistics reports on school, public, and academic libraries may prove useful although they are somewhat dated. The most recent reports are available through the A.L.A. Web site under the association's Web resources section (A.L.A. 2000).

Standards are particularly useful when the team needs to make findings as concrete as possible. In outcome or goal-based settings, a set of concrete written standards to be met at a certain level by a certain date can answer the needs of administrators effectively. Of course, the staff must see the standards as appropriate, feasible, and fully supported by administrative allocations of time, staff, and money. Therefore, this approach is only recommended when a set of clearly agreed-upon standards already exists or when the time necessary to develop such standards is included.

The Needs of the Library

The final framework for sharing the study results is one not commonly considered by librarians when talking to the public and administrators, namely the needs of the library as an institution or organization. The needs assessment provides facts, examples, and other evidence of the value of the library collections, staff, and services. The money required to maintain and to build on that value must be actively sought and persuasively argued for in a variety of forums. Grants, increases in the base budget, special one-time requests, and partnerships can all serve as productive avenues for the assertive CINA team. Several forums are open to the team and/ or library administration, including electronic media, newspapers, group meetings, presentations to decision-making bodies, newsletters, exhibits, and formal reports. Presenting the findings in terms of their impact on the library, at least in part, moves the team toward identifying and locating the resources necessary to make an outstanding effort to truly meet the community's information needs.

Public library teams can benefit from Sally Gardner Reed's solid, if somewhat dated, manual aptly titled *Saving Your Library: A Guide to Getting, Using and Keeping the Power You Need*. Both locally and on the broader stage, her practical techniques for maintaining and even expanding the budget base of public libraries provide tools for change. Weaving the data of a recent information-needs study into her techniques can bolster the efficacy of any program. Certainly the A.L.A.'s annual publication *Great Library Promotion Ideas* is also useful.

In addition to the ever-present need for money, libraries may also need enhanced respect from a higher administrative unit or greater access to a segment of the population. For example, if a school library team wants to convince their principal to institute open scheduling, they might highlight the findings indicative of that scheduling approach. (That assumes that the change really does meet information needs rather than librarian preferences.) The findings should never be modified, exaggerated, or mitigated, but the team can frame and explain them in terms supportive of library needs.

Of course, connecting the library's needs to those of the larger institution is also productive. For example, an academic library that needs more financial support from the university president might emphasize the services supportive of successful faculty grant applications. Additional support could well lead to additional grants. The promise of an impact study to follow needed changes, now that staff are well trained in many of the methods necessary to conduct such a study, is also persuasive. Similarly, a school library team might show that those teachers who used curriculum integrated library materials were able to help their students make higher scores on standardized tests. Tying library success to institutional goals can lead to greater support for the library.

For some of these approaches, the team might need to gather a small amount of additional data. Grant application rates, overall test scores, and similar data may be generally unavailable or even considered confidential. In that case, the team needs to work with administrators to gain permission for one person to handle all transactions so that names are not disclosed, total counts are made available, and appropriate information obtained.

Finally, the team might choose to consider the library's long-range needs in terms of space, technological infrastructure, and staffing. Knowing what the majority needs provides some clues regarding staffing levels and building size. Sometimes it is the cutting-edge few, however, who indicate the need for specific technological developments.

COMMUNICATING WITH ADMINISTRATION, STAFF, AND PUBLIC

Before taking the final public step of communicating with administrators, staff, and the public, the team reviews all decisions made on the basis of the data. Following the old adage of "under-promise and over-deliver," the team members conduct a brief reality check to ensure that no department or individual is being rushed, overwhelmed, pushed, or neglected. For example, the study might determine that a segment of the "potential user" population simply needs to be exposed to some basic PR on the library in order to move them towards making use of the library. The suggested change, therefore, is to conduct such a PR program. The team might notice, however, that if their PR is effective, the current staffing levels could not handle the new workload. In such a case, the initial decision might be revisited before any public announcements are made.

In some large libraries, several community needs will simply be passed on to the individuals or departments responsible for meeting them. This public debriefing of the resultant decisions would, therefore, be the responsibility of those actually doing the work of implementing changes, rather than the work of the CINA team.

At this stage the CINA team prepares to disband. Members brief their colleagues as needed, join initial discussions, and pass along the work to those who will handle the next phases. This may be such a formal transition that the team writes up the first half of a report covering the study and its findings while another group or individual writes up the second half covering the follow-through proposed in response to the findings, with the presentation as a joint effort.

One team member takes primary responsibility for the packaging and layout of the information. Different audiences will need different degrees of detail, ranging from an executive summary to full explanations. The findings mean a great deal more when they are placed in the context of the research methods used, relevant known facts, and affected library functions. Therefore, the final format of the presentations (both written and verbal) should include more than lists of questionnaire responses. Graphs, charts, and other visual elements can be as effective as concise quotes. Brief summations of major findings, concerns, and issues can serve as the foundation to discussion. Since statistics, although often effective and persuasive, may oversimplify complex issues, they are used carefully. Quotations and illustrative examples bring life to cold, formal findings, but confidentiality must always be strictly maintained.

After one team member writes up the reports and presentation handouts, the entire team reviews them for nuance and perspective. The same fact can be presented in different ways in order to emphasize different facets and factors. As the following example illustrates, each word choice has its own nuance.

Watch the Power of Words

As the following example indicates, simple phrasing decisions can have a tremendous impact on the findings report.

"Let us suppose that forty per cent of the sample state that they used the catalogues first when looking for a particular book. This can be reported exactly as it stands. But there are several other possible ways of stating this:

1. Only forty percent of the entire sample consulted the catalogue first;
2. As many as forty percent of the sample consulted the catalogue first;
3. Sixty percent of the sample admitted that they did not consult the catalogue first.

All of these sentences are loaded with the expectations or pre-conceptions of the investigator; 3 carries moral overtones as well."

Line 1967, 105

Having team members read everything for tone as well as accuracy is an essential step. Having someone completely outside the process read it for clarity and organization is quite useful.

One last element requires a bit of team discussion, namely the order of presentation. Obviously, the staff must be fully informed before the public is, but other elements are more flexible. Generally speaking, the presentation order runs as follows: (1) library administration, (2) institution or organization administration, (3) general staff, and (4) the public. Informing administrators first can head off the surprise of changes required for administrative reasons. Generally an oral presentation, with selected handouts, should precede a more complete, formal written report.

The general public is not likely to be interested in an oral presentation of the findings but some feedback is useful, especially for those who actively participated in the study. Where possible, the team looks for ways to combine this feedback with established communications. For example, a newsletter, bookmark, e-mail notice, or newspaper column of library news could take the CINA findings as a theme. Of course, anything special done for participants should maximize cost-effectiveness, such as delaying thank-you letters a bit until a brief findings summary could also be included in the mailing. Naturally occurring forums for public communication, such as an annual report, can also provide an avenue for arousing interest in the results of the study.

Finally, someone on the team should take time to share the methodology and findings with the library community. A revised version of the written report could be submitted as an article to the appropriate journal. Posting the key elements of the report on the library's Web site or sending notice to a few pertinent discussion lists helps put out the word electronically without undue expense. Particularly if little has been published in the area (e.g., elementary-school–needs analyses), it is worth taking some time to share with colleagues via a traditional publication. These articles can be found a decade from now to guide and inform those who will face the same challenges the team faced so successfully.

CHAPTER 9 READINGS

Public Relations

Bajjaly, Stephen. 1999. *The community networking handbook*. Chicago: American Library Association.

Childers, Thomas A., and Nancy A. Van House. 1993. *What's good? Describing your public library's effectiveness*. Chicago: American Library Association.

Flowers, Helen. 1998. *Public relations for school library media programs: 500 ways to influence people and win friends for your school library media center*. New York: Neal-Schuman.

Ross, Catherine Sheldrick, and Patricia Dewdney. 1998. *Communicating professionally: A how-to-do-it manual for library applications*. 2nd edition. How-To-Do-It Manuals for Librarians, number 58. New York: Neal-Schuman.

Turner, Anne M. 1997. *Getting political: An action guide for librarians and library supporters.* New York: Neal-Schuman.

Wolfe, Lisa A. 1997. *Library public relations, promotions, and communications: A how-to-do-it manual.* How-To-Do-It Manuals for Librarians, number 75. New York: Neal-Schuman.

Standards

Van House, Nancy A., Mary Jo Lynch, Charles McClure, Douglas Zweizig, and Eleanor Jo Rodger. 1987. *Output measures for public libraries: A manual of standardized procedures.* 2nd edition. Chicago: American Library Association.

Walter, Virginia A. 1992. *Output measures for public library service to children: A manual of standardized procedures.* Chicago: American Library Association.

An Example of Expertise for Collection Assessment in Schools

Kuhlthau, Carol Collier, ed. 1994. *Assessment and the school library media center.* Englewood, CO: Libraries Unlimited.

An Example of Using the RLG Music Conspectus as a Standard

Gottlieb, Jane. 1994. *Collection assessment in music libraries.* MLA Technical Report, number 22. Canton, MA: Music Library Association.

Suggestions for Effectively Advocating Library Improvement

Reed, Sally Gardner. 1992. *Saving your library: A guide to getting, using and keeping the power you need.* Jefferson, NC: McFarland.

Putting Questionnaire Data to Work

DeCandido, GraceAnne. *After the user survey, what then?* September 1997. Systems and Procedures Exchange Center (SPEC) Kit 226. Julia Blixrud, SPEC Editor. Issues and Innovations in Transforming Libraries. Washington, DC: Association of Research Libraries, Office of Management Services.

Chapter 10

Acting on the Results

Acting on the study's results moves the entire process into a totally new realm. Actions, players, goals, and perspectives shift radically at this time. Some factors in this final stage are well beyond the scope of this book, such as service modification, standards development, and evaluation design. However, this final stage commonly involves six elements: managing data, building the momentum for change, refining priorities, monitoring progress, analyzing change, and making recommendations. Recognizing the all too common problem of lost momentum (see Schlichter and Pemberton 1992), the team must take responsibility for moving from findings to real action.

MANAGING DATA

A simple but essential task is the management of all the data gathered throughout the study. The team member best able to handle detail takes on the responsibility for determining which materials are to be saved in what physical formats under the keeping of which staff member. All confidential material is destroyed, including interview transcripts, lists of subject names, and observation notes. Both electronic and paper files are ruthlessly weeded down to a reasonable, productive minimum. Those who are responsible for acting upon the findings of the CINA must be able to identify and review items in the files readily without any fear of accidentally breaching subject confidentiality or anonymity. All official materials, such as the final reports, are centrally archived with additional copies sent to administrators and staff as needed. Although fairly mechanical, this useful step helps the CINA team bring closure to their work and begins the essential process of moving primary responsibility for the next stages to those who are to direct the change.

BUILDING THE MOMENTUM FOR CHANGE

Of course, the people who direct the change might well be the same people who conducted the CINA. However, in the library with enough staff, those who are invested in the outcome of the work should lead the next stage. For example, if the CINA reveals a need for increased Web access to the reference staff during hours when the academic library is closed, then the head of reference takes charge of that need. Working with the reference staff and/or the local Webspinner to identify the person(s) to be responsible for handling that information need, the department manager directs the change.

Forming an action team (analogous to the CINA team) to spearhead the implementation of major, long-term change is an efficient mechanism for minimizing duplication of effort when two or more information needs cross jurisdictional boundaries, within or beyond the library. The original CINA team members are involved in the early work of this action team, if only as advisors.

Using the final report with its suggested solutions and prioritized information needs, each action team begins moving through the three steps of the implementation process: They revise, if necessary, the library's basic mission; develop new goals and/or revise old goals; and create practical objectives with fairly specific timelines for each goal. These decisions are shared fully with the staff and any appropriate partners or institutional administrative units. In addition, a very generalized statement might be given out to the public in the "under-promise, over-deliver" mode. This is particularly helpful when a subpopulation has participated heavily in the CINA or become the focus of an extended effort.

Getting the action team set up, the staff informed, and any additional groups (e.g., administrative units, subpopulations) on board will begin to build momentum for change. As the process begins, everyone involved must realize that the goals and objectives come directly from the CINA results. General goals (such as "have 100 percent of the potential users make one use of the library in the coming year") may be as inappropriate as they are simple because they fail to make full use of the CINA findings. For example, it is probable that a relatively small portion of the library's potential users may, quite properly, account for most of the library use. Therefore, the action team may want to have 90 percent of that subpopulation using the library regularly and the rest simply aware of possibilities. Recognizing the purpose, background, and validity of the goals helps everyone involved in the process build and maintain momentum.

REFINING PRIORITIES

Generally, the CINA results indicate far more concerns than the action teams can address. The final report on the study, discussed in the previous chapter, set specific priorities to follow, but the action teams often refine those broad priorities in light of opportunities, circumstances, and environmental changes.

Some items must be set aside, even though they are important; others must be pushed to the top despite the fact that they will require a great deal of preparation and effort. For example, a public library with greater connectivity within the community network as a high priority might be willing to wait for the successful grant application required to fund the purchase of essential equipment. The connectivity remains a high priority, but the timing is not artificially forced just to produce a tangible, but inconsequential, effect quickly. In that case, the management action team might well give the goal several incremental objectives, the first of which is the successful submission of a grant application. Realistic timing is essential for top priority goals or else the action teams risk the temptation to cut corners just to be able to report rapid progress on an important initiative. Often, the most important items take the most time.

Finally, partners are involved in the process of setting (or modifying) priorities. If the library gained any new partners or if the team needs to follow through on developing any tenuous connections to new partners, everyone involved must join the discussion of priorities. Sometimes the effort spent on laying groundwork for a new partnership is worth the long-term result, even though the short-term gains will appear to be relatively minimal in light of the information needs identified by the CINA. For example, the P.T.A.'s Library Committee could be involved in discussions of those priorities to which it could most effectively make a contribution, such as the need to create a core of parent volunteers for after-school homework support in the public library. The university's academic computing center could be involved in discussions about ways to increase electronic access to library resources for off-campus students. The local genealogy club might fund the development of a special segment of the library's Web site on genealogy, under the firm direction of the reference staff.

MONITORING PROGRESS

Once the CINA team has bowed out entirely, the action team(s) establishes a simple plan for monitoring progress on the priority concerns. The monitoring comes in two parts: tracking and sharing. Tracking depends on the work to be done, obviously. Staff meetings, departmental or individual monthly reports, and informal conversations help track the steps taken on a project. The point of this work is to provide resources, advice, and other support as needed to maintain momentum.

The sharing, often brief and informal, encourages the interest of both staff and users in the work at hand. While the team monitoring progress does so somewhat formally, they must keep in mind that some members of the staff and public will be doing the same thing on an informal basis. By giving everyone accurate, complete, current information on the work's progress, the team minimizes the inaccuracies fostered by uninformed opinion.

It is particularly important for staff to have everything they need to answer questions from the public about changes of any type. Shifting shelves, modifying the homepage, training staff in new reference interview techniques, and other changes can generate questions from the public. It may therefore be natural to expend some effort on strengthening staff's ability to communicate with patrons.

ANALYZING CHANGE

As members of the action teams implement and monitor the progress on the changes suggested by the CINA team, they must also analyze the effects of those changes. Are the changes meeting the intended needs? Did unexpected problems or side effects occur? Has anything in the informational, institutional, or library environment changed enough to warrant re-evaluation of the priorities set earlier? Do staff responses indicate the need for more training, or have changes moved so smoothly that staff can actually handle more than was originally planned?

Identifying needs and then changing services based on those needs are only two legs of the stool; evaluating the effectiveness of the change is the third leg that stabilizes the process. A recent survey of Association of Research Libraries (A.R.L.) libraries indicates that relatively few librarians work on that third but crucial step (Brekke 1994, 6). At some point a full-scale, formal evaluation of the changes may be appropriate, but even small-scale, informal evaluations can be accomplished with relative ease if the staff involved in the original CINA can employ some of the same skills they developed during the assessment to help conduct the evaluations. Again, consultants can help set up the basics or actually conduct an evaluation in full.

MAKING RECOMMENDATIONS FOR THE NEXT STUDY

Finally, the original CINA team and the action team(s) collaborate briefly on a set of recommendations to be left for the next group that might work on a community information-needs analysis. Building on the recommendations formed earlier by the CINA team, both groups consider priorities, environmental developments, and the early effects of the initial changes. As an addendum to the final report of the CINA team, they write up or modify recommendations regarding the focus and specific elements of the study to follow. Perhaps a limited segment of the recently completed assessment should be updated in a few years or perhaps an entirely new assessment should be conducted with an entirely different focus. The recommendations are not highly specific, of course, but they do provide a sense of continuation by making it clear that future CINAs have their place in the planning cycle.

Looking at the current mechanisms for gathering in-house data on information needs and satisfaction, the group might be able to recommend some simple changes to increase the value of the information. Some pieces of data can be gathered annually, such as students' access to home computers. Some items can be gathered continually by using standard mechanisms such as reference statistics and workshop evaluation forms. For example, if the staff give workshops or one-on-one tutorials for patrons, the group might recommend that everyone include a question in the standard evaluation form to elicit other topics for instructional sessions.

The action team and the CINA team might have one joint meeting about a year after the close of the assessment just to discuss any recommendations on CINA focus and means of gathering information. They could also talk about the pace of environmental and community change. Are things changing rapidly enough to make a new assessment necessary in four years or eight years? Were the changes suggested by this assessment such that they won't be fully in place for four years so that an assessment in ten years would seem more reasonable? No absolute decision must be or should be made. But thinking it through, particularly in terms of implementing techniques for gathering simple data, can help insure that when the next CINA starts, staff will be grateful for the forethought of this group.

CHAPTER 10 READINGS

Forms Useful in Monitoring Staff Relationships with the Public

Hernon, Peter, and Ellen Altman. 1996. *Service quality in academic libraries.* Norwood, NJ: Ablex. See chapter 7.

Evaluating Library Collections and Services

Lancaster, F. W. 1988. *If you want to evaluate your library . . .* Champaign, IL: University of Illinois, Graduate School of Library and Information Science.

Follow-up Work

DeCandido, GraceAnne. *After the user survey, what then?* September 1997. Systems and Procedures Exchange Center (SPEC) Kit 226. Julia Blixrud, SPEC Editor. Issues and Innovations in Transforming Libraries. Washington, DC: Association of Research Libraries, Office of Management Services.

Techniques for Future Use in Other Types of Studies

Nitecki, Danuta. 1996. Changing the concept and measure of service quality in academic libraries. *Journal of Academic Librarianship.* 22: (3, May): 181–190.

Powell, Ronald R. 1997. *Basic research methods for librarians.* 3rd edition. Greenwich, CT: Ablex.

Robbins, Jane, Holly Willett, Mary Jane Wiseman, and Douglas Zweizig, eds. 1990. *Evaluation strategies and techniques for public library children's services: A sourcebook.* University of Wisconsin, Madison: School of Library and Information Studies.

Van House, Nancy A., Mary Jo Lynch, Charles McClure, Douglas

Zweizig, and Eleanor Jo Rodger. 1987. *Output measures for public libraries: A manual of standardized procedures.* 2nd edition. Chicago: American Library Association.

Van House, Nancy A., Beth Weil, and Charles McClure. 1990. *Measuring academic library performance: A practical approach.* Chicago: American Library Association.

Walter, Virginia A. 1995. *Output measures and more: Planning and evaluating public library services for young adults.* Chicago: American Library Association.

Zweizig, Douglas, Debra Wilcox Johnson, Jane Robbins, et al. 1996. *The TELL IT! Manual: The complete program for evaluating library performance.* Chicago: American Library Association.

Appendix A

Academic Library Study

The report of this study consists of the following documents: executive summary, methodology notes, data-gathering instruments, findings highlights, recommendations, and final commentary. The quotations within these documents come from other documents (e.g., meeting minutes and staff memos) used in the study. The librarians involved in the study have graciously given their permission to allow their real names to be used. They may be contacted for more information at the addresses below.

Andy Tucker
Reference Librarian
Blagg-Huey Library
Texas Woman's University
Denton, TX 76204
stucker@twu.edu

Connie Maxwell
Head of Reference
Blagg-Huey Library
Texas Woman's University
Denton, TX 76204
cmaxwell@twu.edu

Executive Summary

The Blagg-Huey Library serves as the primary library for the four campuses of the Texas Woman's University. Serving just under 10,000 students and 370 faculty, the staff of 25 librarians and 20 paraprofessionals provides reference and instructional support. One of the primary reference services is a relatively new, personalized service for faculty known as "FIRST" which includes online searching, document delivery, and alert services. The program developed organically from staff efforts to meet faculty information needs but no formal needs assessment had ever been conducted.

This study was proposed to "to identify the research, information needs of all faculty on each campus of Texas Woman's University." As secondary purposes, the study was also conducted in the expectation that "all staff who are interested in the process of gathering and analyzing data will learn what they need to know" and in an effort to "strengthen public relations with each faculty member on campus."

The methodology required interviews and a questionnaire. Staff training sessions in the former and group development of the latter provided lasting benefits as did the special training offered in narrative data analysis techniques.

The findings were presented to interested librarians in a discussion-centered meeting. Staff from the Assistant Director level down to the front-line reference librarian level met to share ideas, generate responses, and suggest new approaches to meeting faculty information needs.

The final recommendations were presented to the Library administrators who have begun to incorporate them into the strategic planning process.

Methodology Notes

These notes are taken from meeting minutes and provide concrete examples of decision-making.

Stage one: preliminary data gathering

In-house statistics to be considered
- None available now that are really useful
- Suggest that final report include recommendation to keep information requests by subject area, department, owned versus borrowed, format (print versus electronic) and so on

Subpopulations to be considered

- Research Assistants in terms of their support for faculty research; acting as conduits for faculty research needs
- Faculty at various levels of using the five specialized reference services provided for faculty: high-users, low-users, non-users, and ex-users; the five services include document delivery, reference, online searching, TOC, and SDI; define high as using any of the specialized faculty services on a weekly basis (averaged over a year); define ex-users as those who had signed up for one or more of the services then withdrawn but remained at TWU
- Departmental subpopulations: every single department on any of the campuses
- Campus subpopulations: cover Houston, Parkland, Presbyterian, [covers OT, PT, and Nursing] and Denton

Data gathering points to be considered

- Rejected various data-gathering instruments: focus groups (impractical—faculty would not come); paper documents such as journals (no time to gather or analyze such data); exit interviews (too sparse, many faculty not in the library); Web-survey (save for later when more library staff have greater skill in designing such instruments)

- Chose brief interviews (phone and in-person) with faculty selected to represent various levels of use on all campuses and in all types of departments (i.e., social sciences, physical sciences, humanities, and fine arts) followed by a questionnaire to all faculty
- Spend a good deal of time on nonusers and ex-users so use longer interviews for them
- Spend modest amounts of time on low and high users; low will use phone interviews and high will use brief interviews
- Qualifications of staff to be involved in the interviewing: for in-depth interviews with non- and ex-users we want staff who are tactful, not defensive, good at listening, and able to avoid leading questions; for in-person interviews with high users want to avoid assigned librarians (to avoid any hint of evaluation) but do want full-time librarians who will be partially trained by the assigned librarian; for phone interviews with low users want people who are good on the phone, friendly, but quite professional

Interview questions

In each case, set up the focus of the interview on research support. Then some general form of the following questions will be asked. These questions will, of course, be honed and pre-tested prior to actual use.

- Non- and ex- users: 20–30 minutes of an in-person interview
  - Have you ever used or heard of another university's library service which you found useful or interesting?
  - What could the library do to best support your research?
  - Where do you go to or how do you have your research needs met now?
  - In what way has the library met your research needs? In what ways has it NOT met your research needs?
  - What databases do you tend to search most heavily?
  - How do you find out about the latest work in your field?
  - Are there information skills that you'd like to learn?
  - What types of reference/information questions would you

bring to a librarian? What types would you NOT bring to a librarian?

- For what purpose did you last use the library?
- Do you use a research assistant (RA)? If so, in what capacity do you use your RAs?
- Do you regularly search databases or the Web for your information? If so, what works well for you in those searches?
- Are your research needs interdisciplinary? If so, how do you find what you need in various disciplines?

- High users: 5–12 minutes of an in-person interview
  - Have you ever used or heard of another university's library service which you found useful or interesting?
  - What could the library do to best support your research?
  - Where do you go to or how do you have your research needs met now?
  - In what way has the library met your research needs? In what ways has it NOT met your research needs?
  - What types of reference/information questions would you bring to a librarian? What types would you NOT bring to a librarian?
  - Are your research needs interdisciplinary? If so, how do you find what you need in various disciplines?

- Low users: 5–10 minutes of a phone interview
  - Have you ever used or heard of another university's library service which you found useful or interesting?
  - What could the library do to best support your research?
  - Where do you go to or how do you have your research needs met now?
  - In what way has the library met your research needs? In what ways has it NOT met your research needs?
  - Do you use a research assistant? If so, in what capacity do you use your RAs?

Stage two: final data gathering

- Will create a questionnaire based on the findings of the interviews
- Want it to go out to every faculty member on all four campuses and hope to get a 10 percent response rate from each department on each campus
- Need print, personal, and electronic PR on it in advance: use the campus newsletter and a letter from the Library director
- Follow-up with mailed copies of the survey to those who have not responded so keep track by numbering the surveys
- Want to include an offer at the end to have librarians follow-up regarding specific services
- Get basic demographic facts re department, rank, sex, campus from mailing list and other sources so no need to ask for those data points; record those facts on the actual responses once they arrive

Training plans

- Need: phone interview, in-depth interview, and brief interview training, interview data analysis techniques
- Need to identify those who should be included in training but make it open to all staff
- Schedule training right away so that it can run as soon as the final interview questions have been pre-tested and approved by the Library director *{Note: If you'd like further information on the training, please contact the author.}*

Data-Gathering Instruments: Interviews and Questionnaire

A total of 24 faculty were interviewed; 8 members of the library staff, including two paraprofessionals, conducted the interviews following a one-hour training session.

Non-active (i.e. nonusers and ex-users)
20–30 minutes of an in-person interview

1. Think about your latest research project. How do you get the information you need for that work?
2. Do you regularly search databases or the Web? (Why or why not?)
3. Are there information skills that you'd like to learn?
4. How do you find out about the latest work in your field?
5. Have you ever used or heard of another library's service which you considered useful?
6. What could the library do to best support your research?

High users: 5–12 minutes of an in-person interview

1. Think about your primary research interests. How do you get the information you need for that work?
2. Are your research needs interdisciplinary? If so, how do you find what you need in various disciplines?
3. What could the library do to best support your research?

Low users: 5–10 minutes of a phone interview

1. Think about your primary research interests. How do you get the information you need for that work?
2. In what way has the library met your research needs? In what ways has it NOT met your research needs?
3. What types of research questions would you take to a reference librarian?

Research Support Survey

The five minutes you spend on this survey could save you hours later. Please give us the information we need to spend this summer working to serve you better. (This survey applies to your research needs; future studies will focus on your teaching needs.)

1. Which of these library services would effectively support your research? Please check all that apply.
   - ❑ books and journals delivered to my office upon request
   - ❑ 48 hour response to reference questions left by phone, e-mail, or in-person
   - ❑ tables of contents of selected journals sent to me via e-mail
   - ❑ citations to books and journals on set topics sent to me via e-mail weekly
   - ❑ a single librarian assigned to answer my reference questions
   - ❑ a single librarian assigned to monitor the Web for me
   - ❑ a single librarian to help me organize my collection of Web sites
   - ❑ a single librarian to help me organize my books and journals
   - ❑ a single librarian to analyze my information-seeking patterns and help me find any time-saving short cuts that might be available
   - ❑ a single librarian to help me search other libraries
   - ❑ ability to order materials via e-mail or the phone
   - ❑ a set of full-text resources in my field available via the library Web site
   - ❑ a set of authoritative, scholarly Web sites in my field available via the library Web site
   - ❑ identification of scholarly, research-based discussion lists in my field
   - ❑ identification of and contact information for authoritative authors in various fields as needed
   - ❑ notification of new books in my field, whether owned by the library or not

❑ databases and/or Web searched for me on demand with requests left by e-mail or phone
❑ longer library hours, specifically:_____
❑ a drive-by book drop
❑ other, please explain:

2. Which of these faculty development services would effectively support your research? Please check all that apply.
❑ personalized instruction on searching the Web
❑ personalized instruction on searching specific databases
❑ personalized instruction on searching the Web and/or databases either from home or while traveling
❑ written support for searching the Web
❑ written support for searching specific databases
❑ written instruction on searching the Web and/or databases either from home or while traveling
❑ other, please explain:

3. Which of these collections require development to effectively support your research? Please check all that apply.

❑ books in the following area:

❑ reference books in the following area:

❑ journals in the following area:

❑ conference proceedings in the following area:

❑ other, please explain:

4. What else can you tell us about your research information needs?

Please share a little personal information.

Do you use the Internet at home? _____
Do you plan to apply for outside grants next year? _____
Do you plan to conduct research next year?_____

Thank you for your input. Please return this survey to Blagg-Huey Library, care of Andy Tucker, in the enclosed envelope. If you'd like a copy of the study's final executive summary, then please give us your name and address below. Your answers will, of course, be kept completely confidential.

Findings Highlights

Interview highlights

- The continuums along which faculty information needs ran often held a common thread, namely that of personalized, one-on-one service at the time of need. Learning, finding, retrieving, and other information-seeking activities were constant but the need for librarian-support was often seen as specialized, idiosyncratic, and unique.
- Many people expressed various levels of concern about information management from issues with maintaining an awareness of their information options to keeping track of all the useful citations they locate.
- Many people were concerned about the constant need to learn something, usually something technological.
- Awareness of the library's services and of service options in general ranged from fairly complete to virtually nonexistent.
- Many people did not perceive any distinctions between their teaching and research needs or between their electronic and their paper documents. The information need was more important than the context or the format of the answer.

Questionnaire highlights

- Response rates exceeded expectations. At least 30 percent of virtually every department and all four campuses responded, far more than the 10 percent which was all that past studies had led staff to expect.
- Faculty at all ranks want document delivery to their offices (which they have), personalized instruction on electronic information seeking, and in-depth research support for grant applications.
- Faculty are far less concerned with collection development than with interdisciplinary information-seeking.
- Relatively few faculty are concerned about information overload but a noticeable number are concerned about managing the citations they have located.

Recommendations

The library administration is reviewing these recommendations and will assign staff, due dates, and measurement levels as the next phase in this work. The Library has just moved to an entirely new integrated OPAC, is in the midst of building a new instructional lab for the reference area, and is handling the staffing changes common in an academic library. The next stages will be incorporated into all of these changes as part of the Library's overall work.

1. Goal: Develop a cohesive vision for faculty information support services.
   - Objective: Write a mission statement for the FIRST service. (Draft of such a statement is attached.)
   - Objective: Strengthen coordination of FIRST support elements in light of Endeavor, new staff, and other changes by giving one librarian the responsibility for keeping everyone else informed of developments.
2. Goal: Develop a 3-tier approach to FIRST services that maximize existing strengths while minimizing attendant costs. As resources become available, move more faculty up the tiers.
   1. Objective: Combine all specialized faculty services into a seamless, coordinated effort known as FIRST through coordination of existing services.
   2. Objective: Establish a minimal tier of service that is offered to all faculty, namely access to document delivery, automatic alert services, and office/home visits to develop basic familiarity with library databases and the Internet.
   3. Objective: Establish a middle tier of service that is offered on a short-term basis to faculty involved in an intensive project such as the development of a new course, a major course revision, development of a grant application, or work on a major publication. Establish this tier as a research service in which requests for extensive, reiterative searching are met as needed, including requests for

personal instruction on how to improve end-user searching. Market this to new faculty as a way to launch their courses and their research.

4. Objective: Establish a top tier of service that is offered to all faculty on an *as-resources-permit* basis, namely personalized information management service and instruction involving personal bookmark management, use of personalized bibliographic control software (e.g., ProCite or EndNote), and control of personal collections.

5. Objective: Create the public relations resources that must support the tiered system including a Web page, business cards, a brochure, and so on.

6. Objective: Streamline requests, document delivery, and other daily practice elements of the tiered system to maximize automated services, minimize staff impact, and gather useful data on the service.

3. Goal: Establish a long-range plan for increasing base funding for FIRST and its resultant costs.

- Objective: Track the costs of providing document delivery, alert services, and so on.
- Objective: Collect the statistics necessary for a study to document the impact that the program has on publishing, presentations, new course development, distance education, and grant-seeking. (Look at the relationship between providing service and faculty output. An IMLS research and demonstration leadership grant might fund both program development and provide documentation for resource development.)
- Objective: Conduct a satisfaction study once the tiered program has been in place for one academic year.
- Objective: Use the data from the previous 3 objectives to ask for a FIRST librarian (analogous to the Distance Education position) and other budget increases as needed.
- Objective: Encourage (or require) faculty to include FIRST in their grant applications whenever possible.

DRAFT
Mission Statement for the FIRST Program

The FIRST service exists to provide individualized informational and instructional support for faculty research and teaching endeavors. The services provided move beyond basic reference as needed and as opportunities for program development arise. Serving all faculty on all campuses in all disciplines, the service first supports T.W.U. strategic priorities (i.e., distance education, grant-seeking, and scholarly production) and, as resources permit, supports the general on-going development of faculty self-sufficiency in the areas of information retrieval and management. Maximizing use of cost-effective, mass customization resources (e.g., alert services and Web tutorials), FIRST maintains a balance within the mission of the Blagg-Huey Library by minimizing costs wherever possible. While no faculty are expected to move beyond the need for FIRST, the combination of instructional and informational support are expected to continually increase faculty self-sufficiency, confidence, and competence in the face of continual information technology development.

Final Commentary

This study was the first step in a series of studies which will eventually encompass both the undergraduate and graduate student populations. The rapidly increasing number of distance education students may also be a subpopulation with information needs distinct enough to warrant a separate study.

Several members of the library are now able to conduct interviews and a smaller core are able to analyze data in various formats. The administration is aware of the value of this type of study. While it is too soon to judge the impact of the study, preliminary indications are that it will be used to restructure service to faculty.

Partnerships within the library were significant. Staff outside of the reference department took part in training and data gathering, as well as the discussions which followed. A number of faculty expressed an interest in receiving the final report on the study. Many departmental liaisons to the Library expressed a renewed interest in the Library's services as did others who had no formal ties to the Library.

Appendix B

Public Library Study

The report of this study consists of the following documents: executive summary, methodology notes, data-gathering instruments, findings highlights, recommendations, and final commentary. The quotations within these documents come from other documents (e.g., meeting minutes and staff memos) used in the study. The librarian involved in the study has graciously given her permission to allow her real name to be used. Formerly Director of the Hurst Public Library, she may be contacted for more information at the address below.

Danita Barber
Branch Administrator
Fort Worth Public Library
500 W. 3rd St.
Fort Worth, TX 76602
DBarber@pub-lib.ci.fortworth.tx.us

Executive Summary

This executive summary document was presented to the Library Board and the Deputy City Manager at their monthly meeting.

Hurst Public Library Community Information Needs Analysis: Executive Summary

Methodology
Three data gathering techniques produced the data for this study: an extensive series of structured interviews, a two-page survey distributed to a random sampling of households, and an analysis of existing demographic and in-house data. These findings were presented to the library managers who discussed them at great length, generating an array of productive, innovative responses to community information needs. The Library Director then placed the needs in priority order, set four goals, established performance measures, and assigned staff specific objectives to meet by specific dates.

Results
A series of fifty-nine interviews with representatives of ten different subpopulations within the community produced descriptive data. A total of 203 community surveys (18 percent of those distributed) were returned.

Limitations
All studies are limited by the practical necessities of their implementation. The major limitation of this study was the number of surveys returned. The 18 percent response on the community survey produced a great deal of useful data, as did the extensive interviews. They do not, however, provide a fully representative sample of the population therefore the findings are appropriate to a 1–3 year plan but do not support a long-range plan.

Key findings
The primary finding of both the interview and the survey data was the undoubted strength of the library's collections and services. As one respondent put it, "The Hurst Library is an excellent facility. Keep up the good work!"

In addition, several areas of need appeared repeatedly, including the following: the need for a stronger book collection (particularly in adult materials); the need for educational support (in terms of both materials and educational programs, such as workshops) for Hurst children from preschool through high school; the need to know more about the services and collections already provided by the Library; and the need for a warmer, more attentive staff.

Top priorities
Four goals were initially established on the basis of three criteria. Each goal (a) met a major need, (b) was essential to the Library's mission, and (c) would require no major expenditures or staff re-structuring.

1. Improve customer satisfaction with staff service.
2. Develop a well-balanced collection that is well utilized by the community.
3. Strengthen Library ties to all parts of the community through development of a cohesive public relations program on existing services and collections.
4. Improve efforts to meet the educational needs of the children of Hurst from their preschool through their high school years.

Next steps
Each objective under each of the four goals requires a progress report within two to six months. The Library Director will be able to provide concrete measures of progress on each goal within one year although some of them will require up to three years for completion.

Methodology Notes

The quotes herein are taken from meeting minutes. These planning meetings included the Library Director, one paraprofessional staff member, and the author.

Subpopulations

- Since the purpose of the study is to identify the information of the general population, care must be taken to identify and make contacts among the smaller subpopulations which might be overlooked in a generalized survey approach.
- The Director and staff identified the following subpopulations:
  - "racial/ethnic: could reach them via churches, family-owned ethnic restaurants, and ESL classes at a local church; language is the major difficulty in reaching these community members
  - 2-income families: could reach them via the large number of daycare centers in the area; time is the major difficulty in reaching these community members
  - age: we have both ends of the age spectrum to reach; those who are retired could be contacted via the extremely active senior center; children could be contacted via various high-population activities such as scouting, soccer, girls softball, and baseball; teens could be reached via various school-centered activities such as band and sport as well as any other mechanisms which the library's teen volunteers would recommend
  - local government officials
  - school librarians"
- Discussions with staff identified a large number of people from various departments who were interested in learning to conduct interviews and who were willing to take part in the study. By rearranging their workloads, they were able to plan on participating because so many of them were willing to be involved that no one person need take on too much.

- The city administrators would control how many surveys could get out to whom and that information would not be available for some time but the general idea of sending out a written instrument was approved.
- An extensive series of brief interviews with people from the following subpopulations was set up: all local religious leaders (a key way to reach ethnic community gatekeepers), ESL tutors (a useful way to reach into the ESL community considering the lack of language skills available on the library staff), working parents, seniors, teens, school librarians, business owners, government officials, and child care providers
- Based on the findings of the interviews, a postal instrument would be designed and distributed as allowed by the city manager.
- Training would be provided for the interviewers and for the paraprofessional who was interested in narrative data-analysis techniques
- Initial conversations with community leaders opened the possibility of creating a space for a small, business-centered library branch. That led to a particular interest in the needs of the business community.

Data-Gathering Instruments

Slight variations on the following questions were asked of each separate subpopulation. Interviewers were given copies of and were trained in the use of their particular questions. For the other question set, contact the author.

Interview Questions: City Government Officials
- What do you see as the important information needs of city government leaders?
  - Follow-up questions: Does that include professional-casual-personal needs as well? Are there any needs you think might become more important in the next few years?
- How could the library best support your management of city activities?
  - Follow-up questions: What services would you like to see the library develop in this area? What changes in the collections would help?
- How do you usually find the information, books, magazines and so on that you want?
  - Follow-up questions: What do you like most about that? Do others in your community like to do anything different?

Interview Questions: Church Leaders
- What do you see as the important information needs of members of your community?
  - Follow-up questions: Does that include professional-casual-personal needs as well? Are there any needs you think might become more important in the next few years?
- How could the library best help members of your community in their daily lives?
  - Follow-up questions: What services would you like to see the library develop in this area? What changes in the collections would help?
- How do they usually find the information, books, magazines and so on that they want?

- Follow-up questions: What do you like most about that? Do others in your community like to do anything different?

Interview Questions: Retirees
- What do you see as the important information needs of retirees?
- How could the library best support them in handling daily personal needs?
- How do you usually find the information, books, magazines and so on that you want?

Interview Questions: ESL and Recent Immigrants
- What do you see as the important information needs of recent immigrants or those learning English?
- How could the library best support their efforts to become comfortable in Hurst?
- How do they usually find the information, books, magazines, and so on that they want?

This instrument was printed with the Library heading and sent with a cover letter from the Mayor and Library Board Chair.

Public Hurst Library Survey

In order to serve you and your family better, we would like to have your input. Please return this survey by May 30.

1. What kinds of information and materials do you and your family need? Please check all that apply.

   __support for school work   __parenting support
   __medical information   __personal finances material
   __legal forms & information   __travel material
   __recreational reading, adult __recreational reading, children
   __videos for education   __videos for recreation
   __books on tape   __spiritual/religious materials
   __nonEnglish material   __personal growth materials
   __access to professional journals
   __other, please explain below

2. What kinds of services do you see a need for in the Hurst community? Please check all that apply.

   __access to books that Hurst does not own
   __programming for children such as storytelling
   __non-English educational programs
   __GED support programs
   __literacy programs
   __workshops on how to search library computers
   __workshops on how to search the Internet
   __after school homework support for teens
   __Web access to reputable material on educational subjects
   __Web access to reputable material on daily living topics
   __Web access to reputable material on business topics
   __other, please explain below

3. If we opened a small branch in the Mall to focus on information for job seekers and small businesses, what kind of materials and services would you want to find there? Please explain.

4. Think about the information you and your family most need. Think about the needs you see in our community. What are the top two priorities you'd like to suggest to the Hurst Public Library staff?

5. Please tell us anything else you'd like us to know about ways in which we could better serve you and the community at large.

Demographics

Sex:_____number of females   _____ number of males

Ages of those in household:_____

Race/ethnicity of those in household:_____

Home computer access: ____have computer   ____have Internet

Work computer access: ____have computer   ____have Internet

Thank you very much for your input. Please fold this so the Hurst Public Library address is on the outside then mail it or drop it off at the Library. We appreciate your help.

Findings Highlights

"The primary finding of both the interview and the survey data was the undoubted strength of the library's collections and services. As one respondent put it, 'The Hurst Library is an excellent facility. Keep up the good work!'

In addition, several areas of need appeared repeatedly, including the following: the need for a stronger book collection (particularly in adult materials); the need for educational support (in terms of both materials and educational programs, such as workshops) for Hurst children from preschool through high school; the need to know more about the services and collections already provided by the Library; and the need for a warmer, more attentive staff."

Recommendations

The following action plans are based on the data, staff recommen-dations, and Administrator's priorities that resulted from the com-munity user needs analysis. Staff members' names have been removed for privacy reasons but were included on the original document.

Goal I: Significantly improve the customer service skills of all staff and strengthen the customer-orientation of the Library.

Objective 1: Develop a core of volunteer greeters who are (a) carefully trained to provide useful referrals to other departments, (b) carefully trained regarding the limited questions which they can answer, and (c) well supplied with library literature to be distrib-uted to those who are leaving.

> Who: [librarian] and the volunteer who coordinates vol-unteers.
> When: Progress report to the Administrator by 4/30/00.
> Suggestion: When no one is at the Information Desk, a large sign will be displayed, directing people to the Reference Desk. Greeters will walk patrons on to Ref-erence Desk.

Objective 2: Develop a staff-training manual (which can be given to all new staff) with an emphasis on customer service.

> Who: [5 staff members from different departments.]
> When: Report on progress and first draft to the Administra-tor by 2/28/00.
> Suggestion: Introduce new staff-training manual to existing staff at departmental meetings.

Objective 3: Work to change the corporate culture by discuss-ing various means of developing and strengthening the customer service orientation at staff management meetings as well as at de-partmental meetings.

> Who: The Administrator and four department heads.

When: Discuss and compare means of developing and strengthening the customer service orientation at a meeting of the five responsible parties by 4/30/00.

Objective 4:   Send all staff to the North Texas Council of Government customer service training session(s) which are most appropriate to their positions.
Who: The Administrator
When: All staff to at least one workshop by 11/1/00. (The team involved in objective 2 will be sent first.)

Objective 5:   Have all staff wear pins identifying them as staff while on duty.
Who: The Administrator
When: Order new pins by 11/30/99; begin wearing them as soon as they arrive.
Measure: The Administrator will review progress on the goal as a whole on an informal basis in six months, making corrections as needed. The Administrator will assign a management team to design and implement an approved, formal measure of progress on the goal by 11/30/00.

Goal II: Develop a well-balanced collection that is well utilized by the community.

Objective 1:   Add to extremely high-demand sections of the collection and weed extremely low-use areas of the collection according to set criteria. (This is only the first step in an overall effort to manage the collection.)
Who: The Collection Management Committee will create the criteria and have them approved by the Administrator.
When: The criteria will be approved by 12/15/99; individuals in charge of various sections of the collection will provide the Administrator with a written progress report on both selection and weeding on the last Friday of every even numbered month.

Suggestion: Using circulation reports from acquisitions, determine what percentages of owned books were checked out in each section. Apply that data in light of publication date.

Suggestion: Check with local teachers and make a list of annual assignments (Indians, Civil War, leaf identification, etc.) for each grade.

Suggestion: Check with school librarians to see if they use accelerated readers; if they do, are there areas they cannot get that HPL should supplement?

Objective 2: Develop a measure of use which includes in-house use as well as circulation statistics; take those measures for a year and compare with current data to determine the utility of the collection; use those data to design the next steps for collection management.

Who: Collection Management Committee

When: Have the measures approved by the Administrator by 12/15/99. Gather the data throughout 2000 and 2001. Report on the data analysis and design the next steps by 4/30/02.

Suggestion: Establish a year-round pattern to collect data on in-house use on a random, but regular basis; vary by time of day, day of week; make and display "Please Do Not Reshelve" signs during these times.

Objective 3: Develop ties with Texas Woman's University School of Library and Information Studies to recruit strong practicum students who are interested in working on essential collection management projects as a major portion of their practicum.

Who: The Administrator

When: Ongoing

Goal III: Have most members of the community understand and be consistently aware of the Library collections and services which most pertain to their information needs.

Objective 1:   Record ideas and practical plans for any new services that might support public relations in general.
>   Who: All staff
>   When: Collect ideas and hold them until the Administrator calls a staff meeting to discuss them in late 2000.

Objective 2:   Develop a comprehensive public relations plan for the Library as a whole; include procedures for implementing each section of the plan.
>   Who: [four librarians and paraprofessionals from different departments]
>   When: General brainstorming meeting with the Administrator by 11/30/99; written plan with due dates and responsible parties to the Administrator by 12/20/99.
>   Suggestion: Have greeters distribute flyers on current events and new collections.
>   Suggestion: Advertise existing after school hours as homework times, e.g. "Homework Night" and so on.
>   Suggestion: Get more pages in *Inside-Out*.
>   Suggestion: Enhance the Library's Web site by, for example, listing events on a calendar with email links to appropriate staff.
>   Suggestion: Get a cost estimate for an automated phone line.
>   Suggestion: Generate a list of community contacts for whom each librarian is responsible. Contact each person via letter or e-mail at least twice a year.
>   Suggestion: Structure community-wide distribution of library-wide information (e.g., where flyers are distributed and what local Web sites are encouraged to link to the Library Web site).
>   Suggestion: Utilize high school Honor Society students in P.R. efforts, such as greeting, teaching computer classes to seniors, and providing homework help.
>   Suggestion: Create special Web page and flyer series advertising existing collections and services for parents.
>   Suggestion: Make each public relations effort a two-way street

so that people can express their information needs directly to the responsible staff member (e.g., the genealogy club's president requesting reference staff to provide a workshop on using Library resources or gardening club members requesting more books on roses).

Objective 3: Revise and develop in-house data gathering on evidence of public relations efforts (e.g., cards distributed at the end of workshops asking attendees to identify the mechanisms by which they learned of the workshops); incorporate those measures into the overall plan for public relations.
> Who: [four librarians and paraprofessionals from different departments]
> When: 12/20/99

Goal IV: Strengthen services and collections to better serve the educational needs of the children of Hurst.

Objective 1: Encourage use of existing services and collections by developing a plan for closer coordination with those schools which are attended by Hurst children.
> Who: [3 staff members from children's and adult services]
> When: Plan to the Administrator for approval by 12/15/99
> Suggestion: Review the library's mission statement to incorporate the library's educational mission within the community.
> Suggestion: Coordinate with the PR group to make use of suggestions that pertain to children.

GENERAL APPLICATION SUGGESTIONS

1. To serve needs of the visually and physically challenged as well as dyslexics, be sure all children, YA, and adult librarians have forms and information on the National Library for the Blind, Physically Handicapped, and Dyslexic. Per-

haps do an exhibit, have news items, share information with school counselors, share information with senior centers, and so on. Do staff training if necessary.

2. Change room rental policy to allow community volunteers free access to the room when they want to provide free community support classes, e.g. computer workshops for seniors.

Long-term goals, pursued as resources become available:

Goal A: Extend evening hours in support of Hurst children's need for access to homework resources.

Goal B: Analyze the information needs of the business community.

Goal C: Select and provide access for materials in languages other than English, as needed by the community.

Goal D: Explore the options pertaining to the use of institutional cards for teachers (at all levels) who teach in Hurst schools.

Goal E: Explore the options pertaining to increasing access to high demand, best sellers by adjusting the loan period on selected copies.

Goal F: Conduct a follow-up user needs analysis that reaches a fully representative portion of the population of Hurst.

Final Commentary

The staff learned a great deal about data gathering and the general process of a study. People at all ranks were energized by the findings and have begun work on their assigned projects. The brainstorming meeting with staff which followed the data analysis was most productive.

Future studies will need to take into account the generally low response rate which postal questionnaires generate. The various methods planned for increasing response rate (e.g., sending postcards in advance, sending far more than required by the sample size, using other distributions methods in addition to that of postal mail) were not supported by city administration. While the findings were useful, they could have been a great deal more useful had a higher response rate been generated. That fact having been demonstrated, however, future studies should benefit.

The partnerships which were generated by the interviews should continue to yield fruit. The possible branch library requires extensive thought and planning. Community contacts may generate more volunteers and liaisons.

Appendix C

School Library Study

The report of this study consists of the following documents: executive summary, methodology notes, data-gathering instruments, findings highlights, recommendations, and final commentary. The quotations within these documents come from other documents (e.g., meeting minutes and staff memos) used in the study. The librarian and school administrator involved in the study have graciously given their permission to allow their real names to be used. They may be contacted for more information at the addresses below.

Jane Sego
Executive Director
Fairhill School
16150 Preston
Dallas, TX 75248

Karen Sanchez
Librarian
Fairhill School
16150 Preston
Dallas, TX 75248

Executive Summary

This is an excerpt from the final report prepared for the School administration. Fairhill School is a private, no-profit school serving grades 1–12. Focusing on students with special learning needs, the School has small classes, computer facilities, and an attractive library. Automated for the first time in the summer just prior to this study, the library is staffed by a part-time, certified librarian and several parent volunteers.

"A planning session with the three investigators [i.e., the librarian, the School's chief administrator, and the author] led to a two-stage data gathering plan involving representative members of the Fairhill community. Focusing on faculty information needs, the study began with two focus groups in which faculty were clustered by grade levels with the resulting mixture of disciplines. All but two of the invited faculty was able to attend one of these 45–minute sessions. The resulting data were reviewed by Dr. Westbrook to identify key themes, issues, and concerns. Those items were then incorporated into a written questionnaire that was distributed to all faculty. The instrument was tested and reviewed by Ms. Sego and Ms. Sanchez. Twenty-three faculty completed the written survey. These data were analyzed by Dr. Westbrook, leading to an initial list of recommendations. These recommendations were reviewed and accepted by the Librarian and Ms. Sego."

Methodology Notes

General considerations
- Ms. Sanchez was quite interested in the study but did not feel that she had the experience, education, or time to handle the study personally. She did, however, want to learn as much as she could of the general process and the specific techniques.
- Ms. Sego was thoroughly supportive of the study and quite interested in using the findings to further develop the library's role in the School's overall strategic plan, including grant-seeking plans.
- Since faculty had never been studied and since their work served the students' needs, the primary focus of the study was to be the information needs of faculty.

Stage one
- Faculty would be willing to contribute to a focus group meeting since they were used to meeting in small groups, interested in the library, and a time slot could be used which would not impose on their current work schedule.
- After discussion of various ways in which to group faculty for the focus groups, it was decided that more ideas might be generated by contrasting discipline than age group. Therefore, those who taught the same general age groups (i.e., lower school faculty teaching grades 1–6 and upper school faculty teaching grades 7–12) would be used to form the groups. The contrast by subject specialty might lead to varying views being expressed.
- Faculty were to be encouraged to discuss anything that interested them without regard to administrative boundaries between the library and the computer lab technical support services.

Stage two
- Faculty were, given their course development patterns, likely to have additional insights after the focus groups generated

some thought on the issues. Therefore, a follow-up questionnaire would be distributed within a week of completing data
analysis on the focus group notes.

- The timing of the questionnaire was so close to the end of
  the term that a second copy would be sent to everyone in
  the hope of increasing the response rate. Keeping track of
  those who had not completed the instrument might inhibit
  free expression of information needs so the second copy
  would be sent to all with a note of explanation.

Data-Gathering Instruments

All of these questions were covered in the 50–minute sessions, each of which had approximately 15 subjects involved. Everyone spoke on at least two points and many spoke on each item.

1. Think back to the beginning of this school year. You were preparing for classes, writing lesson plans, setting goals. What kind of information did you need at that time?
2. Where do you go for the information you need? Do you browse bookstores, explore the Web, talk to colleagues, visit your local public library, or use your own personal collection?
3. These days it's often not hard to find information; the real problem comes in finding it efficiently then managing it once you've got it. Things change so fast that it's hard to learn what we need to know sometimes. Is there anything you'd like to have support doing, such as using search engines or searching the library's new online catalog?
4. Think about a time when you needed information to help you prepare for a class and you couldn't get it easily. What did you want? What did you do to get it?
5. Part of what you do in the classroom is connect your students to information resources. How do you do that? What would make that task easier?
6. Is there anything else that you'd like to share about your professional information needs?

Faculty Information Needs Survey

Thank you for taking the time to complete this survey. It will help us plan for and develop the library. Please return this to the office by 12/16.

1. Please name the two subject areas which you'd most like to see enhanced in the library's book collection.
   a._____
   b._____

2. Please rank the following equipment requests in terms of their importance to your teaching. Leave blank any items which are not important to you. Add items as needed.
   ___ VCRs with televisions
   ___ Faster printers
   ___ Tape players and headphones for a listening center
   ___ Faster Internet connections
   ___ Library's catalog on a computer in each classroom
   ___ Other:_____

3. Rank the following enhancements in terms of their importance to your teaching. Leave blank any items which are not important to you. Add items as needed.
   ___ Reference materials
   ___ Web sites of proven lesson plans in your area
   ___ Web sites useful for your students' work on specific unit of study
   ___ A Web site covering the day's news in your subject area(s)
   ___ Clearinghouses of Web sites in your subject area(s) and grade level(s)
   ___ Lists of recommended materials commonly available in public libraries and bookstores on the major, repeated themes you use
   ___ Lists of fiction materials by subject, such as myths, folk tales, and science fiction

___ Lists of all types of library materials on various themes commonly repeated in your courses

___ Other:_____

4. Please rank the following service enhancements in terms of their importance to your teaching. Leave blank any items which are not important to you. Add items as needed.

___ An individualized tour of the library which focuses on the resources most pertinent to your subject area(s) and grade level(s)

___ Individual resource meetings each semester with the librarian to highlight new library acquisitions and Internet material pertinent to your subject area(s) and grade level(s)

___ Copies of the table of contents of professional magazines with the chance to order, within 24 hours, copies of the articles you choose

___ News updates covering professional development resources such as Region 10 conferences, good DISD videos available for loan, and practical articles on teaching techniques

___ Routed reviews of software, multimedia kits, and research resources for which you could make requests

___ Other: _____

5. Faculty information needs generally come in three areas: resources needed for the classroom, professional development resources needed to prepare for the classroom, and professional skills to maintain and develop. For each of those three areas, please name your most critical need.

___ Classroom resource:

___ Professional development resource:

___ Professional information skill:

6. Please share any other information needs which haven't been covered.

   _____

   _____

Please return this to the office as soon as possible. Again, thank you very much.

Findings Highlights

The following highlights of the focus group notes were discussed by the three members of the study team. All but two teachers participated in the focus groups.

1st focus group; lower school teachers in reading, AP, math, language arts; needs include the following items

- Personal tour of the library; need depth of the resources; need to know the library well enough to understand what we have that will inspire students and give them immediate gratification
- Learn details of the facility and resources
- A computer into which they can put in a theme from any part of the curriculum then pull up any book including those which do *not* have the theme in the title
- Research material for students beyond encyclopedias
- Ways in which to use SIRS more often and more effectively
- More videos, making sure that they too get full entries in the annotated list right away
- Need OPAC access in the classroom
- Need access to the OPAC, the video list and other library resources on the net
- Library staff who could pull books on demand
- Get multiple printers
- Want to get to the library via the Web
- Use home Web access to get information which both inspires and informs students
- Bookstores (Barnes and Noble, Border's, and Half Price) have books which the library does not; need information on books we don't have even if we can't get them
- Want Web sites for themselves and for students
- Hard copy of various Web pages
- Want to learn to use the Web
- Web sites which have been evaluated for children
- Professional publications

- Need pared down, filtered lists of the best sites for different purposes
- Need help in learning how to search the Web efficiently
- Need sites on specific topics, preferably annotated lists
- Need to have Web sites which have been reviewed by age with notes as to why the sites have been selected as appropriate for a topic and age so they can be recommended to students; not lists but actual sites
- Need help in searching the Web and SIRS, how to do these tasks and how to teach the students to do these tasks
- Need Webliographies or Web collections by topic since there's no time to search for sites using Boolean logic
- Problem with very slow printers; students can't take notes well so they need to print out but the entire class gets backed up due to slow printers
- The excitement of using databases generates ideas and inspiration; want to keep that momentum going; it excites students and engages them but they keep getting stopped by the lack of access
- Want a variety of sources for the same topic so students can compare the quality and relative appropriateness of various sources and types of sources
- Need paper copies of classic reference sources (e.g., encyclopedias and dictionaries) so students can learn to handle them, understand their nature
- Need help in teaching students to cite materials they've obtained from the Web
- Need help in citing sources in general; need examples
- Need help in adhering to copyright laws
- Want lists of sites from which students might get papers in their efforts to plagiarize
- Need media equipment; need a VCR in every room so they can show short segments as needed with flexibility; reserving machines in advance is too tough

2nd focus group; math, health, social studies, history, and science teachers; primarily upper school

- Proven projects that would support lesson plans; help develop, refresh, and integrate them; science and social studies
- Projects which relate the material to students' lives, that make the material obviously useful and real to them; math needs obviously useful projects that show students they need this
- Software which moves beyond drilling and into inspiring; with meaning for now and for future
- Need lower level material; books, kits, tapes, and short videos at their level;
- A great deal of auditory and visual information for students in all areas; multi-sensory approach
- Need extremely current items on all topics, examples actually in the news today
- Need current visuals (videos, slides, photos, etc.) in health, social studies, and history; need to be current in their content but also need to appear current
- Would like to know what students did last year, what skills they need for this year
- Need to see magazines right away, no time to route one copy through so many people
- Taking journals at home since they don't get all that they need here; would help to get more of them
- Need lists of Web sites
- Need someone to filter alert services so they can find useful resources without wading through so much
- Need Web clearinghouses and meta-sites which are well chosen, annotated, and updated
- Need immediate needs filled quickly when class moves in a good direction or goes further than expected; need support
- Need to make effective use of the DISD video library; have to wade through a lot of trash but do have many good items
- Need to know how to search the Web

- Need to capture student questions in the classroom, send out for the answers, and have them during the same period
- Need to organize resources that they do use on a personal basis; information management issues
- Need structure for their lesson plans, filing systems and general organization; need index to their lessons and works
- Want someone reviewing their lesson plans then jumping in with new resources, ideas, and fresh takes
- Need unity in themes across classes so they can all use the same resources to reinforce ideas; work in teams
- When ask for resources on a theme, they need information in all possible formats, not just books; they need videos, latest magazine articles, kits, and Web sites; want this in all areas; want that day's news
- Need support for teaching students' basic, general skills like study habits, study skills, taking notes, recognizing what's important, how to take a test, evaluating materials, questioning what they read, summarizing information, reading for detail, organizing notes, making connections, and applying skills in a new context

Questionnaire findings: A rough draft of the study findings was shared with Ms. Sanchez and Ms. Sego after the 23 (of 32 possible) responses were received. Building on their input, the final report was written in three units: findings, information literacy standards, and grant materials. The latter two pieces consisted of gathered resources presented to supplement the action plans.

Subject areas or types of books requested:
- Sciences/math
  - Science history, science (2), physics, chemistry, earth science, physical science
  - PE games and activities (2), health
  - Math (4), elementary math story books
- Humanities/art
  - Literature: novels for upper grades, adult fiction, myths and legends, beginning/young reader fiction, accelerated readers, novels for middle school, high interest/low ability books
  - Drama, plays for children, monologues, duets
  - Easy reader books, fiction and nonfiction
- Social sciences
  - Specific nonfiction: biographies (2), biographies of Texans, Native American tribes, holidays, Jewish holidays
  - Social studies (2), economics, history, government (United States and foreign), Texas history, world history
  - Reference books for young children, beginning dictionaries, atlases, middle school reference works

Equipment requests:
- VCRs with televisions [1st choice]
- Library's catalog on a computer in each classroom [2nd choice]

Enhancements:
- Reference materials
- Web sites of proven lesson plans in your area [1st choice]

- Web sites useful for your students' work on specific units [2nd choice]
- Web site of the day's news in your subject areas
- Clearinghouses of Web sites in your subject areas and grade levels
- Lists of recommended materials available in libraries and book stores on major, repeated themes
- Lists of fiction material by subject, such as myths, folk tales, science fiction
- Lists of all types of library materials on various themes commonly repeated in your courses [3rd choice]

Service enhancements:
- Individualized tour of the library
- Individual resource meetings each semester [2nd choice]
- Copies of table of contents of professional magazines [3rd choice]
- News updates on professional development resources [1st choice]
- Routed reviews of software, kits, and research resources

Classroom resources:
- Visual resources: VCR tapes; VCRs (6); televisions (6); films; camcorder; videos on the books and stories read in class; laser disks
- Audio resources: cassette players with earphones for *each* classroom; tape recorders with head sets; easy reader books and audio tapes to go with them
- Objects: math manipulatives and activity books; models
- Reading matter: magazines; greater access to reference materials (2); books of monologues, duets, short plays; mixed novels for students 14–16
- Workshops on subject matters
- Guest speakers
- Internet access
- Time to assimilate material

Professional development resources:
- How to get lesson plans and information that is current
- Workshops regarding students' needs; information on LD; math; teacher training
- Magazines: professional math teacher magazines; professional magazines for young children such as *Mailbox*, *Highlights*, and *Ladybug*
- Web sites
- Meetings regarding social studies

Professional information skill:
- Workshops; on higher order thinking; ways to illustrate these skills to LD kids; learning differences; using the Internet (3); students' needs
- Magazines and books on language development
- Instructional videos
- Notification of continuing education opportunities

Additional requests:
- Films of classics
- Written review of library programs for new teachers such as Accelerated Reader
- Notice of professional development opportunities from the National Council for the Social Studies
- Reference materials in the classroom
- More videos for young children
- Videos
- Video/audio tapes with some VCR/TV combinations
- Sport instructional videos
- Taped novel units
- Resources for research college typesetting
- Camcorder

Recommendations

Administration: Each of the collection, service, and capital recommendations made in the sections which follow this one, is based on the assumption that at least some of this additional support has been made available.

1. Recruit a set of library volunteers to manage and execute specific, limited tasks such as setting up a library Web site.
2. Have one faculty member in the Upper School and one in the Lower School act as the library liaison for their schools. These people will act as two-way information conduits and advocates for the library while providing advice and suggestions for the librarian.
3. Identify and apply for grants to fund temporary help for various major projects; hire library studies students to work under the librarian's direction to complete those projects.

Collection: The following recommendations encourage new avenues and propose particular priorities among competing needs based on the intensity of the need and the cost/benefit ratio involved.

1–3 years:
- Use the new OPAC to run an analysis on the collection with reference to each subject area at each grade-level grouping (e.g. social studies for 4–6th graders). Identify gaps and strengths in the collection. Match the major, repeated curriculum units (e.g., Texas history) against the collection reports.
- Build the fiction collection with an emphasis on well-reviewed series, classics, and high-interest/low-reading-skill works.
- Build highly selective nonfiction areas with an emphasis on curriculum support (e.g., science project background works) and high-interest/low-reading-skill topics which support general reading development (e.g., celebrity biographies and joke books).

- Build the periodical collection in the areas of children's magazines and professional reading materials. Determine which titles are needed then ask the parents of each class to contribute to an annual subscription each year.
- Continue to develop the video collection with an emphasis on building a minimal set of resources in each subject area and grade level.
- Collect essential Web sites just as books are already collected. Establish a very basic collection of sites in high-demand areas.

4–6 years:
- Develop a limited set of professional development resources for faculty in multiple formats on topics such as copyright law, working with students who have learning differences, and practical teaching techniques.
- Develop the sciences with an explicit focus on college preparatory works and curricular support works. Build this collection on the repeated units in each grade (e.g., basic parts of the cell) as well as the science themes common to several grades (e.g., conservation of natural resources).
- Develop those areas of the personal reading interest areas of the social sciences and fine arts with an explicit focus on high-interest low-reading-ability materials.
- Develop a deeper collection of Web sites with an emphasis on supporting long-term, repeated homework assignments such as Texas history and math facts. Include sections on interdisciplinary issues such as current events, study skills, and art appreciation.

Services: These recommendations move the library deeper into the mainstream of school activities by tying it more deeply into the curriculum, particularly in the area of developing information literacy skill programs.

1–3 years:
- Publicize new materials in the collection through book talks, book displays, reading lists, the school newsletter, student

reviews, and more. Make this project a post for a volunteer.

- Create a library Web site with selected, high-use resources. Organize the site to support faculty and student information seeking in high-use, commonly needed areas. Encourage students and faculty to share sites which they find useful. Have the Upper School computing classes maintain the site.

4–6 years:
- Begin to formally develop the instructional program so that Fairhill students begin to meet the information literacy standards established by the American Association of School Librarians. Using "Information Power" and "The Big Six," begin to set information literacy goals for each grade, work with teachers to establish cooperative lessons in support of each goal, and devise means of evaluating the efficacy of that instruction. (So labor-intensive a recommendation requires particularly substantial support, perhaps in the form of a grant.)
- Set professional development goals for faculty in the area of information literacy skills. Develop a series of professional development workshops for faculty to help them meet those goals.
- In the Web site, include reference service from an instructional perspective, e.g., accept questions regarding long-term homework questions or topic areas then refer students to sites which guide them through mastery of those issues.

Capital development: In order to meet mounting interest in incorporating multimedia work into the curriculum, funding must be obtained to develop essential infrastructure elements.

1–3 years:
- Develop a plan to maximize funding options in order to obtain more VCR stations for classroom use.
- Develop a modest listening center making full use of the Library for the Blind, Physically Handicapped, and Dyslexic.

4–6 years:
- Obtain funding to network the school with the OPAC and Internet in each classroom.

Final Commentary

A one-librarian library serving so many grades with so many special education needs requires long-term planning. By limiting the focus of the study to faculty, the School and library administrators could make a reasonable start on a daunting task. The open-ended nature of the focus groups and questionnaire items generated a much wider array of information needs than could be met with existing budget constraints but did provide the basis for setting priorities, seeking new partnerships with parents, and seeking specific grants.

Appendix D

Statistical Reports Generated by Various OPACs

Twenty-seven major software companies were contacted and eighteen provided information on their statistical reporting capabilities. That information is reported below in three segments. First, numbered report descriptions describe the statistical report capabilities about which each company was questioned. Second, the company entries identify the capabilities of each system and the preferred company contact data. Third, a matrix of the findings allows ready cross-company comparisons by listing the companies along one axis and the numbered reports along the other. While these capabilities are sure to change over time, this provides both a starting point and a minimal list of questions on this point to be used when contracting for a new system.

Statistical reports:
Companies were asked whether or not their software was capable of providing each of the following reports. If the software were indeed capable of providing the report, the companies were then asked whether or not doing so would incur any additional cost. There are 21 possible reports followed by two additional questions.

Understanding community borrowing patterns

1. Number of items borrowed in a set time period in each call number range, e.g., ability to tell how many items were borrowed from the P 100s (in LC) in a one-week period.

2. Same but in terms of percentages of the total number of items circulated, e.g., ability to tell that 60 percent of the borrowed items during one week were from the P 100s.

3. Number of items borrowed in a set time period in each call number range arranged by patron demographic, e.g., the ability to determine that 509 books in the P 100s were borrowed by undergraduates and 43 books in the Q 700s were borrowed by faculty in a one-week period.

4. Same but in terms of percentages of the total number of items circulated and the total number of registered patrons in each demographic group, e.g., the ability to determine that 20 percent of the faculty borrowed 60 percent of the circulated Q 700 books in one week.

5. The number of times that various numbers of books were borrowed on one day or visit on one card over a set period of time, e.g., the ability to determine that on 43 occasions three books were borrowed on a single day or visit on one card in the month of May.

6. Same but in terms of percentages of the total number of items per visit, e.g., the ability to determine that 20 percent of the time that books were borrowed in May, three books were taken out per visit. (Allows librarians to determine the months or weeks in which patrons are "stocking up" when they visit, e.g., right before vacation.)

7. The number of occasions on which a certain number of books were borrowed on one day or visit on one card over a set period of time in terms of patron demographics, e.g., the ability to determine that 16 times in May three books were borrowed on a single day or visit using a faculty member's card.

8. Same but in terms of percentages of the total number of items per visit in terms of patron demographics, e.g., the ability to determine that in May twenty percent of the time an individual faculty card is used, three books are borrowed simultaneously.

9. The number of days that regular term books are kept out in a set time period, e.g., the ability to tell that 500 books borrowed in the second week of April were kept out for only two days.

10. Same but in percentage, e.g., the ability to tell that 35 percent of the books borrowed were kept out for three weeks.

Understanding community OPAC searching patterns
11. The number of searches conducted using each command (i.e., author, title, subject, keyword, etc.) over a set period of time, e.g., the ability to determine that 150 keyword searches were run in August.

12. Same but in percentages, e.g., the ability to determine that 10 percent of the August searches were keyword.

13. The number of searches resulting in 0 or 5000+ hits over a set period of time, e.g., the ability to determine that 466 August searches resulted in 0 hits and 544 August searches resulted in 5000+ hits.

14. Same but in percentages, e.g., the ability to determine that 54 percent of the August searches resulted in 0 hits and 25 percent of the August searches yielded 5000+ hits.

15. The number of searches resulting in 0 or 5000+ hits over the course of a year by search type, e.g., the same as report number 13 except that it covers an entire year.

16. Same but in percentages, e.g., the same as report number 14 except that it covers an entire year.

17. The number of searches on different help screens over the course of a year, e.g., the ability to determine that in Sep-

tember there were 440 searches for the help screen on doing keyword searching.

18. Same but in percentages, e.g., the ability to determine that in September 11 percent of all searches were for the help screen on doing keyword searching.

19. Can your system generate separate statistics for interlibrary loan, reserves, AV formats, or other special areas?

20. Can your system's reports be generated graphically, e.g., pie charts or histograms or graphs?

21. Can your system create a profile of the user who borrows certain items, e.g., the person who borrows a history book is likely to be a graduate student who keeps the book for three days and checks out four additional books on the same visit?

22. Are there any additional in-house statistical capabilities of your system which have not been covered? Please explain briefly.

23. Are there any major upgrades in this area planned for your program in the next year?

Software reporting capabilities by company:
The following information is available for each responding company: the numbers of available reports and the contact information provided by each company.

Best-Seller, Inc.: A few reports fully available, including 1, 2, and 19. Reports 3–10 available at an additional cost. External reporting package on the type of report needed for 20.
Contact Information: Normand Cardella
                         E-mail: ncardella@bestseller.com

CARL Corporation: Reports 1–10 and 19 fully available. Report module needed for 11–18 and 20 at an additional charge.
Contact Information: Don Kaiser
                      E-mail: dkaiser@carl.org
                      Generic e-mail: info@carl.org

Data Research Associates, Inc: Some reports fully available, including 1, 11, 13, 15, and 19. Support of a third party needed for reports 2–9 and 17. Additional charge assessed for 10, 12, 14, 16, 18.
Contact Information: Jennifer Chilton Kallery
                      E-mail: Jennifer@dra.com

Endeavor Information Systems, Inc.: Reports 1–4, 11–13, 15, 19, and 20 fully available. User-initiated change to prepackaged report for 5–10, 14, 16. WebTrends provides analysis for 17 and 18. Results of 21 obtained by combining results from several reports. Graphical SQL writer needed for report 22.
Contact Information: Cindy Edgington Miller
                      Director of Product Strategy
                      Endeavor Information Systems, Inc.
                      2200 East Devon Avenue
                      Suite 382
                      Des Plaines, IL 60018
                      Telephone: (847) 296–2200, Extn. 2630;
                      (800) 762–6300
                      Fax: (847) 296–5636
                      E-mail: Cindy@endinfosys.com

epixtech, inc.: A few reports fully available, including 1, 11, and 19.
Contact Information: epixtech, inc.
                      (formerly Ameritech Library Services)
                      400 West 5050 North (headquarters)
                      Provo, UT 84604
                      www.epixtech.com
                      800/222–8020 for sales information

ExLibris, Inc.: Reports 1–18 fully available.
Contact Information: Russell McDonald
Vice President of Sales and Marketing
Ex Libris, Inc.
Telephone: (510) 655–0663
Fax: (510) 655–0669
E-mail: russell@exlibris-usa.com

Follett Software Company: Reports 1 and 2 fully available.
Contact Information: Michele Shaw
Product Manager
1391 Corporate Drive
McHenry, IL 60050
Telephone: (815) 344–8700
Fax: (815) 344–8774
E-mail: mshaw@fsc.follett.com

Fretwell-Downing Informatics (USA) Limited: Selected reports currently available with support from third party software. Substantially developed array of reports projected to be available at the end of 2000.
Contact Information: Betsy Larson
Fretwell-Downing Informatics Ltd.
PMB 227
10308 Metcalf
Overland Park, KS 66212
Telephone: (888) 649–6542;
(913) 649–7213
Fax: (913) 649–2271
E-mail: Betsy.Larson@FDGroup.com

Gaylord Information Systems: Polaris has a greater number of reports available than GALAXY, including the following: 1–8, 11–16, 19, 20, and 22. GALAXY provides 1, 2, 11–15, and 22.
Contact Information: Michael Frasciello
Corporate Communications Developer
Gaylord Information Systems

P.O. Box 4901
Syracuse, NY 13221–4901
Telephone: (315) 457–5070
Fax: (315) 457–5883
E-mail: frasciello@gaylord.com

Geac Computers, Inc.: Report 19 fully available. Fees assessed for reports 1–18. The majority of non-Mac computers can handle report 20.
Contact Information: Phil Smith
Marketing Communications Manager
Geac Computer Corporation Limited
11 Allstate Parkway
Suite 300
Markham, Ontario L3R 9T8
Fax: (905) 475–3847
E-mail: p.smith@geac.com

Inmagic, Inc.: Many reports fully available, including 1–16, 19, and 21.
Contact Information: Lynda Moulton
Director of Integrated Library Systems
800 West Cummings Park
Woburn, MA 01801
Telephone: (781) 938–4442, Extn. 273
Fax: (781) 938–6393
E-mail: lmoulton@inmagic.com

Innovative Interfaces: 1, 2, 3, 4, and 9–23 available. Plans include making all statistical reports available on Web browsers with pie charts and graphs.
Contact Information: Frank R. Bridge
Innovative Interfaces, Inc.
5850 Shellmound Way
Emeryville, CA 94608
Telephone: 512/372–0550
Fax: 512/372–0551
E-mail: fbridge@iii.com

International Library Systems Corporation: Some reports fully available, including 1, 3, 5, 9, 11, 16, 18, and 19. Third party tools, such as Excel, required for report 20. Additional charges assessed for reports with percentages.
Contact Information: Noelle Khong
                     E-mail: Helpdesk@ils.ca

Keystone Systems, Inc.: Reports 1, 3, 11–16, 19, and 21 fully available. Reports 2, 4–10, 17–18, and 20 available within some parameters.
Contact Information: David Holloman
                     8016 Glenwood Avenue
                     Raleigh, NC 27612
                     Telephone: (800) 222–9711
                     E-mail: dave@klas.com

Open Text Corporation: Product is called BASIS Techlib, formerly Information Dimensions. A few reports fully available, including 1, 3, and 19. Report writing tool is required to extend reports 2 and 4. Data retained in the system for analysis in reports 5–10. Data for analysis collected by system monitor for reports 11–12
Contact Information: Carol Knoblauch
                     Product Manager
                     Open Text, BASIS Division
                     Telephone: 614/761–7228
                     E-mail: knoblauch@opentext.com

SIRSI Corporation: Product is called Unicorn. Reports 1 and 3 fully available. More reports available within parameters, including 2, 4, 6, 8, 12, 14, 16, and 20. Users can direct report output to disk, e-mail, and desktop applications, including Excel.
Contact Information: Steve Rowley, Manager
                     Sales Support
                     101 Washington Street SE
                     Huntsville, AL 35801–4827

Telephone/Fax: (256) 704–7007
E-mail: stever@sirsi.com

VTLS Customer Support: Some reports fully available, including 1–5, 19, 21, and 22.
Contact Information: Michelle Ervine
Technical Analyst
VTLS Customer Support
E-mail: ervinem@mail.vtls.com

Winnebago Software Company: Report 1 fully available.
Contact Information: Winnebago Software Company
2800 National Drive
Onalaska, WI 54650
Telephone (U.S./Canada): (800) 533–5430
Telephone (Worldwide): (507) 725–5411
E-mail: info@winnebago.com
www.fdusa.com

The following chart provides information regarding the reports made available by each company. The items marked "X" are available without additional cost. The items marked "$" are available but do have an additional cost of some kind.

	1	2	3	4	5	6	7	8	9	10	11	12	13	14	15	16	17	18	19	20	21	22	23
Best-Seller	X	X	$	$	$	$	$	$	$	$									X	$			
Brodart	X		X																X				
CARL	X	X	X	X	X	X	X	X	X	X	$	$	$	$	$	$	$	$	X	$			
Data Research	X	$	X	$	$	$	$	$	$	$	X	X	X	$	X	$	$	$	X				
Endeavor	X	X	X	X	$	$	$	$	$	$	X	X	X	$	X	$	$	$	X	X	X	$	$
epixtech (Ameritech)	X										X								X				
ExLibris	X	X	X	X	X	X	X	X	X	X	X	X	X	X	X	X	X	X					
Follett	X	X														X	X	X					
Gaylord, GALAXY	X	X									X	X	X	X	X	X			X	X	X	X	
Gaylord, Polaris	X	X	X	X	X	X	X	X			X	X	X	X	X	$	$	$	X	$	X	X	X
GEAC	$	$	$	$	$	$	$	$	$	$	$	$	$	$	$	X	X	X	X	$	$	$	$
Inmagic	X	X	X	X	X	X	X	X	X	X	X	X	X	X	X	X			X	X	X	X	X
Innovative Interfaces	X	X	X	X	X					X	X	X	X	X	X	X	X	X	X	X	X	X	X
International Library Systems			X	X	X		X		X	X	X	X						X		$	X	$	$
Keystone	X	$	X	$	X	$	$	$	$	$			X		X	X	X	X	X	X	X		
Open Text	X	X	X	X	X	X	X			X				$		$			X	X			
SIRSI	X	$	X	$	X	X	X	$			$				$		$		X	$		$	
VTLS	X	X	X	X	X														X		X	X	
Winnebago	X																						

Suggested Readings

For All Libraries

Dervin, Brenda, and Kathleen Clark. July 1987. *ASQ: Alternative tools for information need and accountability assessments by libraries.* Belmont, CA; Peninsula Library System. (Obtained as a personal communication from the primary author.)

Fowler, Floyd, Jr. 1993. *Survey research methods.* 2nd edition. Newbury Park, CA: Sage. The chapters on sampling and reducing nonresponse rates provide practical, thorough advice on handling these difficult points of research design. While the book as a whole is meant for those working on substantial research efforts, librarians will find a number of useful elements in each chapter.

Great library promotion ideas. John Cotton Dana Library Public Relations Award Winners and Notables. Chicago: American Library Association. This annual publication of award-winning public relations campaigns sometimes provides interesting ideas for the presentation of some information-needs analysis results.

Hafner, Arthur. 1998. *Descriptive statistical techniques for librarians.* 2nd edition. Chicago: ALA. Lucid yet rigorous, this well-organized volume provides explanations, examples, and commentary on the use of oft-needed analysis techniques. Since all of the examples come from various aspects of librarianship, the usually essential effort to "translate" explanations into the library setting is unnecessary.

Henry, Gary. 1990. *Practical sampling.* Applied Social Science Research Methods Series, volume 21. Newbury Park, CA: Sage. This advanced, well-organized volume illustrates sampling principles with concrete examples. The tables and graphs throughout the work provide concise overviews and clear illustrations of various key points.

Line, Maurice. 1967. *Library surveys: An introduction to their use, plan-*

ning, procedures, and presentation. London: Clive Bingley. Bar the information on punch card computer analysis, this slim volume is still quite useful. Chapters two (planning surveys) and three (collecting information) are particularly productive.

McKillip, Jack. 1987. *Need analysis: Tools for the human services and education*. Newbury Park, CA: Sage. Written for scholars in the social sciences, this compact, practical volume delineates types of needs, steps in needs analysis, and means of gathering information. See particularly the sections on determining readability levels (74–75), designing open-ended questions (74–75), and managing focus groups (87–88).

Powell, Ronald R. 1997. *Basic research methods for librarians*. 3rd edition. Greenwich, CT: Ablex. This standard guide provides the rigor and depth that are essential to high quality studies along with the explanations and examples that are essential to comprehension. Readily understood by competent librarians, the work will guide your choice of data-gathering tools, your sample design, and your data analysis.

Reed, Sally Gardner. 1992. *Saving your library: A guide to getting, using, and keeping the power you need*. Jefferson, NC: McFarland. Written for public librarians, this enjoyable volume provides practical support for almost any librarian. Just substitute the members of your population, power structure, and administrative units and get to work on getting more money. Of particular interest is the text of her telephone questionnaire questions for nonusers.

Sieber, Joan. 1992. *Planning ethically responsible research: A guide for students and internal review boards*. Applied Social Research Methods Series, volume 31. Newbury Park, CA: Sage. The three chapters on social and behavioral research cover all the common issues such as voluntary consent, privacy, and means of assuring confidentiality. While much of it is far more detailed than is likely to be needed, the style is quite comfortable and practical.

Zweizig, Douglas. 1992. Community analysis. In *Keeping the books: Public library financial practices*. Jane Robbins and Douglas Zweizig, eds. Fort Atkinson, WI: Highsmith Press, for the Urban Libraries Council. 225–238. This essential piece provides a vigorous overview of the essential principles of any CINA. The issues of moving from findings to actual change and of the reiterative nature of the work are strongly delineated.

Academic Libraries

Brekke, Elaine. November 1994. *User surveys in ARL libraries*. Washington, DC: Association of Research Libraries. SPEC Kit 205. While many of these user surveys focus on an evaluation of the library rather than on the information needs of users, the wide variety of sample surveys is well worth some time. Postal mail, e-mail, telephone, exit, and general distribution surveys of faculty and students are exemplified with cover letters where appropriate. In addition, service specific questionnaire forms are included. The final section on reporting results includes several different formats for sharing findings with the communities involved. (The predecessor to this item is also useful; see *User Surveys*. October 1988. Washington, DC: Association of Research Libraries. Kit 148.)

Hernon, Peter, and Ellen Altman. 1996. *Service quality in academic libraries*. Norwood, NJ: Ablex. Well organized and written, this practical approach to building accountability and quality keeps the focus strongly on user satisfaction. Chapters five, six, and seven are particularly useful for any academic librarian who contemplates an information-needs analysis. Sample forms and concise descriptions add to the process-oriented explanations.

Kantor, Paul. 1984. *Objective performance measures for academic and research libraries*. Washington, DC: Association of Research Libraries. This classic work on performance measures is particularly useful during the follow-up work of a needs analysis. Measuring the outcome of planned changes can be difficult; the explanations and examples in this concise volume are quite useful.

Kent, Allen, et al. 1979. *Use of library materials: The University of Pittsburgh study*. New York: Marcel Dekker. This landmark study of the "extent to which library materials are used and the full cost of such use" (vi) covers a single significant issue relevant to information-needs analysis. The high proportion of university library budgets that are still being spent on acquisitions (rather than on access) indicates the continued need for this type of analysis. Its detailed explanations of various data-gathering methods include definitions, examples, and advice.

McClure, Charles, and Cynthia Lopata. February 1996. *Assessing the academic networked environment: Strategies and options*. Washington, DC: Association of Research Libraries for the Coalition for Networked Information. This penetrating and innovative analysis of a highly complex and critical component of information provision on today's academic library is well stuffed with explanations and examples. Both the qualitative and quantitative forms of data are considered with the goal of obtaining useful, trustworthy information. Data analysis and collection are skillfully woven together throughout. Productive statistics are identified, sample user questionnaires provided, and topics from satisfaction with networked user support to electronic classrooms are covered. For anyone focusing on networked environment, this is a great book.

Public Libraries

Brawner, Lee, and Donald Beck, Jr. 1996. *Determining your public library's future size: A needs assessment and planning model.* Chicago: American Library Association. While certainly valuable for any needs assessment that relates to library size, the sections on the means of gathering data are likely to be productive for assessments with other foci as well. Telephone questionnaires and focus groups are exemplified.

Cassell, Kay Ann. 1988. *Knowing your community and its needs.* Small Libraries Publications Number 14. Chicago: Library Administration and Management Association, American Library Association. This brief publication includes a useful discussion of using census data to inform and augment user study data by covering demographic variables such as age, housing patterns, and occupational status.

Coughlin, Robert, et al. 1972. *Urban analysis for branch library system planning.* Westport: CT: Greenwood. This detailed volume exemplifies the application of information-needs information to the planning process in the context of an urban system with numerous branch libraries. Although too dated to serve as a road map for conducting an information-needs analysis, it should spark ideas on planning for the special needs of this type of library system.

Durrance, Joan C. 1984. *Armed for action: Library response to citizen information needs.* New York: Neal-Schuman. This well-organized study of citizen action groups should prove useful when identifying stakeholders, analyzing their needs, and creating service-based solutions to their information problems. Many of the problems identified in 1984 still exist over a decade later and have merely been complicated by the increase in electronic information resources.

Durrance, Joan C. 1994. *Meeting community needs with job and career services: A how-to-do-it manual for librarians*, number 42. New York: Neal-Schuman. A thoughtful, useful manual exemplifying the right way to establish a service in response to a need. Based on extensive research and filled with examples of each element, it includes a chapter on evaluating the final product, in this case, a job center.

Focus on the future: Needs assessment and strategic planning for county and regional libraries, a how-to manual. July 1994. Ontario: Ministry of Culture and Communications. Although some of this excellent work requires a bit of cultural translation from the Canadian, it provides readable explanations, proven questionnaire forms, and solid advice for those in public libraries.

Kim, Choong Han, and Robert David Little. 1987. *Public library users and uses: A market research handbook.* Metuchen, NJ: Scarecrow Press. This report of an extensive analysis of information needs at several Indiana public libraries is based on data principally gathered from a walk-in, self-administered questionnaire. Over 90 percent of patrons completed the questionnaire. The volume includes several valuable instruments such as an interview guide for reference librarians to use as an information-needs tool when registering new patrons. User groups and information needs are categorized and analyzed quite thoroughly.

Marchant, Maurice. 1994. *Why adults use the public library: A research perspective.* Englewood, CO: Libraries Unlimited. This concise, readable work by a public librarian of many years' experience ties the users' actions to their motivations. His findings are based on interviews conducted by library science master's students with 200 adults from Provo, Utah, over half of whom were men. The extensive interview instrument, including tallies, is available in the appendix.

Powell, Ronald R. January 1988. *The relationship of library user studies to performance measures: A review of the literature.* University of Illinois, Graduate School of Library and Information Science: Occasional Paper Number 181 (ISSN 0276 1769). This well-organized discussion of the relationships between user studies and evaluations provides a valuable context for discussions of the purpose and methods of a user study. Developing performance measures based on the information gleaned from user studies, as discussed so carefully in this work, exemplifies one of the better uses of data gathering.

Rogers, Clark, and Brian Vidic, with Patricia Callahan. 1995. *Community information service management guidelines.* Foreword by James Welbourne. First Edition, Revision One. Pittsburgh, PA: The infoWorks (*sic*) Partnership. This book provides support for community organizers who want to get on board with the information technology that can help them to meet their goals. On pages 156–161 they have a sample questionnaire to help identify the current state of and desires for future access to various computer elements for the general public. Word processing, communications, spread sheets, graphics, and more are captured. In addition, there's a section of the questionnaire on the kinds of information that community organizers might like to have available such as census statistics, crime indices, and so on.

Stephens, Annabel. 1995. *Assessing the public library planning process.* Norwood, NJ: Ablex. In her 15-year study of the planning process in public libraries, she found that a relatively small number of librarians felt that too much time was spent on identifying information needs. As a study of the planning process, which might or might not be based on an information-needs assessment, this book presents a detailed picture of the problems and concerns librarians generally encounter.

Vavrek, Bernard. 1990. *Assessing the information needs of rural Americans.* Clarion, PA: College of Library Science, Clarion University of Pennsylvania. This report of the first national study of rural public library users includes a discussion of the findings as well as examples of the instruments used. Focusing on users (rather than nonusers), this study provides useful examples of various issues and topics that might be covered. A second national telephone survey reached nonusers as well. For an explanation of both studies, including copies of the questionnaires, see Vavrek, 1995. The sheer scope and depth of these studies make them crucial for rural librarians.

Walters, Suzanne. 1994. *Customer service: A how-to-do-it manual for librarians,* number 41. New York: Neal-Schuman. The book as a whole is useful during the follow-up stage as staff works to design and implement user-centered changes. Chapter nine on market research is an interesting overview of an area that is closely related to the assessment process; it includes sample questionnaire forms.

School Libraries

Flowers, Helen. 1998. *Public relations for school library media programs: 500 ways to influence people and win friends for your school library media center.* New York: Neal-Schuman. A careful and well-exemplified guide to development of a comprehensive public relations plan for a school library, this book provides ideas, advice, and support.

Grover, Robert, and Janet Carabell. 1995. Diagnosing information needs in a school library media center. *School Library Media Activities Monthly.* 11 (January): 32–36+. This lucid piece delineates the elements of a cycle of service design.

Latrobe, Kathy, and W. Michael Havener. 1997. The information-seeking behavior of high school honors students: An exploratory study. *Journal of Youth Services in Libraries.* 10 (2, winter): 188–200. Combining a written questionnaire and individual structured interviews, this study examines both personal and academic information seeking among members of this population. The data analysis and findings segments of this article are useful examples of those often-difficult research stages.

Mancall, Jacqueline, and Carl Drott. 1983. *Measuring student information use: A guide for school library media specialists.* Littleton, CO: Libraries Unlimited. This detailed explanation of a practical, field-tested, productive means of identifying and understanding student information needs should prove useful for many in school libraries. Utilizing interviews, questionnaires, and bibliometrics, this technique identifies what high school students actually do in the library without requiring statistical expertise on the part of the librarian.

Works Cited

Abbey-Livingston, Diane. 1982. *Enjoying research? A "how-to" manual on needs assessment.* Toronto: Ministry of Tourism and Recreation.

Adler, Patricia, and Peter Adler. 1994. Observational Techniques. In *Handbook of qualitative research.* Norman Denzin and Yvonna Lincoln, eds. Thousand Oaks, CA: Sage. 377–392.

A.L.A. 2000. The Library, Web Resources. *www.ala.org/library/weblinks.html.* (accessed 7/5/00).

Assessing your community for library planning. 1987. Ontario: Ministry of Culture and Communications.

Babbie, Earl. 1973. *Survey research methods.* Belmont, CA: Wadsworth.

Babbie, Earl. 1998. *The practice of social research.* 8th edition. Belmont, CA: Wadsworth.

Backstrom, Charles, and Gerald Hursh-César. 1981. *Survey research.* 2nd ed. New York: John Wiley & Sons.

Baker, Lynda. 1996. A study of the nature of information needed by women with Multiple Sclerosis. *Library and Information Science Research.* 18 (1): 67–81.

Barber, Peggy, and Linda D. Crowe. 1993. *Getting your grant: A how-to-do-it manual for librarians.* How-To-Do-It Manuals for Librarians, number 28. New York: Neal-Schuman.

Barron, Daniel, and Charles Curran. 1981. A look at community analysis: Some myths and some realities. In Research in Action. Linda Lucas, column editor. *Public Libraries.* 20 (spring): 29–30.

Barry, Christine. 1997. The research activity timeline: A qualitative tool for information research. *Library and Information Science Research.* 19 (2): 153–179.

Beer, Susan, Rita Macella, and Graeme Baxter. 1998. Rural citizens' information needs: A survey undertaken on behalf of the Shetland Islands Citizens Advice Bureau. *Journal of Librarianship and Information Science.* 30 (4, December): 223–240.

Beheshti, Jamshid. 1989. Beyond circulation statistics: Measuring patterns of book use. *Canadian Library Journal.* 46 (December): 397–398.

Beheshti, Jamshid. 1989. A cross-sectional study of the use of library books by undergraduate students. *Information Processing and Management.* 25 (6): 727–735.

Beheshti, Jamshid. 1989. A longitudinal study of the use of library books by undergraduate students. *Information Processing and Management.* 25 (6): 737–744.

Berelson, Bernard, with the assistance of Lester Asheim. 1975, c. 1949. *The library's public.* Reprint of the edition published by Columbia University Press, New York. Westport, CT: Greenwood.

Berger, Kenneth, and Richard Hines. 1994. What does the user *really* want? The Library User Survey Project at Duke University. *Journal of Academic Librarianship.* 20 (November): 306—309.

Big book of library grant money 1998–99: Profiles of private and corporate foundations and direct corporate givers receptive to library grant proposals. 1998. Prepared by The Taft Group. Chicago: American Library Association.

Bolton, W. Theodore. 1982. Life style research: An aid to promoting public libraries. *Library Journal.* 107 (10, May 15): 963–968.

Bookstein, A., and A. Lindsay. 1989. Questionnaire ambiguity: A Rasch Scaling model analysis. *Library Trends.* 38 (2, fall): 215–236.

Bookstein, Abraham. 1985. Questionnaire research in a library setting. *Journal of Academic Librarianship.* 11 (1): 24–28.

Borko, Harold. 1970. *A study of the needs for research in library and information science education.* Washington, DC: U.S. Department of Health, Education, and Welfare, Office of Education, Bureau of Research.

Borko, Harold. 1970. *Predicting research needs in librarianship and information science education.* Washington, DC: American Society for Information Science.

Brannen, Julia. 1992. Combining qualitative and quantitative approaches: An overview. In *Mixing methods: Qualitative and quantitative research.* Julia Brannen, ed. Aldershot: Avebury.

Brawner, Lee, and Donald Beck, Jr. 1996. *Determining your public library's future size: A needs assessment and planning model.* Chicago: American Library Association.

Brekke, Elaine. November 1994. *User surveys in ARL libraries.* Washington, DC: Association of Research Libraries. SPEC Kit 205.

Bruyn, Severyn. 1970. The methodology of participant observation. In *Reader in research methods for librarianship.* Mary Lee Bundy, Paul

Wasserman, and Gayle Raghi, eds. Washington, DC: Microcard Editions. 172–185.

Bustion, Marifran, et al. 1992. On the merits of direct observation of periodical usage: An empirical study. *College and Research Libraries.* 53 (November): 537–550.

Carlson, Lynda, Dwight French, and John Preston. 1993. The role of focus groups in the identification of user needs and data availability. *Government Information Quarterly.* 10 (1): 89–100.

Cassell, Kay Ann. 1988. *Knowing your community and its needs.* Small Libraries Publications Number 14. Chicago: Library Administration and Management Association, American Library Association.

Cassell, Kay Ann, and Elizabeth Futas. 1991. *Developing public library collections, policies, and procedures: A how-to-do-it manual for small and medium-sized public libraries.* How-To-Do-It Manuals for Librarians, number 12. New York: Neal-Schuman.

Chambers, John, William Cleveland, Beat Kleiner, and Paul Tukey. 1983. *Graphical methods for data analysis.* Belmont, CA: Wadsworth International Group.

Chatman, Elfreda, and Victoria Pendleton. 1995. Knowledge gap, information-seeking and the poor. *Reference Librarian.* 49/50: 135–145.

Cheng-gong, Zhu. 1987. User needs: The principal basis for designing college or university's library buildings. In *Adaptation of buildings to library use.* München, West Germany: Saur.

Cherry, Joan. 1990. Methods of studying database users: The role of surveys, laboratory studies, and field studies. *The Canadian Journal of Information Science.* 15 (3, July): 17–29.

Childers, Thomas A., and Nancy A. Van House. 1993. *What's good? Describing your public library's effectiveness.* Chicago: American Library Association.

Christensen, Larry, and Charles Stoup. 1991. *Introduction to statistics for the social and behavioral sciences.* 2nd ed. Pacific Grove, CA: Brooks/Cole Publishing.

Christensen, Steven, Marsha Broadway, and Holly Garbutt. 1995. Medical information needs and frustrations in a rural community. *Rural Libraries.* 5 (2): 55–72.

Clark, Herbert, and Michael Schober. 1992. Asking questions and influencing answers. In *Questions about questions: Inquiries into the cognitive bases of surveys.* Judith Tanur, ed. New York: Russell Sage Foundation. 15–48.

Clougherty, Leo, John Forys, Toby Lyles, Dorothy Persson, Christine Walters, and Carlette Washington-Hoagland. 1998. The University of Iowa libraries' undergraduate user needs assessment. *College and Research Libraries.* 59 (6): 572–584.

Converse, Jean M., and Stanley Presser. 1986. *Survey questions: Handcrafting the standardized questionnaire.* Quantitative Applications in the Social Sciences, number 63. Newbury Park, CA: Sage.

Coughlin, Robert, et al. 1972. *Urban analysis for branch library system planning.* Westport: CT: Greenwood.

Coursen, Derek. 1996. Community analysis data resources. *The Unabashed Librarian.* 99: 11–12.

Croyle, Robert, and Elizabeth Loftus. 1992. Improving episodic memory performance of survey respondents. In *Questions about questions: Inquiries into the cognitive bases of surveys.* Judith Tanur, ed. New York: Russell Sage Foundation. 95–101.

Curtis, Karen, Ann Weller, and Julie Hurd. 1997. Information-seeking behavior of health sciences faculty: The impact of new information technologies. *Bulletin of the Medical Library Association.* 85: (4, October): 402–410.

DeCandido, GraceAnne. *After the user survey, what then?* September 1997. Systems and Procedures Exchange Center (SPEC) Kit 226. Julia Blixrud, SPEC Editor. Issues and Innovations in Transforming Libraries. Washington, DC: Association of Research Libraries, Office of Management Services.

D'Elia, George. 1980. The development and testing of a conceptual model of public library user behavior. *Library Quarterly.* 50 (4): 410–430.

Denver Public Library management guide to community analysis. 1981. In *Beyond PR: Marketing for libraries.* LJ Special Report 18. New York: *Library Journal,* R. R. Bowker. 28–32.

Dervin, Brenda. 1977. Useful theory for librarianship: Communication, not information. *Drexel Library Quarterly.* 13 (3, July): 16–32.

Dervin, Brenda. 1983. An overview of sense-making research: Concepts, methods, and results to date. A paper delivered at the International Communication Association Annual Meeting, Dallas. May.

Dervin, Brenda, and Kathleen Clark. July 1987. ASQ: Alternative tools for information need and accountability assessments by libraries. Belmont, CA: Peninsula Library System. (Obtained as a personal communication from the primary author.)

Devadason, Francis Jawahar, and Pandala Pratap Lingam. 1997. A methodology for the identification of information needs of users. *IFLA Journal.* 23 (1): 41–51.

DeVellis, Robert F. 1991. *Scale development: Theory and applications.* Applied Social Research Methods Series, volume 26. Newbury Park, CA: Sage.

Dewdney, Patricia, and Roma Harris. 1992. Community information needs: The case of wife assault. *Library and Information Science Research.* 14 (January–March): 5–29.

Downing, Douglas, and Jeff Clark. 1997. *Statistics the easy way.* 3rd edition. Hauppauge, NY: Barron's.

Dresang, Eliza. 1990. Interviewing using micro-moments and backward chaining. In *Evaluation strategies and techniques for public library children's services: A sourcebook.* Jane Robbins, Holly Willett, Mary Jane Wiseman, and Douglas L. Zweizig, eds. University of Wisconsin, Madison: School of Library and Information Studies. 131–134.

Drott, M. Carl. 1969. Random sampling: A tool for library research. *College and Research Libraries.* 30 (March): 119–125.

Durrance, Joan C. 1984. *Armed for action: Library response to citizen information needs.* New York: Neal-Schuman.

Durrance, Joan C. 1994. *Meeting community needs with job and career services: A how-to-do-it manual for librarians,* number 42. New York: Neal-Schuman.

Dyer, Esther. 1979. The Delphi technique in library research. *Library Research.* 1: 41–52.

Evans, G. Edward. 1992. Needs analysis and collection development policies for culturally diverse populations. *Collection Building.* 11 (4): 16–27.

Flanagan, John. 1954. The critical incident technique. *Psychological Bulletin.* 51 (4): 327–358.

Flowers, Helen. 1998. *Public relations for school library media programs: 500 ways to influence people and win friends for your school library media center.* New York: Neal-Schuman.

Focus on the future: Needs assessment and strategic planning for county and regional libraries, a how-to manual. July 1994. Ontario: Ministry of Culture and Communications.

Fontana, Andrea, and James Frey. 1994. Interviewing: The art of science. In *Handbook of qualitative research.* Norman Denzin and Yvonna Lincoln, eds. Thousand Oaks, CA: Sage. 361–376.

Ford, Geoffrey, ed., 1977. *User studies: An introductory guide and select bibliography.* Sheffield, England: University of Centre for Research on User Studies.

Fowler, Floyd, Jr. 1993. *Survey research methods.* 2nd edition. Applied

Social Research Methods Series, volume 1. Newbury Park, CA: Sage.

Fowler, Floyd, Jr. 1995. *Improving survey questions: Design and evaluation*. Applied Social Research Methods Series, volume 38. Thousand Oaks, CA: Sage.

French, Beverlee. 1990. User needs and library services in agricultural sciences. *Library Trends*. 38 (3, winter): 415–441.

Glazier, Jack. 1985. Structured observation. *College and Research Libraries News*. 46 (March): 105–108.

Gold, Raymond. 1969. Roles in sociological field observation. In *Issues in participant observation*. George McCall and J. L. Simmons, eds. Reading, MA: Addison-Wesley: 30–39.

Goldhor, Herbert. 1980. Community analysis for the public library. *Illinois Libraries*. 62 (April): 296–302.

Gonzalez, Michael, Bill Greeley, and Stephen Whitney. 1980. Assessing the library needs of the Spanish-speaking. *Library Journal*. April 1: 786–789.

Gorden, Raymond. 1970. Dimensions of the depth interview. In *Reader in research methods for librarianship*. Mary Lee Bundy, Paul Wasserman, and Gayle Araghi, eds. Washington, DC: NCR. 166–171.

Gorden, Raymond. 1975. *Interviewing: Strategy, techniques, and tactics*. Revised edition. Homewood, IL: Dorsey.

Gottlieb, Jane. 1994. *Collection assessment in music libraries*. MLA Technical Report No. 22. Canton, MA: Music Library Association.

Govan, James. 1976. Community analysis in an academic environment. *Library Trends*. 24 (January): 541–556.

Great library promotion ideas. [annual] John Cotton Dana Library Public Relations Award Winners and Notables. Chicago: American Library Association.

Green, Andrew. 1990. What do we mean by user needs? *British Journal of Academic Librarianship*. 5 (2): 65–78.

Green, Joseph. 1989. The ideal consultant. *Library Journal*. 114 (February 15): 133–135.

Greer, Roger, and Martha Hale. 1981. Appendix A: Data collection. In *Beyond PR: Marketing for libraries*. LJ Special Report 18. New York: *Library Journal*, R. R. Bowker. 30–32.

Greer, Roger, and Martha Hale. 1982. The community analysis process. In *Public librarianship: A reader*. Jane Robbins-Carter, ed. Littleton, CO: Libraries Unlimited. 358–366.

Grover, Robert, and Janet Carabell. 1995. Diagnosing information needs in a school library media center. *School Library Media Activities Monthly*. 11 (January): 32–36+.

Grover, Robert, and Janet Carabell. 1995. Toward better information service: Diagnosing information needs. *Special Libraries.* 86 (1, winter): 1–10.

Güereña, Salvador. 1990. Community analysis and needs assessment. In *Latino librarianship: A handbook for professionals.* Salvador Güereña, ed. Jefferson, NC: McFarland. 17–23.

Hafner, Arthur. 1998. *Descriptive statistical techniques for librarians.* 2nd edition. Chicago: American Library Association.

Haro, Robert. 1981. *Developing library and information services for Americans of Hispanic origin.* Metuchen, NJ: Scarecrow Press.

Harris, Denise. 1989. Community surveys. *The Cape Librarian.* 33: 2–5.

Harris, Donald. 1994. Reassessing user needs. *Journal of the American Society for Information Science.* 45 (5): 331–334.

Harris, Michael, and James Sodt. 1981. Libraries, users, and librarians: Continuing efforts to define the nature and extent of public library use. In *Advances in librarianship.* 11: 110–133. New York: Academic Press.

Hart, Richard. 1998. The relationships between work roles and information gathering of the faculty at SUNY, College at Fredonia. *Library and Information Science Research.* 20 (2): 163–185.

Hedrick, Terry, Leonard Bickman, and Debra Rog. 1993. *Applied research design: A practical guide.* Applied Social Research Methods Series, volume 32. Newbury Park, CA: Sage.

Henry, Gary. 1990. *Practical sampling.* Applied Social Science Research Methods Series, volume 21. Newbury Park, CA: Sage.

Hernon, Peter. 1999. Editorial: Research in Library and Information Science, reflections on the journal literature. *Journal of Academic Librarianship.* 25 (4, July): 263–266.

Hernon, Peter, and Ellen Altman. 1996. *Service quality in academic libraries.* Norwood, NJ: Ablex.

Hildebrand, David, James Laing, and Howard Rosenthal. 1977. *Analysis of ordinal data.* Quantitative Applications in the Social Sciences Series, number 8. Newbury Park, CA: Sage.

Himmel, Ethel, William James Wilson, with the ReVision [*sic*] Committee of the Public Library Association. 1998. *Planning for results: A public library transformation process, The guidebook.* Chicago: American Library Association.

Holt, Cynthia, and Wanda Clements Hole. 1995. Assessing needs of library users with disabilities. *Public Libraries.* 34 (March/April): 90–93.

Jacob, M. E. L. 1990. *Strategic planning: A how-to-do-it manual for librarians.* How-To-Do-It Manuals for Librarians, number 9. New York: Neal-Schuman.

Jacobson, Frances. 1991. Gender differences in attitudes toward using computers in libraries: An exploratory study. *Library and Information Science Research.* 13 (July/September): 267–279.

Johnson, Debra Wilcox. 1992. Keeping things in focus: Information for decision making. In *Keeping the books: Public library financial practices.* Jane Robbins and Douglas Zweizig, eds. Fort Atkinson, WI: Highsmith Press, for the Urban Libraries Council. 405–419.

Jorgensen, Danny. 1989. *Participant observation: A methodology for human studies.* Newbury Park, CA: Sage.

Joyce, Marilyn. 1995. The I-Search paper: A vehicle for teaching the research process. *School Library Media Activities Monthly.* 11 (6, February): 31–37.

Joyce, Marilyn, and Julie Tallman. 1997. *Making the writing and research connection with the I-Search process: A how-to-do-it manual for teachers and school librarians.* How-to-Do-It Manuals for Librarians, number 62. New York: Neal-Schuman.

Kalton, Graham. 1983. *Introduction to survey sampling.* Quantitative Applications in the Social Sciences, number 35. Newbury Park, CA: Sage.

Kantor, Paul. 1984. *Objective performance measures for academic and research libraries.* Washington, DC: Association of Research Libraries.

Kent, Allen, et al. 1979. *Use of library materials: The University of Pittsburgh study.* New York: Marcel Dekker.

Kidston, James. 1985. The validity of questionnaire responses. *Library Quarterly.* 55 (2): 133–150.

Kim, Choong Han, and Robert David Little. 1987. *Public library users and uses: A market research handbook.* Metuchen, NJ: Scarecrow Press.

Kraemer, Helena Chmura, and Sue Thiemann. 1987. *How many subjects?* Newbury Park, CA: Sage.

Krathwohl, David. 1998. *Methods of educational and social science research: An integrated approach.* 2nd edition. New York: Longman.

Krueger, Richard. 1994. *Focus groups: A practical guide for applied research.* 2nd edition. Thousand Oaks, CA: Sage.

Kuhlthau, Carol. 1993. *Seeking meaning: A process approach to library and information services.* Norwood, NJ: Ablex.

Kuhlthau, Carol, ed. 1994. *Assessment and the school library media center*. Englewood, CO: Libraries Unlimited.

Lakner, Edward. 1998. Optimizing samples for surveys of public libraries: Alternatives and compromises. *Library and Information Science Research*. 20 (4): 321–342.

Lancaster, F. W. 1988. *If You Want to Evaluate Your Library . . .* Champaign, IL: University of Illinois, Graduate School of Library and Information Science.

Lange, Janet. 1988. Public library users, nonusers, and type of library use. *Public Library Quarterly*. 8 (1/2): 49–67.

Latrobe, Kathy, and W. Michael Havener. 1997. The information-seeking behavior of high school honors students: An exploratory study. *Journal of Youth Services in Libraries*. 10 (2, winter): 188–200.

Leckie, Gloria, et al. 1996. Modeling the information seeking of professionals: A general model derived from research on engineers, health care professionals, and lawyers. *Library Quarterly*. 66 (2): 161–193.

LeCompte, Margaret, Judith Preissle, and Renata Tesch. 1993. *Ethnography and qualitative design in educational research*. San Diego, CA: Academic Press.

Leedy, Paul. 1989. *Practical research: Planning and design*. 4th edition. New York: Macmillan.

Lewis, Laurie, and Elizabeth Farris. March 1990. *Services and resources for children in public libraries, 1988–89*. Washington, DC: National Center for Education Statistics, Office of Educational Research and Improvement, U.S. Department of Education. NCES 90–098.

Lincoln, Yvonna, and Egon Guba. 1985. *Naturalistic inquiry*. Newbury Park, CA: Sage.

Line, Maurice. 1967. *Library surveys: An introduction to their use, planning, procedures and presentation*. London: Clive Bingley.

Linstone, Harold A. 1975. Eight basic pitfalls: A checklist. In *The Delphi method: Techniques and applications*. Harold A. Linstone and Murray Turoff, eds. Reading, MA: Addison-Wesley. 573–586.

Linstone, Harold A., and Murray Turoff. 1975. Introduction. In *The Delphi method: Techniques and applications*. Harold A. Linstone and Murray Turoff, eds. Reading, MA: Addison-Wesley. 3–16.

Macrorie, Ken. 1988. *The I-search paper*. Revised edition of *Searching Writing*. Portsmouth, NH: Boynton/Cook.

Mancall, Jacqueline, and Carl Drott. 1983. *Measuring student information use: A guide for school library media specialists*. Littleton, CO: Libraries Unlimited.

Marchant, Maurice. 1994. *Why adults use the public library: A research perspective.* Englewood, CO: Libraries Unlimited.

Martin, Lowell. 1944. Community analysis for the community. In *The library in the community: Papers presented before the Library Institute at the University of Chicago August 23–28, 1943.* Leon Carnovsky and Lowell Martin, eds. Chicago: University of Chicago Press, 201–214.

Massey, Morris. 1976. Market analysis and audience research for libraries. *Library Trends.* 24 (3, January): 473–482.

Matthews, Joseph. 1994. The effective use of consultants in libraries. *Library Technology Reports.* 30 (November/December): 745–814.

Maxwell, Joseph. 1992. Understanding and validity in qualitative research. *Harvard Educational Review.* 62 (3, fall): 279–300.

McClure, Charles, and Cynthia Lopata. February 1996. *Assessing the academic networked environment: Strategies and options.* Washington, DC: Association of Research Libraries for the Coalition for Networked Information.

McCracken, Grant. 1988. *The long interview.* Newbury Park, CA: Sage.

McDonald, Lynn, and Holly Willett. 1990. Interviewing young children. In *Evaluation strategies and techniques for public library children's services: A sourcebook.* Jane Robbins, Holly Willett, Mary Jane Wiseman, and Douglas L. Zweizig, eds. University of Wisconsin, Madison: School of Library and Information Studies. 115–130.

McKillip, Jack. 1987. *Need analysis: Tools for the human services and education.* Newbury Park, CA: Sage.

Mellon, Constance. 1990. *Naturalistic inquiry for library science: Methods and applications for research, evaluation, and teaching.* New York: Greenwood.

Miles, Matthew, and Michael Huberman. 1984. *Qualitative data analysis: A sourcebook of new methods.* Newbury Park, CA: Sage.

Mitroff, Ian I., and Murray Turoff. 1975. Philosophical and methodological foundations of Delphi. In *The Delphi method: Techniques and applications.* Harold A. Linstone and Murray Turoff, eds. Reading, MA: Addison-Wesley. 17–36.

Mullaly-Quijas, Peggy, et al. 1994. Using focus groups to discover health professionals' information needs: A regional marketing study. *Bulletin of the Medical Library Association.* 82 (3, July): 305–311.

National Guide to Funding for Information Technology. 1999. 2nd edition. New York: Foundation Center.

National Guide to Funding for Libraries and Information Services. 1999. 5th edition. New York: Foundation Center.

Nelson, Janet. 1992. An analysis of transaction logs to evaluate the educational needs of end users. *Medical Reference Services Quarterly.* 11(4, winter): 11–21.

Neuman, Delia. 1995. High school students' use of databases: Results of a national Delphi study. *Journal of the American Society for Information Science.* 46 (4, May) 284–298.

Nicholas, David. 1997. The information needs interview: A long way from library-use statistics. *Education for Information.* 15 (4, December): 343+.

Nitecki, Danuta. 1996. Changing the concept and measure of service quality in academic libraries. *Journal of Academic Librarianship.* 22: (3, May): 181–190.

Otto, Theophil. 1982. The academic librarian of the 21st century: Public service and library education in the year 2000. *Journal of Academic Librarianship.* 8(2): 85–88.

Palmour, Vernon. 1977. Planning in public libraries: Role of citizens and library staff. *Drexel Library Quarterly. 13: 33–43.*

Palmour, Vernon, et al. 1980. *A planning process for public libraries.* Chicago: American Library Association.

Parrish, Marilyn. 1989. Academic community analysis: Discovering research needs of graduate students at Bowling Green State University. *College and Research Libraries News.* 8 (September): 644–646.

Patten, Mildred. 1998. *Questionnaire research: A practical guide.* Los Angeles: Pyrczak.

Phillips, Sharon, and Margaret Zorn. 1994. Assessing consumer health information needs in a community hospital. *Bulletin of the Medical Library Association.* 82 (3, July): 288–293.

Powell, Ronald R. January 1988. *The relationship of library user studies to performance measures: A review of the literature.* University of Illinois, Graduate School of Library and Information Science: Occasional Paper Number 181.

Powell, Ronald R. 1992. Impact assessment of university libraries: A consideration of issues and research methodologies. *Library and Information Science Research.* 14: 245–257.

Powell, Ronald R. 1997. *Basic research methods for librarians.* 3rd edition. Greenwich, CT: Ablex.

Price, Anna, and Kjestine Carey. 1993. Serials use study raises questions about cooperative ventures. *Serials Review.* 19 (3, fall): 79–84.

Pritchard, Sarah. 1996. Determining quality in academic libraries. *Library Trends.* 44 (3, winter): 572–594.

Reed, Sally Gardner. 1992. *Saving your library: A guide to getting, using and keeping the power you need.* Jefferson, NC: McFarland.

Reigstad, Tom. 1997. I search, you search, we all search for I-Search: Research alternative works for advanced writers, too. ED 412 545.

Reynolds, H.T. 1984. *Analysis of nominal data.* 2nd edition. Quantitative Applications in the Social Sciences Series, number 7. Newbury Park, CA: Sage.

Richmond, Elizabeth, and Michele McKnelly. 1996. Alternative user survey and group process methods: Nominal group technique applied to U.S. depository libraries. *Journal of Government Information.* 23 (2): 137–149.

Robbins, Jane. 1990. Sampling. In *Evaluation strategies and techniques for public library children's services: A sourcebook.* Jane Robbins, Holly Willett, Mary Jane Wiseman, and Douglas Zweizig, eds. University of Wisconsin, Madison: School of Library and Information Studies: 135–138.

Robbins, Jane, Holly Willett, Mary Jane Wiseman, and Douglas Zweizig, eds. 1990. *Evaluation strategies and techniques for public library children's services: A sourcebook.* University of Wisconsin, Madison: School of Library and Information Studies.

Robbins, Jane, and Douglas Zweizig. 1992. Planning. In *Keeping the books: Public library financial practices.* Jane Robbins and Douglas Zweizig, eds. Fort Atkinson, WI: Highsmith Press, for the Urban Libraries Council. 217–223.

Rogers, Clark, and Brian Vidic, with Patricia Callahan. 1995. *Community information service management guidelines.* Foreword by James Welbourne. First Edition, Revision One. Pittsburgh, PA: The infoWorks (*sic*) Partnership.

Ross, Catherine Sheldrick, and Patricia Dewdney. 1998. *Communicating professionally: A how-to-do-it manual for library applications.* 2nd edition. How-To-Do-It Manuals for Librarians, number 58. New York: Neal-Schuman.

Ruccio, Nancy. 1980. The planning process—Is it for me? *Rural Libraries.* 1 (4, fall): 45–87.

Sager, Don. 1995. Public Library Service to Homeschoolers. In the "Perspectives" column. Includes David Brostrom on "Assessing Homeschooler Needs," Dave Dembeck on "A Homeschooler's Perspective," Rosemary Moran on "Planning Homeschooler Services," and Evelyn Vanek on "School and Community Relations." *Public Libraries.* (July/August): 201–205.

Sarling, Jo Haight, and Debra S. Van Tassel. 1999. Community analysis: Research that matters to a north-central Denver community. *Library and Information Science Research.* 21 (1): 7–29.

Savolainen, Reijo. 1995. Everyday life information seeking: Approaching information seeking in the context of "way of life." *Library and Information Science Research.* 17 (3): 259–294.

Schlichter, Doris, and J. Michael Pemberton. 1992. The emperor's new clothes? Problems of the user survey as a planning tool in academic libraries. *College and Research Libraries.* 53 (3): 257–265.

Schuman, Howard, and Stanley Presser. 1996. *Question and answers in attitude surveys: Experiments on question form, wording, and context.* Thousand Oaks, CA: Sage.

Schwartz, Morris, and Charlotte Schwartz. 1955. Problems in participant observation. *American Journal of Sociology.* 60: 343–353.

Scott, Alice. 1981. Marketing as a community analysis goal. In *Beyond PR: Marketing for libraries.* LJ Special Report 18. New York: *Library Journal,* R. R. Bowker. 20–27.

Shilts, Thomas. 1991. A study of rural public library patrons by unobtrusive observation. *Rural Libraries.* 11 (2): 27–48.

Sibia, Ted, et al. March 1993. *Assessment of information services for USDA Agricultural Research Service scientists: Final report on a study conducted by the University of California, Davis General Library and the National Agricultural Library.* Contract No. 58–32U4–9–29.

Sieber, Joan. 1992. *Planning ethically responsible research: A guide for students and internal review boards.* Applied Social Research Methods Series, volume 31. Newbury Park, CA: Sage.

Simpson, I. S. 1988. *Basic statistics for librarians.* 3rd edition. London: Library Association Publishing.

Slonim, Morris. 1990. Introduction to *Sampling in a Nutshell.* In *Evaluation strategies and techniques for public library children's services: A sourcebook.* Jane Robbins, Holly Willett, Mary Jane Wiseman, and Douglas Zweizig, eds. University of Wisconsin, Madison: School of Library and Information Studies: 139–151.

Smith, Mark. 1996. *Collecting and using public library statistics: A how-to-do-it manual.* How-To-Do-It Manual for Librarians, number 56. New York: Neal-Schuman.

Spaeth, Joe. 1992. Perils and pitfalls of survey research. *Applying research to practice: How to use data collection and research to improve library management decision making.* Urbana-Champaign: University of Illinois, Graduate School of Library and Information Science: 63–77.

St. Clair, Guy. 1993. *Customer service in the information environment.* London: Bowker-Saur.

Stenback, Tanis, and Alvin Schrader. 1999. Venturing from the closet: A qualitative study of the information needs of lesbians. *Public Library Quarterly.* 17 (3): 37–50.

Stephens, Annabel. 1995. *Assessing the public library planning process.* Norwood, NJ: Ablex.

Sternstein, Martin. 1994. *Statistics.* Hauppauge, NY: Barron's Educational Series. Barron's EZ-101 Study Keys.

Sudman, Seymour, Monroe Sirken, and Charles Cowan. 1988. Sampling rare and elusive populations. *Science.* 240 (May 20): 991–996.

Tague-Sutcliffe, Jean. 1995. *Measuring information: An information services perspective.* San Diego: Academic Press.

Tearle, Barbara. 1994. Information strategies in the academic law library. *The Law Librarian.* 25 (2, June): 75–79.

Trott, Fiona. 1986. *Information for industry.* British Library Research Reviews, number 7. London: The British Library.

Tuominen, Kimmo. 1996. The public library as information source: Findings of an interview study. *Scandinavian Public Library Quarterly.* 29 (1): 8–10.

Turner, Anne M. 1997. *Getting political: An action guide for librarians and library supporters.* New York: Neal-Schuman.

Tygett, Mary, V. Lonnie Lawson, and Kathleen Weessies. 1996. Using undergraduate marketing students in an unobtrusive reference evaluation. *RQ.* 36 (2, winter): 270–276.

Valentine, Barbara. 1993. Undergraduate research behavior: Using focus groups to generate theory. *Journal of Academic Librarianship.* 19 (5): 300–304.

Van House, Nancy A., and Thomas Childers. 1993. *The public library effectiveness study: The complete report.* Chicago: American Library Association.

Van House, Nancy A., Mary Jo Lynch, Charles McClure, Douglas Zweizig, and Eleanor Jo Rodger. 1987. *Output measures for public libraries: A manual of standardized procedures.* 2nd edition. Chicago: American Library Association.

Van House, Nancy A., Beth Weil, and Charles McClure. 1990. *Measuring academic library performance: A practical approach.* Chicago: American Library Association.

Vavrek, Bernard. 1990. *Assessing the information needs of rural Americans.* Clarion, PA: College of Library Science, Clarion University of Pennsylvania.

Vavrek, Bernard. 1995. Rural information needs and the role of the public library. *Library Trends*. 44 (summer): 21–48.

Voelker, David, and Peter Orton. 1993. *Statistics*. Lincoln, NE: Cliffs Notes.

Waldron, Vincent, and Brenda Dervin. 1988. Sense-making as a framework for knowledge acquisition. Paper delivered at the American Society for Information Science Mid-Winter Meeting, Ann Arbor, Michigan. Text obtained from author.

Walsh, Anthony. 1992. All the World Is Data and We But the Ciphers in It . . . William Shakespere [*sic*]. 1992. *Reference Librarian*. 38: 21–30.

Walter, Virginia A. 1992. *Output measures for public library service to children: A manual of standardized procedures*. Chicago: American Library Association.

Walter, Virginia A. 1994. The information needs of children. *Advances in librarianship*. New York: Academic Press. 18: 111–129.

Walter, Virginia A. 1995. *Output measures and more: Planning and evaluating public library services for young adults*. Chicago: American Library Association.

Walters, Suzanne. 1994. *Customer service: A how-to-do-it manual for librarians*. How-To-Do-It Manuals for Librarians, number 41.New York: Neal-Schuman.

Warncke, Ruth. 1975. Analyzing your community: Basis for building library service. *Illinois Libraries*. 57 (2): 64–76.

Weinberg, Gerald. 1985. *The secrets of consulting: A guide to giving and getting advice successfully*. Foreword by Virginia Satir. New York: Dorset House.

Welch, Lee. 1995. Critical factors in information supply to humanitarian aid agencies: A preliminary survey. *Libri*. 45: 2–10.

Westbrook, Lynn. 1997. Qualitative research. In Ronald Powell's *Basic research methods for librarians*. 3rd edition. Greenwich, CT: Ablex. Chapter 6, 143–164.

Westbrook, Lynn. 1997. Information access issues for interdisciplinary scholars: Results of a Delphi study on women's studies research. *Journal of Academic Librarianship*. 23 (3, May): 211–216.

Westbrook, Lynn. 2000. Analyzing community information needs. *Library Administration and Management*. 14 (1, winter): 26–30.

Whyte, William. 1979. On making the most of participant observation. *American Sociologist*. 14 (1): 56–66.

Wilson, T. D., and D. R. Streatfield. 1981. Structured observation in the investigation of information needs. *Social Science Information Studies*. 1: 173–184.

Wolcott, Harry. 1990. On seeking—and rejecting—validity in qualitative research. In *Qualitative inquiry in education: The continuing debate*. New York: Teachers College Press, 121–152.

Wolfe, Lisa A. 1997. *Library public relations, promotions, and communications: A how-to-do-it manual*. How-To-Do-It Manuals for Librarians, number 75. New York: Neal-Schuman.

Wurzburger, Marilyn. 1987. Conducting a mail survey: Some of the things you probably didn't learn in any research methods course. *College & Research Libraries News*. 11 (December): 697–700.

Zweizig, Douglas. 1980. Community analysis. In *Local public library administration*. 2nd ed. Ellen Altman, ed. Chicago: American Library Association. 38–46.

Zweizig, Douglas. 1992. Community analysis. In *Keeping the books: Public library financial practices*. Jane Robbins and Douglas Zweizig, eds. Fort Atkinson, WI: Highsmith Press, for the Urban Libraries Council. 225–238.

Zweizig, Douglas, and Brenda Dervin. 1982. Public library use, users, uses: Advances in knowledge of the characteristics and needs of the adult clientele of American public libraries. In *Public librarianship: A reader*. Jane Robbins-Carter, ed. Littleton, CO: Libraries Unlimited. 189–205.

Zweizig, Douglas, and Debra Wilcox Johnson. 1996. Observation. In *The TELL IT! Manual*. Douglas Zweizig, Debra Wilcox Johnson, Jane Robbins, and Michele Besant, eds. Chicago: ALA. 213–225.

Zweizig, Douglas, Debra Wilcox Johnson, Jane Robbins, et al. 1996. *The TELL IT! Manual: The complete program for evaluating library performance*. Chicago: American Library Association.

Zweizig, Douglas, and Eleanor Jo Rodger. 1982. *Output measures for public libraries: A manual of standardized procedures*. Chicago: American Library Association.

Glossary

The informal explanations of these terms are all given within the context of community information-needs analysis studies as conducted by librarians.

anonymity: being unknown as when a survey is unsigned and unconnected to the name of the subject who completed it; contrast this with "confidentiality"

code: a carefully defined, unique word or phrase which is consistently applied to interview, survey, observation, or other narrative data

codeable: data to which codes can be applied

confidentiality: keeping information private and secret; for example, interviewing someone means that anonymity is no longer possible since the subject must be known to the researcher but confidentiality can be offered if the researcher never shares the subject's name or other information with anyone else; contrast this with "anonymity"

ethics: the rules of good conduct and the moral expectations involved in intruding on the lives of others; confidentiality, protection of minors, and a total lack of coercion are the three principal ethical considerations of most research projects in library studies

evaluation study: an examination of the extent to which a library meets its standards or, if standards are lacking, its purpose

exit interview: usually brief, these interviews are administered at the end of a specific segment of a library visit such as a reference interview or an OPAC search

impact study: an analysis of the effect of a library on its community or some portion of the community

in-depth interview: usually lasting about an hour, these interviews are extensive and often exploratory in nature; details and examples are garnered

invisible users: people who enter libraries, either physically or electronically, but who do not approach staff at any service point; their use of the library may be completely undetectable

I-Search: a type of paper assigned in high school and college in which students record their thoughts and actions during their search for information on a topic; if well done and if all ethical concerns can be met, these papers often reveal the information needs of these students in some depth

Likert scale: a set of options for use in a survey that provides ordinal data such as "perfect—good—acceptable—poor—awful"

needs assessment: a study of the information required by all or part of a library's population

nominal data: categorized but nonhierarchical data as in sex, female versus male; contrast with "ordinal"

nonusers: people who are allowed to but choose not to use the library

ordinal data: data that are strictly sequential so that the same difference is found between each consecutive value as in the number of books borrowed; these data have a true zero

remote-site users: individuals who reach a library electronically through telnet or Web sites; they do not come into the physical building but they do make use of library services and/or resources

response rate: the proportion of responses as compared to the number of requests for response; for example, if 100 surveys are sent out and 50 are returned, then a 50 percent response rate has been achieved

statistical significance: an objective measure of the relative importance of a numerical finding; a finding that could not be explained as resulting from chance

transaction log: the automatically recorded usage records of a database; OPAC transaction logs, for example, often record the number of searches by type (e.g., keyword, title) as well as the number of results by type (e.g., zero hits, over 5,000 hits)

triangulation: the purposeful combination of sampling methods, data-gathering techniques, and research questions with the goal of producing a broader, more in-depth, more accurate understanding of the situation

use: in this context, use may be defined as any interaction with any aspect of the library, its resources, its services, or its staff; some use is productive and some is not, some focuses on the library as an institution providing service (e.g., borrowing a book or using the library's Web site from home) and some focuses on the library as a physical space (e.g., meeting a friend in the lobby)

user: one who makes use of the library

user need: a library-supportable informational gap experienced by a user or potential user; some library might reasonably be expected to meet an information need as a normal part of supplying resources and services

user want: an information gap that is not the purview of a library

Index

About the Author

Jo Lynn Westbrook received her MA in Library Studies from the University of Chicago in 1982 and her Ph.D. in Library and Information Studies from the University of Michigan in 1995. Her work in user needs was recognized by the Association of College and Research Libraries Women's Studies Section, which awarded her book, *Interdisciplinary Information Seeking Women's Studies*, the Award for Significant Achievement in Women's Studies Librarianship in 2000. She has published over 15 journal articles, in addition to her book, as well as monographs on preservation and evaluation techniques. Dr. Westbrook served as an adult services librarian in the Hillside Public Library, as a reference/instruction librarian at the University of Georgia, and as head of reference and instruction at the Undergraduate Library of the University of Michigan. She currently teaches courses in research methods, information professions, information storage and retrieval, community information needs analysis, and reference at Texas Woman's University's School of Library and Information Studies.